Operation Desert Storm

Operation Desert Storm

Evaluation of the Air Campaign

GOVERNMENT REPRINTS PRESS
Washington, D.C.

© Ross & Perry, Inc. 2002 on new material. All rights reserved.

No claim to U.S. government work contained throughout this book.

Protected under the Berne Convention.

Printed in The United States of America
Ross & Perry, Inc. Publishers
216 G St., N.E.,
Washington, D.C. 20002
Telephone (202) 675-8300
Facsimile (801) 459-7535
info@RossPerry.com

SAN 253-8555

Government Reprints Press Edition 2002

Government Reprints Press is an Imprint of Ross & Perry, Inc.

Library of Congress Control Number: 2001093419
http://www.GPOreprints.com

ISBN 1-931641-29-3

Book Cover designed by Sapna/sapna@rossperry.com

Image on cover provided by www.af.mil

♾ The paper used in this publication meets the requirements for permanence established by the American National Standard for Information Sciences "Permanence of Paper for Printed Library Materials" (ANSI Z39.48-1984).

All rights reserved. No copyrighted part of this publication may be reproduced, stored in a retrieval system, or transmitted, in any form or by any means, electronic, photocopying, recording, or otherwise, without the prior written permission of the publisher.

Preface

The Gulf War, also known as "Operation Desert Storm," took place in 1991. Five years later, in July 1996, the US General Accounting Office (GAO) released a summary report on Desert Storm's air campaign. A year later, the GAO published a more detailed version of the same report. After all this time, why should anyone care about—let alone read—an old report on an even older air war? What more is there to tell?

The story that remains is the attempt to suppress and, once it was released, to discredit the GAO report. The attempts at suppression and discrediting tell you everything you need to know about how Washington, D.C. handles defense issues. The story is one of a Defense Department preoccupied with preserving its own image and dogma; of journalists and commentators manipulating and ignoring the facts; of a congressional "watchdog" that often squelches, rather than promotes, independent defense research; and of a Congress almost completely asleep at the switch.

Summary of GAO's Report

The GAO report was unique as an analysis of the Desert Storm air campaign. When the report was initially released in 1996, the overwhelming image of the Gulf War air campaign was one of the spectacular success of "silver bullet" weapon systems. Who can forget the constant images of bombs guiding precisely into targets, which immediately disappeared in a fireball of explosion? The list of accolades from media talking heads, expert pundits, and senior military officers was endless.

F-117s were the unquestioned star of the war. Their special black coating, their novel shape, and their "stealth," gave them a mystique which meshed perfectly with their spectacular "proven" performance. With few exceptions, pundits, generals, DoD briefers, and the media embraced a well circulated Air Force report that during the first hours of the first night of the war, the F-117 "revolutionized warfare"[1] by flying into the teeth of Saddam's highly sophisticated integrated air defense system (IADS) and surgically dispatched it,[2] thereby opening up all of Iraq for conventional aircraft to attack with relative ease.[3] A "force multiplier" if ever there was one.

Older aircraft, such as the F-111F, infused with new precision weapons, "plinked" Saddam's tank force with laser-guided bombs (LGBs) that were so effective and reliable that "one bomb, one target"[4] became a mantra for the advocates of the newly proclaimed "revolution in warfare."

BBC cameras recorded Tomahawk cruise missiles navigating over Baghdad highways unerringly finding their way to pinpoint targets[5] in all forms of weather[6] against the heaviest defenses[7] and, according to estimates from the Joint Chiefs of Staff, achieved a hit rate of 85 percent.[8]

| What really happened? | When GAO looked into the data, recorded by the U.S. Air Force and other DoD agencies, GAO found that the vast majority of the spectacular claims were bogus. America's "silver bullet" weapons performed well, but not nearly as well as the world was told. Furthermore, the low tech weapons—B-52s, A-10s, and even dumb bombs that you almost never heard about—often performed as well and sometimes even better. The proclaimed success of complex weapons was little more than an ad campaign by senior DoD bureaucrats and "milicrats," the defense manufacturing community, and private sector swamis of high tech. The overwhelming popular belief in the triumph of "high tech" was a direct result of the repetitive airing on CNN and other media outlets of carefully selected video tapes of LGB's and other guided munitions unerringly hitting their targets dead-center. The public was never shown any of the several thousands of taped misses. At times, it also required inaccurate narration from ill-informed "talking heads" and from misinformed or misinforming military commanders. A dramatic example, by no less than the Chief of the Staff of the Air Force, was that the F-117 had a 80 percent hit rate against its targets. The Air Force's own bomb-by-bomb data based showed that the highest "hit rate" that could be verified was about 60 percent, and if sorties that were aborted due to weather, reliability failures, and other factors are included, the proven hit rate was about 40 percent.

That so much baloney was coming from the manufacturers should surprise no one; that it was also coming from official military documents and senior military commanders, demonstrates just how pervasive situational ethics have become in Washington, D.C. |
|---|---|
| The "Revolution in Warfare" was actually a Rebellion against Truth | On the first night of the war, according to Air Force's records, 17 F-117s were assigned to destroy 15 Iraqi Integrated Air Defense System (IADS) targets. To begin with, F-117s aborted their attacks on four of these targets. Of the 11 IADS targets attacked, two were simply missed. Just nine were actually struck with laser guided bombs (LGBs) from F-117s. Defense Intelligence Agency (DIA) battle damaged assessments (BDA) found that |

two of those targets were damaged sufficiently to require no more attacks; eight others were still functioning and required re-strikes on later nights. One target could not be assessed. Thus, contrary to the well-orchestrated version of the F-117's spectacular success rate on the first night of the war, either two or three targets were both hit and destroyed, for a less than stunning 13 to 20 percent success rate.

Furthermore, contrary to characterization of F-117's acting "alone and unafraid," they were not the only aircraft attacking air defense targets on that first night. Air Force tasking data show that 167 additional, non-stealthy aircraft including A-10s, F-4Gs, and F/A-18s attacked 18 air defense targets that same first night. Whatever was accomplished against the Iraqi air defense was the result of more than just a few "silver bullet" F-117s.

IADS takedown rate

Just what did all those aircraft accomplish? Air Force intelligence assessed the effectiveness of the Iraqi IADS on a daily basis. By day three, daily intelligence summaries ("DAISUMS") described the IADS as "evidence of degradation ... is beginning to show." By day five, they said "In general, the Iraqi IADS is down but not out."

F-117s demolished the Iraqi IADS in the first hours of the first night? Single-handed force multiplier? "Revolution in warfare?" Give me a break! For the complete discussion of what the F-117 did and did not do, check out pages 85-92 and 125-139 of the report that follows this preface.*

Plinking plucked

Well, you might be asking, if the F-117 did not live up to the hype, at least the assertions about precision weapons, as demonstrated by the F-111F's tank-plinking efforts, was true, wasn't it? After all, the Air Force said it wiped out the Iraqi tank force.

Unfortunately, the number of valid Iraqi tank targets hit and killed (i.e. "plinked") by LGBs is a number known but to God. For tank kills, good data are pretty sparse. Of the 163 Iraqi tanks the Army's Foreign Science and Technology Center inspected on the battlefield after the war (a small and

---

* For an assessment of the Iraqi IADS, the F-117's ability to survive those defenses literally unscratched, and the survivability of other aircraft, see pages 92-106, 137-138, 205-206, and 225-226. While there remains no independent, reliable assessment of Operation Allied Force over Yugoslavia in 1999, it is also worth mentioning in this context that a F-117 was shot down by Serbian air defenses, and another was rumored to have been significantly damaged. Operation Allied Force resulted in only one other aircraft being shot down, a F-16.

non-random sample which is not conclusive), only 28 (17 percent) were assessed as having been hit from the air. The CIA looked more broadly at armor kills. Its analysis found that the air campaign was responsible for immobilizing 1,135 of 2,665 tanks (43 percent) in nine regular Iraqi armored or mechanized divisions. In the key target set of the three Republican Guard divisions in theater, the air campaign immobilized just 13 to 30 percent of the tanks (see pages 146-148). None of the CIA's analyses show how many were hit by LGBs, Mavericks, A-10 gun passes, dumb bombs, Rockeyes or anything else.

Tomahawks taking wrong turns

What about those pin point attacks by Tomahawks? The Navy's Center for Naval Analysis wrote a multi-volume review of Tomahawk's Desert Storm performance. The Defense Department classified most of the GAO report's summary of CNA's work. DoD did, however, permit a statement that about half of the Tomahawks launched hit their targets. The other half were "no shows," and, of them, how many were shot down, got lost, or hit the wrong thing is unknown (see pages 139-143).

It gets worse

After spending billions of dollars in the 1970s and 1980s for "all-weather" aircraft and weapons, we learned in Desert Storm that DoD's "all-weather" sensors and guidance systems could only function in clear, dry air (see pages 78-82). The stand-off systems, designed to keep the operators far from the threat of ground fire, did not eliminate the need to identify the target. Thus, if the operator wanted to have a good chance to identify what he was shooting at, he had to shorten the distance to improve sensor resolution, only to have the benefits of "stand-off" sharply reduced, if not eliminated (see same pages).

But to some, the most disturbing news was the report's findings on the relationship between cost and performance of American weapons systems. For years the Department of Defense (DoD) and the advocates of cost and complexity had nurtured the conventional wisdom that "high tech" systems were, regrettably, more expensive, but the additional cost brought a major pay-off in the form of better performance. The GAO report took a hard look at this entrenched conventional wisdom. GAO was unable to confirm it with the data from Desert Storm. While there were some performance measures where high cost aircraft performed better, i.e., better accuracy in limited circumstances, there were also areas where low cost systems performed better: availability, sortie rate, and cost per sortie.

For most measures, however, there was no correlation between aircraft cost and performance, including targets destroyed, survivability and, tonnage of munitions delivered. For munitions, the study found about as many advantages for low cost dumb bombs as for high cost guided munitions (see pages 162-193).

Washington Reacts to the Report

When both the 1996 and 1997 versions of GAO's report hit the street, they received plenty of media coverage. I had never seen as much press for any GAO report on a defense subject. My incomplete files show 22 straight news articles and 19 editorials or "op ed" commentaries in major newspapers and defense journals. Most of the articles pursued the theme "Weapons Were Overrated,"[9] "Debate Swirls Around F-117,"[10] and "GAO Study Takes Aim At Gulf War Weapons."[11] As stories and commentary like these poured out, the advocates of complexity, cost, and conventional wisdom realized they had a problem on their hands. Both DoD and its "Think Tanks" brought out the damage control teams. Here is how they reacted.

Control the Facts and Bluster

The first reaction was internal before the report went public. The perception among the public is that the General Accounting Office is a stand-offish, independent auditor looking out only for the public. On the contrary, the relationship between DoD and GAO is often much more cozy than it should be. The reasons for this are complex and are worthy of serious focus elsewhere, but suffice it to say here that DoD is accustomed to GAO's changing its findings and conclusions pretty much whenever DoD says it wants a change.

This publicly unrecognised cooperative relationship starts when early drafts of GAO reports are quietly brought over to DoD by GAO staff (on instructions from their superiors) for "fact checking" and "editing" before the first official draft of a report is finalized. Later, when a draft report is formally sent to DoD for official comments, the sharp edges are usually removed, and if for any reason some remain, DoD will meet with GAO staff and tell them where GAO is wrong, and more grinding down usually occurs. This course of conduct over the years has let the Department of Defense become accustomed to GAO's toning down or changing its findings and conclusions pretty much whenever DoD asks.

But accommodating the Department of Defense for its own sake did not happen on this report. The GAO team that produced the initial draft report was from a different GAO division than the one where managers insisted that early drafts be ferreted over to DoD for corrections. This team refused to be party to the "under the table" alterations. When, for example, the GAO authors of this report met with DoD officials to formally start another study, a DoD official asked when he would be receiving his "under the table" copy of the draft study for his revisions. Another DoD official, who had worked with both GAO divisions on previous studies, explained with some embarrassment, "this isn't that division."

He further explained DoD could expect no such favor from the team that was present, which the GAO team further explained was a violation of GAO procedures.

Rather than just take good notes and fold when DoD staff complained about findings they didn't like, this GAO team asked for documentation of the newly asserted facts. When a DoD staff member claimed to have a document that refuted the GAO position, this GAO team had the temerity to ask for a copy of the report—not just excerpts, the whole thing. This sometimes resulted in DoD staff accusing GAO of questioning their honor. Sometimes these DoD staff complained to senior GAO managers that the GAO staff were being a "problem." In some places in GAO, that would take care of the "problem" and, while no new documents would be provided, the report would change.

Unfortunately for DoD, the GAO team assigned to this report kept on asking for documentary evidence of DoD's assertions. Little, if anything, changed in the GAO report when DoD was unable or unwilling to document its assertion.

After the first version of the report was published, in July 1996, one senior DoD manager wrote to the supervisor of the GAO team that wrote the report complaining that "The Department ... is disturbed that the final report reflects few of the Department's technical corrections and concerns regarding the overall construct of the report."[12] To his credit, the GAO manager declined the implied advice to deal with "the problem" and continued to compliment the report team for a job well done.

Suppress the Facts

The Department of Defense's failure to get all its required changes evoked a new tactic: suppression. When GAO finished the report, it was about 250 pages in length. The Department of Defense did what it frequently does when it wants to suppress bad news: it classified massive amounts of the report. It eliminated so much that what finally passed the DoD classifiers' review was a mere 13 pages of vague summary with so little data to substantiate it that it became easy prey for attack by pundits sympathetic to DoD's positions. That ploy was only temporarily successful.

Democratic Senator David Pryor from Arkansas, one of the Members of Congress who had requested the report, had good contacts with another Arkansan in the White House. Senator Pryor saw the dramatic difference between the classified version of the report and DoD's emasculation of it.

In response, he pointed out to the press that GAO was permitted to say that the Department of Defense and defense manufacturers made public claims that were "overstated, misleading, inconsistent with the best available data, or unverifiable,"[13] but that GAO was not permitted to say what DoD and manufacturer statements were false and what the truth was.

Employing his constitutional immunity, Senator Pryor made clear just how disengenous the Department of Defense was being. DoD had classified manufacturer newspaper ads, public statements made by the Secretary of the Air Force and other officials, and previously unclassified passages in the Air Force's contract study on the war and in the Air Force's own "White Paper" on the war.[14] In other words, DoD officials and reports could make inaccurate statements to the public and cite selected data, but it was deemed a threat to national security for GAO to point out what statements were misleading and what data made that clear. Once the base immorality of the DoD position was apparent, the building capitulated, and in 1997, a 235 page version of the report was released. (It is this more complete edition that is reprinted after this preface.)

"One bomb, one target" Bombs Out

Before the publication of the GAO report, "one bomb, one target" had become a Desert Storm mantra. It was repeated by the advocates of guided weapons and was the theme song of the "revolution in warfare." The hymn had become so commonplace that it appeared in advertisements by manufacturers of guided munitions, and it was frequently invoked by pundits in articles.[15]

The GAO report looked closely at how many bombs it actually took in Desert Storm to destroy a target. GAO combined the available strike, target, and Bomb Damage Assessment (BDA) data to tabulate the tonnages used against point targets, area targets, and categories of targets. "One bomb, one target" it wasn't. A better mantra might have been, "a baker's dozen, one target." On average, across all targets in Desert Storm, 11 tons of guided munitions and 44 tons of unguided munitions were needed to destroy a target. Against point targets, bridges for example, where the Center for Naval Analysis (CNA) assessed Navy strikes, it took, on average, 11.3 laser guided bombs to drop a bridge span* (see page 189). GAO's own analysis of Air Force and Navy data found that it took, on average, 10.8 tons of guided munitions and 18.2 tons of unguided munition to destroy a bridge (see page 190).

---

* Different analyses use tonnage or number of bombs. Laser-guided bombs (LGBs) typically weigh 500 or 2,000 pounds.

Faced with this and much more employment and target damage data, DoD folded again. Rather than attempt to find some small number of isolated cases where one bomb did destroy one target in just one try—a set of data that in Desert Storm would likely have been so limited as to prove the opposite—DoD reversed its position and asserted to GAO, "No one has ever seriously attempted to argue that one-shot, one-kill is a realistic expectation for our platforms and weapons."[16] While the statement was included in an official DoD letter to GAO, it was not released to the public, and senior DoD officials continued to make the same statements to the public as before: the "one bomb, one target" mantra continued. In one case, it was merely modified to "The accuracy of our precision-guided munitions is good enough when it takes only two or three weapons to destroy a target."[17] In another case, the mantra was simply changed to "one target, one weapon."[18]

DoD failed to reverse the tide of press coverage on the GAO report. Articles and editorials continued saying that DoD had played fast and loose with the facts. Help was needed from outside the Pentagon. It came in the form of editorials and commentary from pundits not directly attributable to DoD.

Rally 'round the Dogma

While my sympathies are with the commentators who favored the report, it must be said that some of these took considerable liberties with the report. Despite frequent quotes from the report, one commentary bent it into a reason to vote against Bob Dole for President.[19] Another had the "Gingrich Congress" punishing GAO for the report by abolishing the division responsible for the report. (The division was abolished, but not by the "Gingrich Congress.")[20] Another over-generalized the report's finding on non-stealthy aircraft survivability at night,[21] and even the New York Times overstated at least one finding and addressed issues not in the report.[22]

The excessive exuberance of the favorable commentary paled in comparison to the selectivity and inventiveness of the negative commentary. In some cases, the critics hatched new findings and attributed them to GAO; others seemed to borrow information from the report, without attribution, to show how knowledgeable they were; and others almost certainly read only parts of the report, if any at all. None of them sought clarification or explanation from the GAO authors before they launched their attacks. Most focused on one theme: defending the "high tech" weapons they asserted GAO was wantonly trashing.

Washington Post Declares Reports to Public Don't Have to be Accurate

In an editorial, the Washington Post yawned at the GAO finding that DoD overstated the performance of guided munitions in the war—information its own reporters had largely missed.[23] To the Post's editorial writer, it seemed OK for the Pentagon to boast of 40 hits in 40 attempts just so long as there was at least one valid hit against a major target—a rather strange approach to accuracy in reporting for a newspaper. While the editorial conceded that the GAO study may have helped the US learn some lessons, it complained that the report somehow lacked the facts and was "weak on questions of context and comparison." While it is true that the Post had available to it only the early, short, highly-censored version of the report, it is also true that the Post's editorial writers did not make a single inquiry to the report's authors to determine just what facts, context, and comparisons were behind the report.

The Pundits

An op ed commentary in the Washington Times defended the Pentagon. It, too, minimized the report's statement that "the Pentagon did overstate the effectiveness of its Gulf War performance."[24] The main theme was that "high tech" weapons deserved more credit in winning the war than GAO allowed. The Times did this without a careful reading of the report or any discussion with the report's authors. The Times' commentator cited the standard myths about the uniqueness of F-117 and Tomahawk operations over Baghdad (see pages 90-106 & 125-143 of the report), tank plinking (see pages 146-148), and the destruction of the Iraqi air defense system (see pages 135-137). It appeared as if GAO had overlooked these issues, and therefore did not know just how well high tech had performed. When this commentary appeared in the Times, one of the GAO authors contacted the writer and pointed out that several examples of successful high tech operations cited in his commentary were factually incorrect. The GAO author offered to go over everything the report addressed and the DoD data behind it all. The offer was declined.

Remedial Reading Course Needed

Perhaps the most Orwellian commentary appeared in the Washington Post by one of the six outside reviewers GAO contracted to read and comment on draft of the Desert Storm report. This reviewer was retained because of his direction of another multi-volume study of the Gulf War. His scathing commentary in the Post came as a surprise for the simple reason that it was quite inaccurate in describing the report and the circumstances surrounding it.

For example, the commentator asserted that GAO had released its report "with considerable fanfare." That was not true. The GAO issued the report without so much as a press release. The first public notice of the report was based on an unauthorized leak before the report was officially released. The consultant misinterpreted: once they became aware of the controversial report, journalists flocked to it on their own.

The commentator also wrote that the GAO concluded that "the F-117 stealth fighter ... simply did not do very well." That was not the report's conclusion. The report stated that the Department of Defense and contractors vastly overstated the performance of the F-117 (see pages 19 and 24). On the contrary the GAO report stated up front that "although some claims for some advanced systems could not be verified, their performance in combat may well have been unprecedented" (see page 2). The pundit also asserted that "GAO further implies that the $58 billion ... spent on precision guided munitions ... is wasted or excessive." Again, the writer mischaracterized the GAO's comparison of the cost and performance of precision and unguided munitions, as well as the comparison of the performance advantages and limitations of both (see pages 177-193).

What the commentator ignored was that the report constantly attempted to articulate a balance about "high tech" and "low tech" weapons. The 1996 public version of the report to which the reviewer had access and presumably was the object of his criticism, stated prominently, "the success of the sustained air campaign resulted from the availability of a mix of strike and support assets. Its substantial weight of effort was made possible, in significant part, by the variety and number of ... platforms capable of delivering guided munitions, such as the stealthy F-117, to high-sortie-rate attack aircraft such as the A-10."[26] Rather than arguing that money spent for guided munitions was "wasted," the report presented "recommendations [to] help ensure that high-cost munitions can be employed more efficiently at lower risk to pilots and aircraft and that the future mix of guided and unguided munitions is appropriate and cost-effective...."[27]

What seemed to bother this commentator was that GAO had pointed out that there were down sides to the cost and performance of "high tech" weapons and that there were up-sides to the cost and performance of "low tech" weapons. The attempt at balance by GAO was taken by the advocates of "high tech" as a slander against it. To cite both sides of the story was tantamount to being one-sided and was, in the words of the commentator, "not merely incorrect but, if taken to heart, down right dangerous."

Such contrived logic was a skilful manipulation, but it also required ignorance, if not distortion, of the contents of the GAO report. How could a paid reviewer of the report not know of its contents? When contacted to review the 250 page draft, the reviewer/commentator spent only three hours reading it. With this hasty incomplete review, he harshly and universally denounced the draft as, among other things, "tendentious." Based on his comments to the GAO staff, it was obvious to them that there were long and important passages in the draft report he had either not read or badly misinterpreted. However, because of the prominence and authority of the commentator, GAO spent about a year responding to his comments. (GAO also spent this time responding to other outside reviewers, but their comments were far more positive.)

When the revised draft was complete, the reviewer/commentator was asked to read it again, but he refused. His public comments may well have been based just on his hasty, incomplete reading of the early draft of the report. Had he read the final draft, especially in connection with the published unclassified summary, he would have found his criticisms to be directed at a report that did not exist and that would have excluded his argument that GAO was being one-sided.

This experience with Washington, D.C. punditry on defense would seem to reveal two cardinal rules: first, no tarnish is to be allowed on the luminous sheen so carefully applied to high cost, complex ("high tech") weapons. Second, not collecting all the information about the subject at hand—even when it is literally in front of your eyes—makes punditry immeasurably easier.

Who's Watching the Watchdog

Many in Congress and the press adore GAO because when GAO looks into something it is virtually certain to find something wrong. These findings make instant grist for politicians' press releases and journalists' news articles. Furthermore, because it's GAO—the ever-reliable congressional "watchdog"—there is little need to double check the facts or to report the other side of the argument in any but the most cursory manner.

But there is another side. To many, GAO is a joke. It's not that GAO always finds something wrong; it's that on defense subjects GAO is frequently wrong. The reason for this is based on a management-induced bureaucratic culture that discourages truly independent studies and in the poor research and investigatory skills that management fosters among many—but certainly not all—of GAO's auditors and evaluators.

Reasons for the GAO's Poor Results

The bureaucratic culture in GAO requires that its components maintain what GAO management calls a "positive relationship with the agency." Among other things, this can mean that GAO personnel are prohibited from obtaining the very data they need to perform their research.

When they ask for data, they are to accept what they get. While it does not happen on every project, DoD may want to withhold sections of a document, or the whole thing altogether, especially if GAO is on the trail of documents that will reveal things DoD wanted withheld. GAO personnel are allowed to ask again for the documentation, but when the final answer is no, GAO almost always accepts that result. GAO researchers may instead get the agency's description of the withheld document or carefully selected example. This occurs even though GAO has statutory authority to demand any and all documents it deems necessary. Sadly, this unique authority is used only in the rarest cases when DoD refuses to cooperate. The division in GAO responsible for defense matters has virtually never exercised it.*

The deeper you dig into GAO, especially on defense issues, the worse it gets. Despite a large and active training program, many GAO managers and workers know little but the most elementary research techniques. This is evidenced by the "Scope and Methodology" sections of most GAO reports on defense. The section will basically read: "we spoke to a bunch of officials and a few experts; we collected a bunch of documents; we went to a bunch of places; we began on this date, and we ended on this date."

How does GAO confirm it had collected all the available data on the subject? How did GAO work around limitations in the data? How did GAO cross-validate the data, especially officials' statements compared to other data? Did DoD deny access to any data, and what was done about that? Why did the GAO authors select one form of data for one part of the study and another for a different part? When personnel were interviewed, were their superiors present? How were all the data analyzed? What are the strengths and weaknesses of that form of analysis in the context of this study? What were the overall limitations to the study? You get the idea. If you don't see answers to these and other relevant questions, don't bother reading any more, unless you just want to collect anecdotal trivia with a critical bias on the subject of the study.

GAO combines a management culture that seeks to avoid a major conflict with the defense agency being investigated with a lack of strong research techniques. This basically puts GAO at the mercy of DoD. Smart DoD officials know this, and will not stonewall GAO; they will cooperate, but only up to a point. They know that GAO will persist until they find something negative to report. The smart DoD managers throw GAO a bone: that is, hand over enough information so that GAO's need for a critical report is satisfied, but not so much that every element—both positive and negative—of an issue is fully probed.

---

* One exception was the GAO's insistence that Vice President Cheney turn over records of the people with whom he met to discuss energy policy. See, E.J. Dionne Jr., "What's Cheney Hiding?" Washington Post, (Jul 20, 2001) : A31; and Dana Milbank, "Cheney Records Demanded," Washington Post, (Jul 19, 2001) : A01. Note, however, that this "document demand" was from a GAO division different from the division that does defense work.

Every Rule Has an Exception

You might be asking, why should anyone give this GAO study on the Gulf Air War any respect? Isn't it written to the same sorry standard? The answer is, this report wasn't written by GAO's division that normally writes defense reports. That division is the National Security and International Affairs Division, or "NSIAD." This report was written by GAO's Program Evaluation and Methodology Division, or "PEMD."* The culture and skills in PEMD were very different. The staff and managers were extensively trained in evaluation and research techniques. But the more important difference was in the culture. DoD officials were expected to hand over all documents requested, and if they weren't, the process to legally extract the documents was usually started. PEMD was not interested in nurturing a "positive relationship with the agency;" it was interested in documents and research and acted accordingly.

Green Eyeshade Wars

The differences between these two GAO divisions made for poisonous bureaucratic relations. This was made evident at the very beginning of the Desert Storm study; PEMD learned from DoD of an important Air Force data base that identified essential information about every U.S. aircraft strike against all stationary Iraqi targets in the air campaign. PEMD also learned from DoD that GAO already had the data base. It was in NSIAD. The PEMD researchers went to the NSIAD manager who controlled the data base and he informed PEMD that it was his and another manager's "personal property." No, PEMD could not have it. After several days that foolishness went away, but the same official then tried to argue the data base was so complex and messy it was unusable. But after months of work and various reliability and validity tests, PEMD made the information useable, and it became a key part of the report.

In addition to being obstructionist, senior bureaucrats in NSIAD were reluctant to permit the publication of any report that had not been tacitly endorsed by DoD. When the first draft of the report was finished in 1994, GAO procedures required that NSIAD managers also approve it. They were aghast. How could any of these things be true? DoD said the weapons were "all weather;" so what more was there to assess? If an Air Force study said the F-117 had a 80 percent hit rate, why would anyone want to challenge that? Half the Tomahawks missing their targets? That's not what their friends in the Navy said. Literally, they could not believe what they were reading. During one strained meeting where the data in the report were being debated, one frustrated NSIAD manager blurted out, "That's what the data say, but what does DoD say?"

---

* Neither of these divisions currently exist in GAO. As discussed below, PEMD has been eliminated. NSIAD has been reorganized into two new "teams" ("Defense Capabilities and Management" and "Acquisition Sourcing Management"). However, nothing of significance has changed from the previous NSIAD way of doing things.

As a result, NSIAD and PEMD entered an endless editing loop. The former would seek changes in the draft to grind the report's findings down to their own comfort level, sometimes to meaninglessness. PEMD was willing to edit the mode of expression but not the substance. After two years of bureaucratic agony, this back and forth resulted in a final report that retained most of its content, but which was written and re-written again and again to accommodate bureaucratic, political, and cultural preferences.

The result was often stylistic mush, particularly in the parts of the report GAO management though people might actually read. Thus, an extraordinarily long, "executive summary" has many vague, garbled articulations of the report's findings, but it's 23 pages contains little hint of the mountain of details that make a clear understanding of those findings truly compelling. On the other hand, while they contain some pedantic and plodding portions, the report's appendices were—relatively speaking—left free of the tender mercies of GAO management's editorial depredations.

After DoD's first censorship-via-classification of the report, the first, short, vague version finally came out in 1996. After Senator Pryor cowed the DoD censors into submission, the more complete, long version came out in 1997.

GAO Solves the "Problem"

PEMD may have won the battle by persisting with its report through two rounds of publication, but it lost the war. It had been fighting other skirmishes with NSIAD on other defense reports, and PEMD had similar fights with virtually all other GAO divisions. That PEMD could make most of its substantive arguments stick in bureaucratic fights—based on the data and the analysis in the reports—was more than some senior GAO managers could bear.

The first blow was the Comptroller General's forcing into retirement PEMD's highly intelligent and assertive—but also extremely acerbic—division director. After she was removed, top GAO management got braver, and the rest was easy. Shortly after the first version of the air war study was released, PEMD was formally abolished, and its staff was absorbed by the rest of GAO.* When pressed on the matter by the small number of press who took notice, budget cuts imposed by the "Gingrich Congress" were blamed.[28] It was a convenient excuse, but it was not the real reason. Thus, while the air war report did not result in any DoD programs being killed, it did rack up one "kill:" the only division in GAO capable of and willing to write the report.

---

*This bureaucratic change explains why PEMD is listed on the 1996 report, and a NSIAD report number on the second, longer 1997 report.

Shooting Blanks

There is an epilogue to the demise of PEMD. In September 1999, Congressman Denis Kucinich (D., OH) wrote to GAO asking for an analysis of the 1999 NATO air campaign over Yugoslavia (Operation Allied Force). He specifically asked that the same team who performed the Desert Storm study be assigned to this new study. Although PEMD had been disassembled, most of the original report's staff remained in GAO. GAO refused and assigned the new report to normal NSIAD-types.

Knowing full well NSIAD's reputation, Congressman Kucinich wrote again to GAO on November 16 and pointed out that the previous PEMD team had "defined its own study parameters; it conducted its own data collection and analysis, and it did not confer with or seek the pre-approval of the DoD before the official comment period," a subtle but stinging rebuke to NSIAD. He withdrew his study request and asked that his name be removed from any GAO publication on the subject of Operation Allied Force issued subsequent to his original request.

Reaffirming NSIAD's independence and competence, GAO's Comptroller General responded to Congressman Kucinich that it would proceed with the study nonetheless.[29] One product came out in March 2001; it purported to address the Army's deployment and humiliating inability to use Apache helicopters to support the air campaign over Kosovo.[30] It was a typical NSIAD product: extremely narrow focus, woefully incomplete data collection, feeble data analysis, dependence on DoD for drawing conclusions, and hardly any indication that anything of real significance went wrong when the Army tried and failed to employ its primary attack helicopter in a major combat operation.*

Congressional Non-Reaction

Except for Senator Pryor, who skilfully maneuvered DoD into releasing the detailed version of GAO's Desert Storm report in 1997, almost no other Member of Congress showed any awareness that the GAO report even existed.† Copies of the study were sent to the relevant congressional committees.

---

*As I write this preface, GAO was processing a second report on the air campaign over Kosovo. One individual who read a draft of this new report commented that it was even weaker than the earlier report on the Apache deployment.

† There are three minor exceptions. Congressman Andy Ireland (R., FL) and Senator Tim Wirth (D., CO) originally requested the study, and Congressman Ireland and his staff evidenced interest in the study as it progressed. However, both congressman Ireland and Senator Wirth left Congress before the study was finished. Also, Congressman John Dingle (D., MI) joined as a later requestor for the study, and his staff asked for and was given a briefing on the study's results.

Just as articles, editorials, and commentary for and against the study were hitting major newspapers throughout the country, a member of the report team contacted the House and Senate Committee staffers responsible for tactical aircraft and munitions issues. Yes, they had read about the study in the newspapers; no, they had not read the study itself; they had no time to read a 235 page GAO report. A briefing was offered; it would take as little as 30 minutes. They remained uninterested—all of them.

This seemed bizarre. A GAO report was contradicting huge portions of the conventional wisdom on the Gulf War, the report was fuel for numerous news articles in major newspapers, and it was fodder for feisty commentary for and against. Joining this debate—on either side—would be an opportunity for Congressmen and Senators to get lots of public exposure, which they usually craved. Not only were the congressional staffers not interested in a hearing to evaluate the study, they weren't even interested in a short briefing! What on earth was going on? Three possible explanations come to mind.

GAO: Watchdog or Chihuahua?

The first possible explanation is the contempt that many professional staff in Congress' defense committees hold for much of GAO's work. Given the volume of NSIAD's work, it is surprising how seldom GAO testifies to the Armed Services Committees or the Defense Appropriations Subcommittees. In half a dozen years of observing the Senate's Defense Appropriations Subcommittee holding scores of hearings, I recall, two with GAO as a witness. In the Senate Armed Services Committee, GAO testifies more frequently. The records show that, for example, in the year 2000 GAO testified to that committee nine times. During that year, the Armed Services Committee held over 60 hearings,[31] and NSIAD produced 141 reports on "National Defense."[32] That would appear to mean that just 15 percent of the time GAO is considered a useful witness to hear and that six percent of NSIAD's reports were deemed worthy of testimony to the committee. Not a convincing indicator of respect for Congress' self-appointed investigator, evaluator, and auditor.

Conversations with the staffers on those committees reinforce this impression. GAO and its management are not held in high regard. The work is often regarded as too narrow or marginally relevant, unconvincing, and/or easy to pull apart. When the report seems adequate, some of GAO's senior managers who testify on behalf of GAO do not know the subject matter of the report to respond effectively to critical questions, especially when DoD or other critics feed Senators with unfriendly, detailed questions. In sum, GAO is not regarded as a serious player on most defense issues.*

---

*One area where GAO is regarded with more respect on defense issues is in the area of financial management problems in DoD. This GAO work is not, however, preformed by NSIAD or its successor "teams."

Given the low regard generally accorded to GAO, there would be little reason for most congressional staff to think anything different about this GAO report.[*]

Is the Best News No News?

A second possible explanation for Congress' disinterest in the air campaign report is that it went against the general bias in Congress regarding weapon systems. For years, Members of Congress had been hearing from DoD and advocates of "high tech" (and from campaign contributing manufacturers) that there was a major pay off for expensive, complex weapons in the form of better performance. The myths emanating from Desert Storm about "silver bullets" and "one bomb, one target" reinforced that conventional wisdom and provided validation for profoundly held beliefs. Now, along comes an upstart GAO report that asks Members of Congress to revise their thinking: high cost weapons did not perform measurably better in many respects than low cost ones. The same senior generals, admirals, and top bureaucrats who had assured them of the righteousness of their views either did not know what they were talking about or, if they did, had been misleading. Rather than engage this difficult, if not embarrassing, debate, it was a lot easier to ignore the report. A decision on whether to hold briefings or hearings on this report was a no-brainer for most in Congress: why probe an issue that might result in the embarrassment of the boss, or the embarrassment of the staffer whose advice was not validated by the report?

Lousy Report?

There is a third possibility for Congress' ignoring this report: it was a lousy report and the data behind it is trash and/or the analysis weak. While a prolonged debate is possible, the best way to test the quality of the report is to read it. The reader should judge the report on its own merits.

Conclusions

There are highly positive elements to real technological advances, but there are also often negative consequences DoD, the pundits, and Congress ignore or gloss over. The most obvious negative attribute to contemporary technological advance in military hardware is the ever-higher cost, even though civilian "high tech" often comes at lower cost. The growing cost for military systems means fewer are available.

---

[*] One exchange occurred to indicate that the PEMD Desert Storm air campaign report did, indeed, suffer from NSIAD's overall low reputation. One defense committee staffer was familiar with the dynamics between NSIAD and PEMD inside GAO. When told that the report was a not a NSIAD but instead a PEMD product, he showed immediate recognition of the implications and interest in the study. However, when told more about the study's contents, he responded that it would be a waste of time for him to receive a briefing on the study because his boss would be disturbed by the report's findings about the veracity of contractors' and senior military officers' assertions on the performance of certain weapon systems.

And, because the expensive new equipment is often poorly tested to "save" money, the performance limitations become fully known only when the military is forced to use them in combat. So far, the consequences of keeping ourselves in the dark about just how well U.S. weapons will perform in combat have not been catastrophic. We have been running this string of luck for a long time. But, as shown by our experiences in Vietnam and Mogadishu, just having the high tech advantage and being a superpower does not always save us.

Something Even Worse than Santayana's Condemnation

To truly understand the nature of twenty-first century warfare, it is necessary to accurately understand previous events. Slogans and glossy brochures not only don't help, they impede a profound understanding of past events. Without understanding, what has already happened will mean that our adaptations will be based on illusion, not reality. We will not be just forgetting the past; we will be distorting it. Rather than just repeating past mistakes, we may be inventing new ones.

Shooting the Messenger

The GAO report and its authors suffered the consequences of attempting to better inform decision-makers in Washington, D.C. because they did not want to disturb their belief system. The authors can have some level of satisfaction that their report provided the fodder for considerable media coverage and to some extent impacted the public conventional wisdom about Desert Storm. Yet, ten years after the Persian Gulf War, there appears to have been two "rewards" for the GAO team that wrote this report: 1) their parent organization, the division in GAO that provided the environment and the tools to write a report like this, was abolished with nary a whimper of protest from anyone; and 2) not wanting to hear the message, Washington D.C. chose to ignore the report.

Green Eyeshades' Revenge

That may not be a particularly uplifting denouement to the study, but it is not the end of the story. Our constitutional system is one of "checks and balances." For every pundit happy to ignore the data, there is someone else working away on that data (somewhere—maybe even at GAO), trying to make sense of it; they will find a way to lay it before the a public. For every politician asleep at the switch and bureaucrat pushing management-preferred agendas, the real world has the nasty habit of biting them in the butt. If we are lucky, our ignoring the lessons of history will only cost money. We'll see.

How Best to Read this report

Don't read the not-very-short executive summary on pages 14-42. It's long, too vague, and too bereft of data to give you the best information.

If you are looking for GAO's data and analysis on a specific issue, turn first to the table of contents on pages 6-8 and review what's in the various appendices, especially Appendices II, III, IV, V, and XI. Find what interests you and go directly to those pages.

If you want a GAO-style narrative on the air campaign, start at Appendix II on page 60 and proceed to the end. If you find yourself in the middle a discussion of something that strikes you as pointless or boring, skip it and press on to the next subheading that recaptures your interest. While there are a number of pedantic sections, subheadings are very frequent, and it shouldn't require you to turn many pages before you stop and find something that interests you.

When you are finished, you will understand why you may have never heard of this report or if you have, why you were told it was "dangerous." It contradicts not just what DoD would prefer you to think about the performance of its "silver bullets" in Desert Storm; it also argues with the way entire Washington D.C. defense community thinks, acts, and spends money. If you come away with anything from this report, I would only ask that the next time you hear a senior military leader stand in front of the cameras and describe in glowing flames how well his services' equipment performed, just say to him (or think to yourself), "That's all very interesting, general, but show us the data."

by Spartacus[*]

---

[*] The author is a national security analyst who has worked on Capitol Hill and for GAO for 30 years. He has worked in this capacity for both Democrats and Republicans and for liberals, moderates, and conservatives. In order to avoid any association between his views and analysis expressed here and the author's current employer, he has used a pseudonym.

End Notes

[1] "Reaching Globally, Reaching Powerfully: The United States Air Force in the Gulf War," US Air Force, September 1991, page 55.

[2] "We Own the Night," <u>Lockheed Horizons</u>, Issue 30, May 1992, page 57.

[3] Testimony of CINCCENTAF, Department of Defense Appropriations for 1992, hearings of the Subcommittee on Defense of the Committee on Appropriations, House of Representatives, April 30, 1991, page 468.

[4] While numerous sources asserted the achievement of "one bomb, one target" effectiveness, prominent claimants included defense manufacturers, such as Texas Instruments, which produced LGBs, and Lockheed, which produced the F-117. Such claims were made in both advertisements and in annual ("10-K") reports to stock holders.

[5] Author's recollection of BBC TV reporting from Baghdad during the war, as rebroadcast by CNN.

[6] An assertion in "Tomahawk: A Total Weapons System," a brochure produced by McDonnell-Douglas.

[7] See <u>Conduct of the Persian Gulf War, Final Report to Congress pursuant to Title V of the Persian Gulf Conflict Supplemental Authorization and Personnel Benefits Act of 1991</u>, Appendix T, "Performance of Selected Weapons Systems," April 1992, page T-201.

[8] Joint Chiefs of Staff estimate from April, 1991, according to Joint CNA/DIA Research Memorandum 93-49, <u>TLAM Performance During Operation Desert Storm: Assessment of Physical and Functional Damage to the TLAM Aimpoints</u>, Vol. I: Overview and Methodology, March 1994, page 21.

[9] "'Smart Weapons Were Overrated, Study Concludes," <u>New York Times</u>, July 9, 1996.

[10] "Debate Swirls Around F-117," <u>Defense News</u>, September 23-29, 1996.

[11] "GAO Study Takes Aim At Gulf War Weapons," <u>Washington Post</u>, July 1, 1997.

[12] Letter of Deputy Assistant Secretary of Defense Requirements and Plans, Office of the Assistant Secretary of Defense, Strategy and Requirement, to Acting Assistant Comptroller General, Program Evaluation and Methodology Division, General Accounting Office, dated September 4, 1996, page 1.

[13] See first released GAO report, "Operation Desert Storm: Evaluation of the Air War," GAO/PEMD-96-10, page 5.

[14] See "Senator Calls for Declassification of GAO Data on Gulf War Munitions," Inside the Air Force, July 12, 1996, pages 10-11; and "DoD Officials Promise Secrecy Review of Gulf War Report," Defense Week, July 15, 1996, page 2.

[15] See advertisements in Aviation Week and Space Technology in 1991: e.g: "TI Paveway III: One Target, One Bomb," cited on page 145 of report. For pundit articles, see Aerospace America, October 1994 and "Defense in an Age of Hope," by former Secretary of Defense William Perry, Foreign Affairs, November/December, 1996, page 77-78.

[16] Letter of Deputy Assistant Secretary of Defense, Requirements and Plans, DoD to Acting Assistant Comptroller General, Program Evaluation and Methodology Division, GAO, dated 4 September 1996, page 2.

[17] Letter of the Under Secretary of Defense, Acquisition and Technology, DoD to Assistant Comptroller General, National Security and International Affairs Programs, GAO, dated July 29, 1996, page 3.

[18] See "One Target, One Weapon," Paul Kaminski, Air Force Magazine, August 1996, page 80, and Mr. Kaminski's May 2, 1996 Ira C. Eager Distinguished Lecture on National Defense Policy at the US Air Force Academy, Colorado Springs, CO.

[19] "High-tech military boondoggles won't protect America," Milwaukee Journal Sentinel, July 14, 1996.

[20] "The Aliens Are Coming! Pass the Cash," Los Angeles Times, July 16, 1996.

[21] "Weapons hype meets the truth of real combat," New York Daily News, November 3, 1997.

[22] "Stealth, Lies, and Videotape," New York Times, July 14, 1996, and "Get Smarter on Smart Weapons," New York Times, July 11, 1996.

[23] "'Smart' Bombs, Smart Choices," Washington Post, July 15, 1996.

[24] "Dumbing down defense debates," Washington Times, July 19, 1996.

[25] "A Bad Rap on High Tech," Washington Post, July 16, 1996.

[26] "Operation Desert Storm: Evaluation of the Air War," GAO/PEMD-96-10 (July 2, 1996): 4

[27] Ibid., page 12.

[28] See "Cuts Kill GAO Evaluation Division," Roll Call, July 18, 1996.

[29] See correspondence between Congressman Dennis J. Kucinich and GAO Comptroller General David Walker, dated September 28, 1999, November 16, 1999, and December 8, 1999.

[30] See "Kosovo Air Operations: Army Resolving Lessons Learned Regarding the Apache Helicopter," GAO-01-401, March 2001.

[31] Counted from the Senate Armed Services Committee's website at http://www.senate.gov/~armed_services/.

[32] See GAO's website at http://www.gao.gov/.

United States
General Accounting Office
Washington, D.C. 20548

National Security and
International Affairs Division

B-276599

June 12, 1997

The Honorable John D. Dingell
Ranking Minority Member
Committee on Commerce
House of Representatives

Dear Mr. Dingell:

This report is the unclassified version of a classified report that we issued in July 1996 on the Operation Desert Storm air campaign.[1] At your request, the Department of Defense (DOD) reevaluated the security classification of the original report, and as a result, about 85 percent of the material originally determined to be classified has subsequently been determined to be unclassified and is presented in this report. The data and findings in this report address (1) the use and performance of aircraft, munitions, and missiles employed during the air campaign; (2) the validity of DOD and manufacturer claims about weapon systems' performance, particularly those systems utilizing advanced technology; (3) the relationship between cost and performance of weapon systems; and (4) the extent that Desert Storm air campaign objectives were met.

The long-standing DOD and manufacturer claims about weapon performance can now be contrasted with some of our findings. For example, (1) the F-117 bomb hit rate ranged between 41 and 60 percent—which is considered to be highly effective, but is still less than the 80-percent hit rate reported after the war by DOD, the Air Force, and the primary contractor (see pp. 125-132); (2) DOD's initially reported 98-percent success rate for Tomahawk land attack missile launches did not accurately reflect the system's effectiveness (see pp. 139-143); (3) the claim by DOD and contractors of a one-target, one-bomb capability for laser-guided munitions was not demonstrated in the air campaign where, on average, 11 tons of guided and 44 tons of unguided munitions were delivered on each successfully destroyed target (with averages ranging from 0.8 to 43.9 tons of guided and 6.7 to 152.6 tons of unguided munitions delivered across the 12 target categories—see p. 117); and, (4) the all-weather and adverse-weather sensors designed to identify targets and guide weapons were either less capable than DOD reported or incapable when employed at increasing altitudes or in the presence of clouds, smoke, dust, or high humidity (see pp. 78-82).

---

[1]In July 1996, we also issued a report entitled Operation Desert Storm: Evaluation of the Air War (GAO/PEMD-96-10), that set forth our unclassified summary, conclusions, and recommendations.

B-276599

The report also now includes analyses of associations between weapon systems and target outcomes (see pp. 112-118); selected manufacturers' claims about product performance in Desert Storm (see pp. 143-146); the air campaign's effectiveness in achieving strategic objectives (see pp. 148-159); and the costs and performance of aircraft and munitions used during the campaign (see pp. 162-193). Although some initial claims of accuracy and effectiveness of these weapon systems were exaggerated, their performance led, in part, to perhaps the most successful war fought by the United States in the 20th century. And though some claims for some advanced systems could not be verified, their performance in combat may well have been unprecedented.

While this report reveals findings that were not previously publicly available, our analyses of the air campaign's success against nuclear, biological, and chemical (NBC) targets predates recent revelations regarding suspected locations and confirmed releases of chemical warfare material during and immediately after the campaign. In our report, we indicate that available bomb damage assessments during the war concluded that 16 of 21 sites categorized by Gulf War planners as NBC facilities had been successfully destroyed. However, information compiled by the United Nations Special Commission (UNSCOM) since the end of Desert Storm reveals that the number of suspected NBC targets identified by U.S. planners, both prior to and during the campaign, did not fully encompass all the possible NBC targets in Iraq.[2] Thus, the number of NBC targets discussed in the report is less than the actual suspected because (1) target categorizations were based on the predominate activity at the facility that may not have been NBC-related (i.e., a major air base or conventional weapons storage depot may have contained a single chemical or biological weapons storage bunker); (2) target categorizations were inconsistent across agencies; and (3) the intelligence community did not identify all NBC-related facilities.

UNSCOM has conducted investigations at a large number of facilities in Iraq, including a majority of the facilities suspected by U.S. authorities as being

---

[2]In the CIA Report on Intelligence Related to Gulf War Illnesses, dated 2 August 1996, the number of sites suspected to have been connected to Iraq's chemical warfare program alone, totaled 34 (p. 6). UNSCOM has conducted chemical weapons-related inspections at over 60 locations and investigations continue.

B-276599

NBC-related.[3] With three exceptions, Khamisiyah, Muhammadiyat, and Al Muthanna, UNSCOM found no evidence that chemical or biological weapons were present during the campaign; and only at Muhammadiyat and Al Muthana did UNSCOM find evidence that would lead them to conclude that chemical or biological weapons were released as a result of coalition bombing. Post-war intelligence compiled by the Central Intelligence Agency indicates some releases of chemicals at Muhammadiyat and Al Muthanna; however, both are in remote areas west of Baghdad, and each is over 400 kilometers north of the Saudi Arabian border and the nearest coalition base. Regarding the few suspected chemical weapon sites that have not yet been inspected by UNSCOM, we have been able to determine that each was attacked by coalition aircraft during Desert Storm and that one site is located within the Kuwait Theater of Operations in closer proximity to the border, where coalition ground forces were located.[4] However, we have yet to learn why these facilities have not been investigated. We are seeking additional information on these sites.

As agreed with your office, unless you publicly announce its contents earlier, we plan no further distribution of this report until 15 days from its issue date. At that time, we will send copies to the Chairmen and Ranking Minority Members of the Senate and House Committees on Appropriations and their respective Subcommittees on National Security and Defense; Senate Committee on Governmental Affairs; House Committee on Government Reform and Oversight; and Senate and House Committees on the Budget. We will also make copies available to others upon request.

---

[3] UNSCOM and the International Atomic Energy Agency have had responsibility to investigate Iraq's NBC weapons programs since the cease-fire and the number of suspected chemical weapons-related facilities investigated by UNSCOM far exceeds the number of sites originally suspected (or attacked) by the United States. For example, Khamisiyah, which was first inspected by UNSCOM in October 1991, was not identified as an NBC air campaign target during the war and, thus, is not among the 21 NBC sites evaluated in our report.

[4] The Kuwait Theater of Operations is generally defined as Kuwait and Iraq below 31 degrees north latitude.

B-276599

This report was prepared under the direction of Kwai-Cheung Chan, Director, Special Studies and Evaluation, who may be reached on (202) 512-3092 if you or your staff have any questions. Other major contributors are listed in appendix XIII.

Sincerely yours,

Henry L. Hinton, Jr.
Assistant Comptroller General

Contents

Letter		1
Original Letter		14
Appendix I Scope and Methodology		44
	Scope	44
	Methodology	45
	Strengths and Limitations	58
Appendix II The Use of Aircraft and Munitions in the Air Campaign		60
	Operating Conditions: Time, Environment, and Enemy Capability	60
	Air-to-Ground Weapon Systems: Planned Versus Actual Use	64
	Combat Operations Support	82
	Aircraft Survivability	92
	Summary	107
Appendix III Aircraft and Munition Effectiveness in Desert Storm		110
	Effectiveness Data Availability	111
	Associations Between Weapon Systems and Outcomes	112
	Target Accuracy and Effectiveness as a Function of Aircraft and Munition Type	118
	LGB Accuracy	122
	F-117 Effectiveness Claims	125
	TLAM Effectiveness Claims	139
	Weapon System Manufacturers' Claims	143
	Air Campaign Effectiveness Against Mobile Targets	146
	Air Campaign Effectiveness in Achieving Strategic Objectives	148
	Summary	159
Appendix IV Cost and Performance of the Aircraft and Munitions in Desert Storm		162
	Cost and Performance of Aircraft	162
	Cost and Effectiveness of Munitions	177
	Summary	192

Appendix V
Operation Desert Storm Objectives

	194
Desert Storm Campaign Objectives	194
Discussion	200
Summary	203

Appendix VI
Basic Structure of the Iraqi Integrated Air Defense System

	205
Evidence on IADS Capabilities	205

Appendix VII
Pre-Desert Storm Missions and Actual Use

207

Appendix VIII
Weight of Effort and Type of Effort Analysis

	210
WOE Platform Comparisons	210
TOE Platform Comparisons	217

Appendix IX
Target Sensor Technologies

	221
Radar	221
Electro-optical	221
Infrared	221
Other Sensor Systems	221

Appendix X
Combat Support Platforms

	223
Reconnaissance Platforms	223
Surveillance Platforms	223
Electronic Combat Platforms	223
ABCCC	224

Contents

Appendix XI The Experience of F-16s and F-117s at the Baghdad Nuclear Research Facility	225
Appendix XII Comments From the Department of Defense	227
Appendix XIII Major Contributors to This Report	233
Glossary	234

Tables		
	Table 1: Manufacturers' Statements About Product Performance Compared to Our Findings	26
	Table I.1: Twelve Strategic Target Categories in the Desert Storm Air Campaign	45
	Table I.2: Organizations We Contacted and Their Locations	47
	Table I.3: AIF Target Categories and Target Types	49
	Table I.4: Definition of Composite Variables for WOE and TOE Measures	52
	Table I.5: Examples of Phase III BDA and Our FS or NFS Assessments	57
	Table II.1: Air-to-Ground Combat Mission Categories Attributed to Selected Aircraft Before Desert Storm Versus Those Actually Performed	65
	Table II.2: Number and Percent of Coalition "Shooter" Aircraft	75
	Table II.3: Coverage of Strategic Target Categories, by Aircraft Type	77
	Table II.4: BE-Numbered Targets Assigned Exclusively to One Type of Aircraft	78

Contents

Table II.5: Official Public Descriptions of the Prewar and Desert Storm Capabilities of Air-to-Ground Aircraft Sensors	79
Table II.6: Percent of Total Known Refueling Events for Selected Air-to-Ground Platforms	84
Table II.7: Type of Coalition Aircraft Lost or Damaged and Attributed Cause	94
Table II.8: Desert Storm Aircraft Casualty Rates	100
Table II.9: Aircraft Casualties in Day and Night	101
Table II.10: Number and Location of Iraqi SAM Batteries	102
Table III.1: Number of Targets Assessed as Fully Successful and Not Fully Successful by Platform	113
Table III.2: Number of FS and NFS Targets by Platform and Target Type	114
Table III.3: Average Guided and Unguided Tonnage Per BE by Outcome by Category	117
Table III.4: F-117 and F-111F Strike Results on 49 Common Targets	119
Table III.5: F-117 and F-111F Strike Results on 22 Common Targets With GBU-10 and GBU-12 LGBs	120
Table III.6: Outcomes for Targets Attacked With Only MK-84 Unguided Bombs	121
Table III.7: Outcomes for Targets Attacked With Only MK-84s Delivered by F-16s and F/A-18s	121
Table III.8: List of DMPIs and Identifying Information	123
Table III.9: Reported F-117 Hits Lacking Corroborating Support or in Conflict With Other Available Data	128
Table III.10: Examples of Remarks Indicating Nonsupporting Video	129
Table III.11: Examples of Remarks in Conflict With Reported Hits	130
Table III.12: Failures That Prevented Bombs From Being Dropped on F-117 Primary Strikes	132
Table III.13: 37th TFW Data on Bombs Dropped by F-117s During the First 24 Hours	134
Table III.14: F-117 Hit Rate on Strategic Integrated Air Defense Targets on the First Night	136
Table III.15: TLAM Performance in Desert Storm	142
Table III.16: Manufacturers' Statements About Product Performance Compared to GAO Findings	144
Table III.17: Targets Categorized as Fully Successfully Destroyed and Not Fully Successfully Destroyed	149
Table III.18: Desert Storm Achievement of Key Objectives	150

Contents

	Table IV.1: Cost and Performance of Major U.S. and U.K. Desert Storm Air-to-Ground Aircraft and TLAM	166
	Table IV.2: Desert Shield and Desert Storm Air-Related Ordnance Expenditures by U.S. Forces	178
	Table IV.3: Relative Strengths and Limitations of Guided and Unguided Munitions in Desert Storm	179
	Table IV.4: Unit Cost and Expenditure of Selected Guided and Unguided Munitions in Desert Storm	181
	Table IV.5: Number and Cost of Munitions Expended by Target Category and Success Rating	183
	Table IV.6: Munition Costs Associated With Successfully and Not Fully Successfully Destroyed Targets	186
	Table IV.7: Number and Cost of Munitions Used in Naval Air Attacks on 13 Bridges in Desert Storm	189
	Table IV.8: Munitions Costs to Attack 24 Bridges in Desert Storm	190
	Table V.1: Desert Storm Theater Objectives and Phases	197
	Table V.2: Operational Strategic Summary of the Air Campaign	199
	Table V.3: Target Growth, by Category, From the Initial Instant Thunder Plan to January 15, 1991	201
	Table V.4: Number and Percent of Inventory of U.S. Air-to-Ground Aircraft Deployed to Desert Storm	203
	Table XI.1: Number of Days, Total Aircraft, and Total Bombs Employed Against the Baghdad Nuclear Research Center During Desert Storm	225
Figures	Figure II.1: BE-Numbered Targets Assigned to Aircraft	68
	Figure II.2: Percent of Day and Night Strikes for Selected Aircraft	71
	Figure II.3: Strike Support Missions by Week	87
	Figure II.4: " The Value of Stealth"	89
	Figure II.5: Combat Aircraft Casualties From Radar SAMS	97
	Figure II.6: Daytime Combat Aircraft Casualties From All Threats	98
	Figure II.7: Radar-Guided SAM Locations in the Baghdad Area	103
	Figure II.8: AAA Deployment in Iraq	105
	Figure III.1: Paveway III LGBs Delivered Against Selected Point Targets	124
	Figure VI.1: The Iraqi Air Defense Network	205
	Figure VIII.1: Target Category Strikes, by Platform	211
	Figure VIII.2: Target Category Strikes, by Platform, Excluding KBX Targets	212
	Figure VIII.3: Bombs Delivered, by Platform	213

Contents

Figure VIII.4: Bombs Delivered, by Platform, Excluding KBX Targets		214
Figure VIII.5: Bomb Tonnage Delivered, by Platform		215
Figure VIII.6: Bomb Tonnage Delivered, by Platform, Excluding KBX Targets		216
Figure VIII.7: PGM Tonnage Delivered, by Platform		218
Figure VIII.8: Unguided Tonnage Delivered, by Platform		219
Figure VIII.9: Unguided Tonnage Delivered, by Platform, Excluding KBX Targets		220

Abbreviations

AAA	antiaircraft artillery
ABCCC	airborne battlefield command, control, and communications
AC	aircraft
ACTD	Advanced Concept Technology Demonstration
ADOC	air defense operation center
AI	air interdiction
AIF	automated intelligence file
ALCM	air-launched cruise missile
AOB	air order of battle
APC	armored personnel carrier
ATO	air tasking order
ATODAY	air tasking order day
AWACS	airborne warning and control system
BDA	battle damage assessment
BE	basic encyclopedia
BUR	Bottom-Up Review
C^2	command and control
C^3, CCC	command, control, and communications
CALCM	conventional air-launched cruise missile
CAP	combat air patrol
CAS	close air support
CBU	cluster bomb unit
CENTAF	Air Force Component, Central Command
CENTCOM	Central Command
CEP	circular error probable
CIA	Central Intelligence Agency
CINC	commander in chief
CNA	Center for Naval Analyses
COG	center of gravity
CSAR	combat search and rescue

Contents

CW	continuous wave
D-day	first day of Operation Desert Storm (17 January 1991)
DAISUM	daily intelligence summary
DAWMS	Deep Attack/Weapons Mix Study
DCA	defensive counterair
DIA	Defense Intelligence Agency
DLIR	downward-looking infrared
DMA	Defense Mapping Agency
DMPI	desired mean point of impact
DOD	Department of Defense
DS	Desert Storm
DSCS	Defense Satellite Communication System
DSMAC	Digital Scene Matching Area Correlator
ELE	electrical facilities
EO	electro-optical
EW	electronic warfare
FLIR	forward-looking infrared
FOV	field of view
FS	fully successful
FSTC	Foreign Science and Technology Center
G-day	first day of the ground campaign (24 February 1991)
GBU	guided-bomb unit
GOB	ground order of battle
GPS	global positioning system
GVC	government centers
GWAPS	Gulf War Air Power Survey
HARM	high-speed anti-radiation missile
IADS	integrated air defense system
IDA	Institute for Defense Analyses
IFF	identification of friend or foe
IOC	intercept operations center
IR	infrared
JCS	Joint Chiefs of Staff
JEWC	Joint Electronic Warfare Center
JMEM	Joint Munitions Effectiveness Manual
JMO	joint maritime operations
JSTARS	Joint Surveillance Target Attack Radar System
KBX	kill box
KTO	Kuwait theater of operations
LANTIRN	low-altitude navigation and targeting infrared for night
LGB	laser-guided bomb

Contents

LOC	lines of communication
MAP	Master Attack Plan
MIB	military industrial base
MTL	Master Target List
NAV	naval
NBC	nuclear, biological, and chemical
NFS	not fully successful
NMAC	near midair collision
OCA	offensive counterair
OIL	oil refining, storage, and distribution
OPORD	operation order
PD	probability of destruction
PGM	precision-guided munition
P(k)	probability of kill
POL	petroleum, oil, and lubricants
PWD	programmed warhead detonation
RCS	radar cross-section
RG	Republican Guard
RGFC	Republican Guard Forces Command
RP	reporting post
SAD	strategic air defense
SAM	surface-to-air missile
SCAP	surface combat air patrol
SCU	Scud missile
SEAD	suppression of enemy air defenses
SOC	sector operations center
SOF	special operations forces
SPEAR	Strike Projection Evaluation and Anti-Air Research
SSPH	single-shot probability of hit
TALD	tactical air-launched decoy
TERCOM	Terrain Contour Matching
TFW	tactical fighter wing
TLAM	Tomahawk land attack missile
TOE	type of effort
TOT	time on target
TRAM	target recognition and attack multisensor
USAF	U.S. Air Force
WOE	weight of effort

United States
General Accounting Office
Washington, D.C. 20548

**Program Evaluation and
Methodology Division**

B-260509

July 2, 1996

The Honorable David Pryor
Committee on Governmental Affairs
United States Senate

The Honorable John D. Dingell
Ranking Minority Member
Committee on Commerce
House of Representatives

This report responds to your request that we comprehensively evaluate the use and effectiveness of the various aircraft, munitions, and other weapon systems used in the victorious air campaign in Operation Desert Storm in order to aid the Congress in future procurement decisions.

Over 5 years ago, the United States and its coalition allies successfully forced Iraq out of Kuwait. The performance of aircraft and their munitions, cruise missiles, and other air campaign systems in Desert Storm continues to be relevant today as the basis for significant procurement and force sizing decisions. For example, the Department of Defense (DOD) Report on the Bottom-Up Review (BUR) explicitly cited the effectiveness of advanced weapons used in Desert Storm—including laser-guided bombs (LGB) and stealth aircraft—as shaping the BUR recommendations on weapons procurement.[1]

Background

Operation Desert Storm was primarily a sustained 43-day air campaign by the United States and its allies against Iraq between January 17, 1991, and February 28, 1991. It was the first large employment of U.S. air power since the Vietnam war, and by some measures (particularly the low number of U.S. casualties and the short duration of the campaign), it was perhaps the most successful war fought by the United States in the 20th century. The main ground campaign occupied only the final 100 hours of the war.

The air campaign involved nearly every type of fixed-wing aircraft in the U.S. inventory, flying about 40,000 air-to-ground and 50,000 support sorties.[2] Approximately 1,600 U.S. combat aircraft were deployed by the end of the war. By historical standards, the intensity of the air campaign

---

[1]Department of Defense, Report on the Bottom-Up Review (Washington, D.C.: Oct. 1993), p. 18.

[2]Support sorties comprised missions such as refueling, electronic jamming, and combat air patrol.

B-260509

was substantial. The U.S. bomb tonnage dropped per day was equivalent to 85 percent of the average daily bomb tonnage dropped by the United States on Germany and Japan during the course of World War II.

Operation Desert Storm provided a valuable opportunity to assess the performance of U.S. combat aircraft and munitions systems under actual combat conditions. Unlike operational tests or small-scale hostilities, the air campaign involved a very large number of conventional systems from all four services used in tandem, which permits potentially meaningful cross-system comparisons. The combat data in this report can be seen as an extension of the performance data generated by DOD's operational test and evaluation programs that we have previously reviewed.[3]

Objectives, Scope, Methodology

To respond to your questions about the effectiveness of the air campaign; the performance of individual weapon systems; the accuracy of contractor claims, particularly in regard to stealth technology and the F-117; and the relationship between the cost of weapon systems and their performance and contributions to the success of the air campaign, we established the following report objectives.

1. Determine the use, performance, and effectiveness of individual weapon systems in pursuit of Desert Storm's objectives and, in particular, the extent to which the data from the conflict support the claims that DOD and weapon contractors have made about weapon system performance.

2. Describe the relationship between cost and performance for the weapon systems employed.

3. Identify the degree to which the goals of Desert Storm were achieved by air power.

4. Identify the key factors aiding or inhibiting the effectiveness of air power.

5. Identify the contributions and limitations of advanced technologies to the accomplishments of the air campaign.

---

[3]See Weapons Acquisition: Low-Rate Initial Production Used to Buy Weapon Systems Prematurely (GAO/NSIAD-95-18, Nov. 21, 1994); Weapons Acquisition: A Rare Opportunity for Lasting Change (GAO/NSIAD-93-15, Dec. 1992); Weapons Testing: Quality of DOD Operational Testing and Reporting (GAO/PEMD-88-32BR, July 26, 1988); Live Fire Testing: Evaluating DOD's Programs (GAO/PEMD-87-17, Aug. 17, 1987); and How Well Do the Military Services Perform Jointly in Combat? DOD's Joint Test and Evaluation Program Provides Few Credible Answers (GAO/PEMD-84-3, Feb. 22, 1984).

B-260509

6. Determine whether the unique conditions of Desert Storm limit the lessons learned.

We compared the performance of nine fixed-wing air-to-ground aircraft and assessed several major guided and unguided bombs and missiles used in the war, including Tomahawk land attack (cruise) missiles (TLAM), laser-guided bombs (LGB), Maverick missiles, and unitary unguided bombs.[4] The primary focus of our analysis was on the use of these weapon systems in missions against targets that war planners had identified as strategic.[5]

Historically, studies of air power have articulated differing points of view on the relative merits of focusing air attacks on targets deemed to be strategic (such as government leadership, military industry, and electrical generation) and focusing them on tactical targets (such as frontline armor and artillery). These contending points of view have been debated in many official and unofficial sources.[6] In this study, we did not directly address this debate because data and other limitations (discussed below) did not permit a rigorous analysis of whether attacks against strategic targets contributed more to the success of Desert Storm than attacks against tactical targets.

A primary goal of our work was to cross-validate the best available data on aircraft and weapon system performance, both qualitative and quantitative, to test for consistency, accuracy, and reliability. We collected and analyzed data from a broad range of sources, including the major DOD databases that document the strike histories of the war and cumulative damage to targets; numerous after-action and lessons-learned reports from military units that participated in the war; intelligence reports; analyses performed by DOD contractors; historical accounts of the war from the media and other published literature; and interviews with participants,

---

[4]The aircraft included the A-6E, A-10, B-52, F-16, F-15E, F/A-18, F-111F, and F-117 from the U.S. air forces, as well as the British GR-1. The AV-8B, A-7, and B-1B were not included. Both the AV-8B and the A-7 were excluded because of their relatively few strikes against strategic targets. The B-1B did not participate in the campaign because munitions limitations, engine problems, inadequate crew training, and electronic warfare deficiencies severely hampered its conventional capabilities.

[5]Campaign planners categorized all strategic targets into 1 of 12 target sets: command, control, and communication (C^3); electrical (ELE); government centers or leadership (GVC); lines of communication (LOC); military industrial base (MIB); naval (NAV); nuclear, biological, and chemical (NBC); offensive counterair (OCA); oil refining, storage, and distribution (OIL); Republican Guard (RG) or ground order of battle (GOB); surface-to-air missile (SAM); and Scud missile (SCU).

[6]Examples include Edward C. Mann, III, Thunder and Lightning (Maxwell Air Force Base, Ala.: Air University Press, Apr. 1995); John A. Warden, III, The Air Campaign (Washington, D.C.: Pergamon-Brassey's, 1989); and Richard T. Reynolds, Heart of the Storm: The Genesis of the Air Campaign Against Iraq (Maxwell Air Force Base, Ala.: Air University Press, Apr. 1995).

B-260509

including more than 100 Desert Storm pilots and key individuals in the planning and execution of the war.[7] And after we collected and analyzed the air campaign information, we interviewed DOD, Joint Chiefs of Staff (JCS), and service representatives and reviewed plans for the acquisition and use of weapon systems in future campaigns to observe how the lessons learned from Desert Storm have been applied.

To compare the nature and magnitude of the power that Operation Desert Storm employed against strategic targets to the nature of outcomes, we analyzed two databases—the "Missions" database generated by the Air Force's Gulf War Air Power Survey (GWAPS) research group to assess inputs and the Defense Intelligence Agency's (DIA) phase III battle damage assessment (BDA) reports to assess outcomes. While this methodology has limitations, no other study of Desert Storm has produced the target-specific, input-outcome data that can be derived by merging these databases.

The data we analyzed in this report constitute the best information collected during the war.[8] We focused our analyses on data available to commanders during the war—information they used to execute the air campaign. These data also provided the basis for many of the postwar DOD and manufacturer assessments of aircraft and weapon system performance during Desert Storm.[9]

Data Limitations

The best available data did not permit us to either (1) make a comprehensive system-by-system quantitative comparison of aircraft and weapon effectiveness or (2) validate some of the key performance claims for certain weapon systems from the war. However, we were able to compare aircraft and munition performance in Desert Storm using a combination of quantitative and qualitative data. There are major

---

[7] We interviewed pilots representing each type of aircraft evaluated, with the exception of British Tornados. The British government denied our requests to interview British pilots who had flown in Desert Storm.

[8] We also sought data and analyses collected and conducted after the war. We used these data to check the reliability and validity of information collected earlier.

[9] Constraints in the reliability and completeness of some important portions of the data imposed limitations on our analysis of the air campaign. For example, relating specific types of aircraft or munitions to target outcomes was problematic because BDA reports provided a comprehensive compilation of damage on strategic targets at given times during the campaign—not necessarily after each strike against the targets. Therefore, we balanced data limitations, to the extent possible, through qualitative analyses of systems, based on the diverse sources cited above. For example, we compared claims made for system performance and contributions to what was supportable given all the available data, both quantitative and qualitative. (See app. I for additional information on the study methodology and the strengths and limitations of the data.)

B-260509

limitations in the available data pertaining to the effects of aircraft and munitions on targets. At the same time, DOD successfully collected a large amount of data across a wide range of issues, including weapon use, aircraft survivability, sortie rates, and support needs. With the caveats stated above, these data permitted us to analyze aircraft and weapon system performance, performance claims, and the effectiveness of air power.[10]

Results in Brief

Air power clearly achieved many of Desert Storm's objectives but fell short of fully achieving others.[11] The available quantitative and qualitative data indicate that air power damage to several major target sets was more limited than DOD's title V report to the Congress stated.[12] These data show clear success against the oil and electrical target categories but less success against Iraqi air defense; command, control, and communications, and lines of communication. Success against nuclear-related, mobile Scud, and RG targets was the least measurable.

The lessons that can be learned from Desert Storm are limited because of the unique conditions, the strike tactics employed by the coalition, the limited Iraqi response, and limited data on weapon system effectiveness. The terrain and climate were generally conducive to air strikes, and the coalition had nearly 6 months to deploy, train, and prepare. The strong likelihood of campaign success enabled U.S. commanders to favor strike tactics that maximized aircraft and pilot survivability rather than weapon system effectiveness. In addition, the Iraqis employed few, if any, electronic countermeasures and presented almost no air-to-air opposition. As a result, Desert Storm did not consistently or rigorously test all the performance parameters of aircraft and weapon systems used in the air

---

[10]See appendix I for an expanded discussion of our methodology. Appendixes II through XI present the analyses in support of our findings. A description of aircraft and munition use is presented in appendix II. Appendix III discusses aircraft and munition performance and effectiveness. Cost and performance of aircraft and munitions are analyzed in appendix IV. The development of air campaign objectives and the Iraqi air defense system are described in appendixes V and VI, respectively. Appendix VII compares the design mission of aircraft with their actual use, while the weight and types of effort expended are summarized in appendix VIII. Supplementary information on target sensor technologies and combat support platforms are presented in appendixes IX and X. Finally, an examination of the employment of the F-16 and F-117 against the Baghdad Nuclear Research Facility is presented in appendix XI.

[11]The initial objectives of the strategic air campaign were to (1) disrupt the Iraqi leadership and command and control; (2) achieve air supremacy; (3) cut supply lines; (4) destroy Iraq's nuclear, biological, and chemical capability; and (5) destroy the Republican Guard. Destroying Scud missiles and mobile launchers became a priority early in the air campaign.

[12]Department of Defense, Conduct of the Persian Gulf War, Final Report to Congress Pursuant to Title V of the Persian Gulf Conflict Supplemental Authorization and Personnel Benefits Act of 1991 (P.L. 102-25), April 1992.

B-260509

campaign. Moreover, as we noted above, data are not available to fully assess the relative or absolute effectiveness of aircraft and weapon systems in the war. This combination of factors limits the lessons of the war that can be reasonably applied to future contingencies.

Many of DOD's and manufacturers' postwar claims about weapon system performance—particularly the F-117, TLAM, and laser-guided bombs—were overstated, misleading, inconsistent with the best available data, or unverifiable.

Aircraft and pilot losses were historically low, partly owing to the use of medium- to high-altitude munition delivery tactics that nonetheless both reduced the accuracy of guided and unguided munitions and hindered target identification and acquisition, because of clouds, dust, smoke, and high humidity. Air power was inhibited by the limited ability of aircraft sensors to identify and acquire targets, the failure to gather intelligence on critical targets, and the inability to collect and disseminate BDA in a timely manner. Similarly, the contributions of guided weaponry incorporating advanced technologies and their delivery platforms were limited because the cooperative operating conditions they require were not consistently encountered.

DOD did not prominently emphasize a variety of systems as factors in the success of the air campaign. The important contributions of stealth and laser-guided bombs were emphasized as was the need for more and better BDA; less attention was paid to the significant contributions of less-sophisticated systems and the performance of critical tasks such as the identification and acquisition of targets. For example, more than is generally understood, the air campaign was aided by relatively older and less technologically advanced weapon systems and combat support aircraft, such as unguided bombs, the B-52, the A-10, refueling tankers, and electronic jammer aircraft. There was no apparent link between the cost of aircraft and munitions, whether high or low, and their performance in Desert Storm.

After our analysis of the air campaign, we performed a review of the actions taken by DOD to address the lessons learned from our findings. While we found that several lessons were being addressed by DOD, we also found that others have not been. The lessons that have not been fully or appropriately addressed are the subject of three recommendations at the conclusion of this letter.

Principal Findings

Use, Performance, and Effectiveness of Aircraft and Weapon Systems

Aircraft and Weapon Systems Used as Designed

In general, the actual use of aircraft and weapon systems in the conflict was consistent with their stated prewar capabilities. (App. II compares in detail the combat mission categories attributed to each aircraft before Desert Storm and those actually performed during the campaign.) Most targets were attacked by several types of aircraft or weapon systems. However, from strike data and pilot interviews, we did find that certain aircraft were somewhat preferred in certain target categories. The F-117 was the preferred platform against fixed, often high-value C^3, leadership, and NBC targets; against naval targets, the A-6E and F/A-18 were preferred; and against fixed Scud missile targets, the F-15E. (The distribution of strikes by each type of aircraft across each of the strategic target categories is discussed in app. II.)

Support aircraft, including refueling tankers, airborne intelligence-gathering aircraft, reconnaissance aircraft, and strike support aircraft like the F-4G, F-15C, EF-111, and EA-6B flew more than 50,000 sorties and were instrumental in the successful execution of the air campaign. Each type of strike aircraft, conventional and stealthy, received support—such as jamming and refueling—although not necessarily on each mission. (See app. II for a discussion of the support provided to both conventional and stealth aircraft.)

Aircraft Survivability Enhanced by Tactics

The aircraft casualty rate (that is, aircraft DOD identified as lost to Iraqi action or damaged in combat) for the aircraft we reviewed was 1.7 aircraft per 1,000 strikes. This rate was very low compared to planners' expectations and historic experience. The combination in the first week of the war of a ban on low-level deliveries for most aircraft and a successful effort to suppress enemy air defenses (SEAD) that greatly degraded radar surface-to-air (SAM) missiles and the Iraqi integrated air defense system (IADS) resulted in a reduction in the average number of aircraft casualties per day from 6.2 during the first 5 days to about 1.5 for the remaining 38 days of the campaign. If the aircraft combat casualty rate for the first 5 days had continued throughout the war, a total of about 267 coalition aircraft would have been casualties. Avoiding low altitudes, 48 aircraft were actually damaged in combat during the entire war, and an additional 38 were combat losses.

The attrition rate (including both loss and damage) of all combat aircraft was especially low when they flew at medium and high altitudes and at night. For example, only one-third of the Air Force casualties occurred above 12,000 feet, and only one-quarter of the coalition aircraft casualties occurred at night. The attrition rate at low altitudes was notably higher because of the continuing presence of antiaircraft artillery (AAA) and portable infrared (IR) SAMs—systems that are also generally less effective at night. Nonetheless, AAA and IR SAMs, perceived before the campaign to be lesser threats than radar-guided SAMs, were responsible for four times more casualties than radar SAMs. (See app. II for additional information and analysis on aircraft losses and damage.)

One of the stated advantages of stealth technology is that it enhances survivability, and in Desert Storm, the stealthy F-117 was the only aircraft type to incur neither losses nor damage. However, these aircraft recorded fewer sorties than any other air-to-ground platform and flew exclusively at night and at medium altitudes—an operating environment in which the fewest casualties occurred among all types of aircraft.[13] Moreover, given the overall casualty rate of 1.7 per 1,000 strikes, the most probable number of losses for any aircraft, stealthy or conventional, flying the same number of missions as the F-117 would have been zero. (See app. II for more information on the tactics and support used by F-117s to minimize their exposure to air defense threats.)

Guided and Unguided Munitions Revealed Strengths and Weaknesses

While higher altitude deliveries clearly reduced aircraft casualties, they also caused target location and identification problems for guided munitions and exposed unguided bombs to uncontrollable factors such as wind. Medium- and high-altitude tactics also increased the exposure of aircraft to clouds, haze, smoke, and high humidity, thereby impeding IR and electro-optical (EO) sensors and laser designators for LGBs. These higher altitude tactics also reduced target sensor resolution and the ability of pilots to discern the precise nature of some of the targets they were attacking. While pilots and planners reported that unguided bombs were substantially less accurate and target discrimination problems were sometimes severe, these unguided bombs were employed with radar against area targets in poor weather.

---

[13]For example, nonstealthy aircraft, such as the F-111F and F-16, also suffered no losses when operating at night, and the A-10s experienced neither damage nor losses at night. Each of these three aircraft types flew at least as many night strikes as the F-117.

B-260509

Our interviews with pilots also revealed a mix of concerns about survivability with guided and unguided munitions. Pilots pointed out that in some circumstances, guided munitions permitted the aircraft to "stand off" at relatively long distances from targets and their defenses, which was not possible with unguided munitions, while retaining accuracy. [DELETED] (See apps. II and IV for more pilot views on the use of guided and unguided munitions.)

Guided bombs were the weapon of choice against small, point targets, such as reinforced bunkers, hardened aircraft shelters, and armored vehicles. However, from high altitude, unguided bombs were the weapon of choice against area targets, such as ammunition storage facilities and ground troop emplacements. In addition, pilots, especially of the F-16, remarked to us that they believed their high-altitude unguided bomb deliveries were ineffective against point targets such as tanks.

Over the course of the campaign, the overall ratio of guided-to-unguided munitions delivered (1 to 19) did not significantly change from week to week. This and other data—such as interviews with campaign planners and pilots—indicate that there was no discovery of a systematic failure of either type of munition or any broad effort to change from one type of munition to another. (Patterns of munition use are discussed in app. II.)

Aircraft and Munition Effectiveness Measures Developed

Despite data limitations in some instances, sufficient data were generated to permit a limited analysis of the relative effectiveness of aircraft and munitions. We developed a surrogate effectiveness measure by calculating the ratio of fully successful (FS) to not fully successful (NFS) target outcomes for the set of strategic targets attacked by each type of weapon system.[14] By comparing these ratios, we found that effectiveness varied by type of aircraft and by type of target category attacked. For example, the F-111F participated in a higher ratio of FS versus NFS (3.2:1) than any other aircraft type. The F-117 and the F-16 performed next best and at about the same ratio (1.4:1 and 1.5:1, respectively), and the F-15E and the A-6E both participated in about the same number of successfully attacked targets as

---

[14]Using intelligence gathered during the war from multiple sources, DIA conducted BDA on 357 of the 862 strategic targets in the GWAPS Missions database. We categorized the outcomes for these 357 strategic targets as being either fully successful or not fully successful. We classified a target outcome as FS if the last BDA report on that target stated that the target objective had been met and a restrike was not necessary. We classified all other target outcomes as NFS. DIA produced BDA during the war at the request of U.S. Central Command (CENTCOM). Thus, although the representativeness of the targets assessed by DIA is unknowable, these 357 do represent the set of targets of greatest interest to the commanders in the theater. (See app. I for a more detailed discussion of our BDA classification methodology.)

B-260509

not fully successfully attacked (1.0:1 and 1.1:1 respectively).[15] Only the B-52 and the F/A-18 participated in more NFS target outcomes than FS (with ratios of 0.7:1 and 0.8:1, respectively). Data were not available for the A-10.

The effectiveness of aircraft and munitions in aggregate varied among the strategic target sets.[16] While the attainment of strategic objectives is determined by more than the achievement of individual target objectives, the compilation of individual target objectives achieved was one tool used by commanders during the war to direct the campaign. Among strategic targets for which BDA were available, the percent of targets where objectives were successfully met ranged from a high of 76 percent among (known) nuclear, biological, and chemical (NBC) targets to a low of 25 percent among fixed Scud-related strategic targets.[17]

No consistent pattern indicated that the key to success in target outcomes was the use of either guided or unguided munitions. On average, targets where objectives were successfully achieved received more guided and fewer unguided munitions than targets where objectives were not determined to have been fully achieved. In comparing the use of guided munitions to unguided munitions, on average, approximately 11 tons of guided munitions were delivered against FS targets and over 9 tons were released against NFS targets. Fewer unguided munitions were used against FS targets (44 tons) than NFS (54 tons). However, neither pattern held across all target categories. In four target categories, NFS targets received more tons of guided munitions than successful ones, and in six categories, successful targets received more unguided munitions than the NFS ones. (Our complete analysis of air campaign inputs [that is, numbers and types of aircraft and munitions] and target outcomes [that is, successfully or not fully successfully met target objectives] is presented in app. III.)

Some DOD and Contractor Claims Overstated

As requested, we analyzed numerous Desert Storm performance claims and found from the available data that DOD, individual military services, and manufacturers apparently overstated the Desert Storm performance of certain aircraft and weapon systems that used advanced technologies. We

---

[15]Although the F-111F participated in the highest ratio of FS to NFS target outcomes, the F-117 participated in the highest number of successful outcomes. The F-117 participated in 122 FS outcomes (as well as 87 NFS); the next 2 aircraft with the highest participation in successful outcomes were the F-16, with 67 (and 45 NFS), and the F-111F, with 41 (and 13 NFS).

[16]The number of targets in each strategic target set where the target objectives had been successfully met was used as a measure of the effectiveness of aircraft and munitions in the aggregate. Whether a target objective had been met was determined from the final DIA phase III BDA report written on a target during the campaign.

[17]Less than 15 percent of the nuclear-related facilities were identified before the end of the air campaign.

B-260509

found justification in several instances for the congressional concern that some contractor claims may have been overstated. For example, some key claims concerning the F-117, the TLAM, and LGBs, among other advanced systems, were either misleading, inconsistent with available data, or unverifiable because of the absence of data.

F-117s. DOD's title V report stated that 80 percent of the bombs dropped by F-117s hit their target—an accuracy rate characterized by its primary contractor, Lockheed, as "unprecedented." However, in Desert Storm, (1) approximately one-third of the reported F-117 hits either lacked corroborating support or were in conflict with other available data; (2) the probability of bomb release for a scheduled F-117 mission was only 75 percent; and (3) for these reasons and because of uncertainty in the data, the probability of a target's being hit from a planned F-117 strike in Desert Storm ranged between 41 and 60 percent.[18] Similarly, (1) F-117s were not the only aircraft tasked to targets in and around Baghdad where the defenses were characterized as especially intense, (2) F-117s were neither as effective on the first night of the war as claimed nor solely responsible for the collapse of the Iraqi IADS in the initial hours of the campaign, (3) F-117s did not achieve surprise every night of the campaign, and (4) F-117s occasionally benefited from jammer support aircraft. (Analyses of F-117 bomb hit data are presented in app. III; the ability of F-117 stealth fighters to achieve tactical surprise is discussed in app. II.)

TLAMs. While TLAMs possess an important characteristic distinct from any aircraft in that they risk no pilot in attacking a target, they can be compared to aircraft on measures such as accuracy and survivability. Their accuracy was less than has been implied. The DOD title V report stated that the "launching system success rate was 98 percent." However, this claim is misleading because it implies accuracy that was not realized in Desert Storm. Data compiled by the Center for Naval Analyses (CNA) and DIA in a joint study revealed that only [DELETED] percent of the TLAMs arrived over their intended target area, and only [DELETED] percent actually hit or damaged the intended aimpoint.[19] From [DELETED] TLAMs were apparently lost to defenses or to system navigation flaws. Thus, the

---

[18]A planned strike is the tasking of one or more bombs against a specific aimpoint or target on a scheduled F-117 mission as recorded in the official 37th Tactical Fighter Wing (TFW) Desert Storm database.

[19]This analysis addresses TLAM C and D-I models only; data on the D-II model were excluded because of classification issues.

B-260509

TLAMs experienced an en route loss rate as high as [DELETED] percent.[20] (See app. III for a more detailed analysis of TLAM performance.)

LGBs. The manufacturer of the most advanced LGB guidance system (Paveway III) claimed that it has a "one target, one bomb" capability. DOD officials adopted the phraseology to demonstrate the value of advanced technology in Desert Storm. We sampled Paveway III LGB targets and found that the "one target, one bomb" claim could not be validated, as no fewer than two LGBs were dropped on each target. Six or more were dropped on 20 percent of the targets, eight or more were dropped on 15 percent of the targets, and the overall average dropped was four LGBs per target. And larger numbers of Paveway III and other LGB types were dropped on other targets. Moreover, as noted earlier, an average of approximately 11 tons of guided munitions—most of them LGBs—were used against targets that DIA's phase III BDA messages showed were successfully attacked. This notwithstanding, the number of LGBs required for point targets was clearly less than the number of unguided munitions needed in this and previous wars, especially from medium and high altitudes. (See app. III for our analysis of the "one target, one bomb" claim.)

Table 1 shows some of the discrepancies between the claims and characterizations of manufacturers to the Congress and the public about the actual and expected performance of weapon systems in combat and what the data from Desert Storm support. (App. III contains additional examples of discrepancies between manufacturers' claims and our assessment of weapon system performance in Desert Storm.)

---

[20]Beyond TLAM's [DELETED]-percent miss rate against intended targets, it demonstrated additional problems. The relatively flat, featureless, desert terrain in the theater made it difficult for the Defense Mapping Agency (DMA) to produce usable Terrain Contour Matching (TERCOM) ingress routes, and TLAM demonstrated limitations in range, mission planning, lethality, and effectiveness against hard targets and targets capable of mobility. Since the war, the Navy has developed a Block III variant of the TLAM. Its improvements include the use of Global Positioning System (GPS) in TLAM's guidance system. With GPS, TLAM route planning is not constrained by terrain features, and mission planning time is reduced. However, some experts have expressed the concern that GPS guidance may be vulnerable to jamming. Thus, until system testing and possible modifications demonstrate TLAM Block III resistance to electronic countermeasures, it is possible that the solution to the TERCOM limitations—GPS—may lead to a new potential vulnerability—jamming. Moreover, the Block III variant continues to use the optical Digital Scene Matching Area Correlator (DSMAC), which has various limitations. [DELETED]

B-260509

Table 1: Manufacturers' Statements About Product Performance Compared to Our Findings

Manufacturer	Their statement	Our finding
General Dynamics	"No matter what the [F-16] mission, air-to-air, air-to-ground. No matter what the weather, day or night."	The F-16's delivery of guided munitions, such as Maverick, was impaired and sometimes made impossible by clouds, haze, humidity, smoke, and dust. Only less accurate unguided munitions could be employed in adverse weather using radar.
Grumman	"A-6s . . . [were] detecting, identifying, tracking, and destroying targets in any weather, day or night."	The A-6E FLIR's ability to detect and identify targets was limited by clouds, haze, humidity, smoke, and dust; the laser designator's ability to track targets was similarly limited.[a] Only less accurate unguided munitions could be employed in adverse weather using radar.
Lockheed	"During the first night, 30 F-117s struck 37 high-value targets, inflicting damage that collapsed Saddam Hussein's air defense system and all but eliminated Iraq's ability to wage coordinated war."	On the first night, 21 of the 37 targets to which F-117s were tasked were reported hit; of these, the F-117s missed 40 percent of their air defense targets. BDA on 11 of the F-117 strategic air defense targets confirmed only 2 complete kills. Numerous aircraft, other than the F-117, were involved in suppressing the Iraqi IADS, which did not show a marked falloff in aircraft kills until day five.
Martin Marietta	Aircraft with LANTIRN can "locate and attack targets at night and under other conditions of poor visibility using low-level, high speed tactics."[b]	The LANTIRN can be employed below clouds and weather; however, its ability to find and designate targets through clouds, haze, smoke, dust, and humidity ranged from limited to no capability at all.
McDonnell Douglas	TLAMs "can be launched . . . in any weather."	The TLAM's weather limitation occurs not so much at the launch point but in the target area where the optical [DELETED].
Northrop	The ALQ-135 "proved itself by jamming enemy threat radars"; and was able "to function in virtually any hostile environment."	[DELETED]
Texas Instruments	"TI Paveway III: one target, one bomb."	Of a selected sample of 20 targets attacked by F-117s and F-111Fs with GBU-24s and GBU-27s, no single aimpoint was struck by only 1 LGB—the average was 4, the maximum 10.

[a]Forward-looking infrared (FLIR).

[b]Low-altitude navigation and targeting infrared for night (LANTIRN).

Data Inadequate for Comprehensive Aircraft and Weapon System Comparisons or Validation of Some Claims

The data compiled on campaign inputs (that is, use of weapon systems) and outcomes (that is, battle damage assessments) did not permit a comprehensive effectiveness comparison of aircraft and weapon systems. The most detailed Desert Storm strike history summary is less than complete, does not provide outcome information consistently, and does not provide strike effectiveness information. For example, because data on a large number of A-10 strike events were unclear or contradictory, we

B-260509

found it impossible to reliably analyze and include A-10 strike data.[21] In addition, the most comprehensive BDA database is less than complete, is constrained by technological limitations associated with imagery intelligence, and in most cases did not benefit from ground verifications or damage updates after the war. Because multiple aircraft of different types delivered multiple bombs of different types, often on the same aimpoint, and because damage was often not assessed until after multiple strikes, it is not possible to determine for most targets what effects, if any, can be attributed to a particular aircraft or particular munition. Moreover, DIA conducted BDA on only 357 of the 862 strategic targets in our analysis for which strike data were available. Therefore, many questions on the effectiveness of aircraft and missile strikes could not be answered nor could some effectiveness claims. (For additional information on data limitations, see apps. I and III.)

Relationship Between Cost and Performance

Data limitations did not permit a systematic comparison of weapon system cost and performance; where data were available, our analysis results either were ambiguous or revealed no consistent trends.

Performance of High-Cost Compared to Low-Cost Aircraft

The cost of aircraft was not consistently associated with performance for several measures such as effectiveness, adverse weather capability, sortie rate, payload, and survivability. Survivability was consistently high for all types of aircraft and therefore indistinguishable for high- and low-cost aircraft.[22] The high-cost F-117 stealth fighter and the low-cost A-10 both experienced 100-percent survivability when operating at night. Although the data on some measures were ambiguous (such as survivability and effectiveness), differences in performance or capabilities between high- and low-cost aircraft were evident for some measures.

Depending on the measure one uses, aircraft types with different costs can be characterized as more, less, or equally capable. For example, in Desert Storm, average sortie rates and payloads for different aircraft showed an inverse relationship between cost and performance. Moreover, during the campaign, high- and low-cost aircraft were often employed against the same targets. Nearly 51 percent of the strategic targets attacked by the

---

[21]This was significant for two reasons. First, the data that are available on the A-10 imply that it may have performed even more than the large number of sorties currently attributed to it. Second, because the A-10 was a major participant in the air war and because it performed at relatively high levels on measures such as sortie rate and payload, it would have been useful to be able to compare its success rate, particularly as a low-cost aircraft, against targets to the other aircraft under review.

[22]Survivability depends on numerous factors, including assistance from support aircraft, quantity and quality of air defenses, size of strike package, altitude, and tactics. In Desert Storm, neither cost nor stealth technology was found to be a determinant of survivability.

B-260509

stealthy F-117s were also attacked by less costly, conventional aircraft—such as the F-16, F-15E, and F/A-18. The incompleteness of A-10 strike data prevents our identifying the extent, if any, to which A-10 and F-117 target taskings overlapped. However, according to GWAPS, both aircraft performed over 40 strikes in the C^3, offensive counter (OCA), SAM, and Scud missile (SCU) strategic target categories. In regard to other aircraft, the available strike data reveal that the F-117 and the F-16 were tasked to 78 common targets, the F-117 and the F/A-18C/D to 62, and the F-117 and the F-15E to 49.

Advocates of the F-117 can argue, based on its performance in Desert Storm, that it alone combined the advantages of stealth and LGBs, penetrated the most concentrated enemy defenses at will, permitted confidence in achieving desired bombing results, and had perfect survivability. Advocates of the A-10 can, for example, argue that it, unlike the F-117, operated both day and night; attacked both fixed and mobile targets employing both guided and unguided bombs; and like the F-117, suffered no casualties when operating at night and at medium altitude. Similarly, other aircraft also performed missions the F-117 was unable to and were used successfully—and without losses—against similar types of strategic targets. Each aircraft of the various types has both strengths and limitations; each aircraft can do things the other cannot. Therefore, despite a sharp contrast in program unit costs, we find it inappropriate, given their use, performance, and effectiveness demonstrated in Desert Storm, to rate one more generally "capable" than the other.

We also found no consistent relationship between the program unit cost of aircraft and their relative effectiveness against strategic targets, as measured by the ratio of FS to NFS target outcomes for the set of strategic targets that each type of aircraft attacked. The high-cost F-111F participated in proportionately more successful target outcomes than any other aircraft type, but the low-cost F-16 participated in a higher proportion of successful target outcomes than either the F-117 or the F-15E, both much higher cost aircraft. However, the F-117 and the F-111F, two high-cost, LGB-capable aircraft, ranked first and third in participation against successful targets.[23] (The complete analysis of the performance of low- and high-cost aircraft is presented in app. IV.)

---

[23]Participation by each type of air-to-ground aircraft against targets assessed as FS targets was as follows: F-117 = 122; F-16 = 67, F-111F = 41, A-6E = 37, F/A-18 = 36, F-15E = 28, B-52 = 25, and GR-1 = 21. No data were available for the A-10. TLAM participated against 18 targets assessed as FS. Participation against FS targets by type of aircraft is a function of two factors—the breadth of targets tasked to each type of aircraft (see app. III) and their FS:NFS ratio as presented previously.

Guided Munitions Compared to Unguided Munitions

In Desert Storm, 92 percent of the munitions expended were unguided. On the assumption that this tonnage contributed to the successful outcome of the entire campaign—at a minimum by permitting nearly continuous attacks against both ground force and strategic targets for 38 days—it is evident that the same campaign accomplishments would have been difficult or impossible with aircraft dropping comparatively small numbers of precision-guided munitions (PGM).

Although only 8 percent of the munitions used against planned targets were guided, they represented approximately 84 percent of the total cost of munitions. The difference in cost between various types of guided and unguided munitions was quite substantial: the unguided unitary bombs used in the air campaign cost, on average, $649 each, while the average LGB cost more than $30,000 each—a ratio of 1:47.[24] IR Maverick missiles cost about $102,000 each—a cost ratio to the unguided bombs of 1:157.

Although cost ratios between guided and unguided weapon systems used in Desert Storm can be readily calculated, data on the relative accuracy or effectiveness of the systems in Desert Storm are limited and often ambiguous. For example, guided and unguided munitions were often used against the same targets. Therefore, given shortfalls in BDA, a precise probability of kill for munitions could not be determined in most instances. However, CNA found a small number of bridges where conditions and data enabled an assessment of effectiveness. These bridges had been attacked with either guided or unguided bombs, and BDA had been performed in time to distinguish which type of munitions were successful. While the sample is small and cannot be generalized, these data show that (1) substantially more unguided bombs than either LGBs or Walleyes were required to successfully destroy a bridge and (2) the cost of the guided munitions used was substantially higher.[25] (See app. IV.)

Cost appears to have been a factor in the selection of munitions by Desert Storm campaign commanders. For example, some pilots we interviewed were instructed to use LGBs and Mavericks only against high-value targets such as tanks, armored personnel carriers, and artillery (rather than trucks

---

[24] All munitions costs are presented in 1991 dollars.

[25] Depending on the platforms involved, the delivery of unguided munitions would (in some cases but not all) require more aircraft sorties than would the delivery of guided munitions. This would increase the cost of the unguided delivery, and it would expose a larger number of aircraft to defenses. However, guided munition delivery requires more straight and predictable flight time and greater pilot workload, thus making guided munition aircraft vulnerable to defenses. In short, the cost and survivability trade-offs between guided and unguided munitions are not simple, and the cost difference, if any, can be assessed only on the basis of specific delivery circumstances.

B-260509

or other GOB targets). If they could not hit these targets, they were not able to use these munitions. They could, however, drop unguided bombs on other targets before returning to base. Similarly, the employment of TLAMs was terminated after February 1. GWAPS reported that Gen. H. Norman Schwarzkopf, commander in chief of U.S. Central Command, approved no additional TLAM strikes because either (1) television coverage of daylight strikes in downtown Baghdad proved unacceptable in Washington or (2) their use was deemed too expensive given the TLAM's relatively small warhead and high cost. Thus, this high-cost munition was not used during the latter two-thirds of the war.

Increasing the proportion of the U.S. weapons inventory comprised of high-cost munitions has potential implications for the future effectiveness and employment of air power. First, for a given level of resources, much higher costs limit the number of weapons that can be procured. With fewer weapons, the priority attached to the survival and successful employment of each high-cost bomb is likely to be high, as demonstrated in Desert Storm. Second, Desert Storm revealed that a focus on increasing aircraft and pilot survivability may have reduced mission effectiveness, thereby increasing the number of munitions required to destroy or damage a target. Third, Desert Storm showed that commanders were less willing to permit the widespread use of very expensive munitions; the value of the target had to be sufficient to justify the cost of a guided weapon.

Thus, an increasing dependence on high-cost weaponry can lead to three types of concerns: limitations in the availability and use of high-cost systems, the need to increase the munition expenditure rate per target to compensate for lessened effectiveness when emphasizing survivability, and a diminished ability to attack large numbers of targets (such as lower priority GOB).[26] (See app. IV for further discussion of the performance of high- and low-cost munitions in Desert Storm.)

Achievement of Campaign Objectives by Air Power

Air power was clearly instrumental to the success of Desert Storm, yet air power achieved only some of its objectives, and clearly fell short of fully achieving others. Even under generally favorable conditions, the effects of air power were limited. Some air war planners hoped that the air war alone would cause the Iraqis to leave Kuwait (not least by actively targeting the regime's political and military elite), but after 38 days of

---

[26]These implications need to be considered within a wider array of issues not discussed here, such as delivery platform cost and survivability as well as munition capabilities and effectiveness.

B-260509

nearly continuous bombardment, a ground campaign was still deemed necessary.

There were some dramatic successes in the air campaign. It caused the collapse of the national electric grid and damaged up to 80 percent of Iraq's oil-refining capacity. At the end of the campaign, only about 40 percent of the Iraqi air force survived.

While air supremacy was achieved within the first week of the campaign, delivery at low altitudes remained perilous throughout the war because of the ever-present AAA and IR SAMs. Iraq's C³ and LOC capabilities were partially degraded; although more than half of these targets were successfully destroyed, Saddam Hussein was able to direct and supply many Iraqi forces through the end of the air campaign and even immediately after the war.

Lack of intelligence about most Iraqi nuclear-related facilities meant that only less than 15 percent were targeted. The concerted campaign to destroy mobile Scud launchers did not achieve any confirmed kills. Central Intelligence Agency (CIA) analysis showed that more than 70 percent of the tanks in three Republican Guard divisions located in the Kuwait theater of operations (KTO) remained intact at the start of the ground campaign and that large numbers were able to escape across the Euphrates River before the cease-fire. (Our assessment of the degree to which the objectives were achieved is in app. III; the development of the Desert Storm objectives is described in app. V.)

Factors Affecting the Effectiveness of Air Power

Success Attributable to Weight and Type of Effort Expended

The mix of available aircraft types enabled the United States and the coalition to successfully attack or put pressure on a variety of targets and target types; at various times of the day and night; in urban, marine, and desert environments; with various guided and unguided munitions. Even including the platform and munition preferences discussed above, no target category was exclusively struck by a single type of aircraft, and no type of aircraft or munition was exclusively used against a single type of target or target category.

Older, less costly, and less technologically advanced aircraft and weapon systems made substantial contributions to the air campaign as did the

B-260509

newer, more technologically advanced systems.[27] No particular weapon system—whether of low or high technology, new or old, single or multirole, high or low cost (or in between on any of these criteria)—clearly proved more effective than another or demonstrated a disproportionate contribution to the objectives of the campaign. For example, while the F-117 carried more tonnage per day than the F-111F, the latter reported a higher rate of success hitting the same targets using the same munitions; the F-16 had only a slightly higher success rate than the F/A-18 when using the unguided MK-84 against similar types of targets. The B-52 and F-16 dropped the largest known bomb tonnages, the F-16 and A-10 had the highest sortie rates, and the B-52 and A-10 were cited by Iraqi prisoners of war as the most feared of the coalition aircraft. (The weight of effort (WOE) and type of effort (TOE) that proved successful in the air campaign are in apps. II and VIII; specific weapon system comparisons are in apps. III and IV.)

Intelligence Needs Not Fully Met

Intelligence shortfalls led to an inefficient use of guided and unguided munitions in some cases and a reduced level of success against some target categories. The lack of sufficient or timely intelligence to conduct BDA led to the additional costs and risks stemming from possibly unnecessary restrikes. For example, BDA was performed on only 41 percent of the strategic targets in our analysis. Restrikes were ordered to increase the probability that target objectives would be achieved. This may partly account for the high tonnage of munitions expended on strategic targets—averaging more than 11 and 44 tons of guided and unguided munitions, respectively, for successful outcomes and more than 9 and 53 tons of guided and unguided munitions, respectively, for less than fully successful outcomes.

Insufficient intelligence on the existence and location of targets also inhibited the coalition's ability to perform necessary strikes and achieve campaign goals. The lack of target intelligence meant that [DELETED] major Iraqi nuclear-related installations were neither identified nor targeted, and no mobile Scud launchers were definitively known to have been located and destroyed. (See apps. I and III.)

Limitations in Target Sensors Inhibited Effectiveness

The capabilities of target location and acquisition sensors were critical to the effectiveness and efficiency of the air campaign. IR sensors allowed night operations, and although pilots praised many sensor systems, they also pointed out numerous shortcomings. IR, EO, and laser systems were all

---

[27]The Desert Storm air campaign may have been the last large-scale employment for several of the older types of aircraft. For example, the A-6E fleet is scheduled to be retired by 1998; the F-4G and F-111 fleets by fiscal year 1997; and all but two wings of the A-10 fleet by the end of fiscal year 1996.

B-260509

seriously degraded by weather conditions such as clouds, rain, fog, and even haze and humidity. They were also impeded by dust and smoke. At high altitudes and even at low altitudes in the presence of high humidity or other impediments, pilots were unable to discriminate targets effectively. They reported being unable to discern whether a presumed target was a tank or a truck and whether it had already been hit by a previous attack.

Radar systems were less affected by weather, but the poor resolution of some radars made it impossible to identify targets except by recognizing nearby large-scale landmarks or by navigating to where the target was presumed to be. Radar systems specifically designed for target discrimination and identification suffered reduced resolution at the higher altitudes (and greater standoff distances) where they were operating. Pilots told us that the F-15E's high-resolution radar, while designed to detect an object as small as [DELETED] at a distance of [DELETED], could actually discriminate only between a tank and a car at a range of about [DELETED]. (Target identification and weapon system sensor issues are discussed in app. II.)

Campaign Planning Failed to Anticipate the BDA Limitations

The kinds of constraints encountered in Desert Storm do not appear to have been adequately anticipated in planning the air campaign. The air campaign planners were overoptimistic concerning the number of days that each phase of the campaign would require and the level of damage each objective would require. Moreover, many of the early missions were canceled because of adverse weather, and after the initial strikes were conducted, the BDA was neither as timely nor as complete as planners had apparently assumed it would be.

Contributions and Limitations of Advanced Technologies

Desert Storm demonstrated that many newer systems incorporating advanced technologies require specific operating conditions for their effective use. However, these conditions were not consistently encountered in Desert Storm and cannot be assumed in future contingencies. Therefore, the level of success attained by various costly and technologically advanced systems in Desert Storm may not be replicated where conditions inhibit operations even more.

Although much of what has been written about Desert Storm has emphasized advanced technologies, many of these were subject to significant operating constraints and a lack of flexibility that limited their contributions and effectiveness. [DELETED] While the TLAM risks no pilot, it achieved a hit rate that CNA and DIA estimated at [DELETED] percent,

B-260509

and it is costly. [DELETED] (Limitations on weapon system performance are discussed in app. II.)

These limitations need to be recognized and anticipated when planning air strikes or estimating the likely effectiveness of air power—particularly for a short conflict, when there may not be opportunities to restrike missed or partially damaged targets. Even in Desert Storm—with months of planning and a vast array of in-theater resources available from the very start—uncertainties and unknowns were typical rather than the exception.

Desert Storm's Uniqueness Limits Lessons Learned

The relevance of the air campaign in Desert Storm to likely future contingencies depends at least partially on how closely its operating conditions can be judged to be representative of future conditions. In this respect, Desert Storm's lessons are limited in some regard because the environmental and military operating conditions for aircraft and weapon system performance are unlikely to be repeated outside southwest Asia and because future potential adversaries—not least, Iraq itself—are likely to have learned a good deal about how to reduce the effectiveness of guided weapons, such as LGBs.[28] At the same time, performance in Desert Storm can be highly instructive about the performance and outcomes that can be expected with existing technologies under conditions like those encountered over Iraq.

Combat Conditions Over Iraq and Kuwait

The terrain and climate in Iraq and Kuwait were generally conducive to the employment of air power. The terrain was relatively flat and featureless as well as devoid of vegetation that would obscure targets. Although the weather was the worst in that region in 14 years, weather conditions even less conducive to an air campaign would be expected in many other locations of historic or topical interest such as Eastern Europe, the Balkans, or North Korea.[29] (See app. II.)

Six-Month Period to Deploy, Train, and Prepare Forces

The success of the air campaign is also attributable, in part, to the 6 months of planning, deployment, training, and intelligence-gathering preceding Desert Storm. During this interval, President Bush assembled a coalition of nations that augmented U.S. resources and isolated Iraq. War preparations were also aided by preexisting facilities in the region and the

---

[28]It is appropriate to note that "aggression by a remilitarized Iraq against Kuwait and Saudi Arabia" was one of two scenarios envisioned in planning strategy, force structure, and modernization programs in DOD's BUR report.

[29]For example, the average percentage of time that the cloud ceiling over Baghdad is less than or equal to 3,000 feet is, historically, only 9 percent; comparable percentages over Beirut, Lebanon; Osan Air Base, Korea; and St. Petersburg, Russia; are 17, 33, and 64, respectively.

B-260509

lack of Iraqi interventions to slow or deter the buildup of forces. (See app. II.)

Some Enemy Capabilities Overstated or Poorly Employed

Contrary to widespread prewar and postwar claims, the Iraqi IADS was not "robust" or "state of the art." Rather, its computers were limited in their capacity to monitor incoming threats; the system was vulnerable to disruption by attacks on a relatively few key nodes; and its design was [DELETED]. IADS had been designed to counter limited threats from the east (Iran) and west (Israel), not an attack from a coalition that included nearly 1,600 U.S. combat aircraft primarily from the south, hundreds of cruise missiles, and the most advanced technologies in the world.

On various dimensions, the Iraqi armed forces were not well disposed to effectively counter the coalition's armed response to the Iraqi seizure of Kuwait. After U.S. and coalition aircraft dominated early air-to-air encounters, the Iraqi air force essentially chose to avoid combat by fleeing to Iran and hiding its aircraft or putting them in the midst of civilian areas off-limits to attack by coalition aircraft. Except for the failed Iraqi action directed at the town of Khafji, the Iraqis did not take any ground offensive initiative throughout the air campaign, and the coalition was able to repeatedly attack targets, including those missed or insufficiently damaged on a first strike. As a result, when the ground war began, Iraqi ground forces had been subjected to 38 days of nearly continuous bombardment. Evidence from intelligence analyses and prisoner-of-war interviews also indicated that many Iraqi frontline troops had low morale and were prone to heavy desertions even before the air bombardment started.

During the war, the Iraqis were unable to effectively resist coalition air attacks from medium and high altitudes. While the Iraqis maintained a potent AAA and IR SAM threat to aircraft below 10,000 feet, the lack of an active Iraqi fighter threat (especially after the first week); the coalition's suppression of most radar-guided SAM defenses in the early days of the war; and the Iraqi use of many of the remaining radar SAMs in an ineffective, nonradar mode created a relative sanctuary for coalition aircraft at medium and high altitudes. Moreover, Iraq employed few potential countermeasures (such as jamming) against coalition strikes. (See app. II.)

Likelihood of Victory Allowed Emphasis on Survivability

Given the overwhelming nature of the coalition's quantitative and qualitative superiority, the conflict was highly asymmetric. U.S. and coalition commanders controlled strike assets that were numerically and technologically superior to the capabilities of the enemy. They expressed

B-260509

little doubt of a victory. One result of this was a command emphasis on aircraft and pilot survivability. The philosophy was "No Iraqi target was worth an allied pilot or aircraft."[30]

Other operating decisions were also taken to increase survivability. For example, after two F-16 losses on day three in the Baghdad area, the Air Force ceased tasking large package daylight strikes of F-16s against metropolitan Baghdad targets. Similarly, after A-10 attacks on the Republican Guard, during which two aircraft were hit while operating at lower altitudes, the A-10s were ordered to cease such attacks. Instead, much higher altitude attacks by F-16s and B-52s, with unguided bombs, were used. (See apps. II and III.)

Some Aircraft and Weapon System Performance Dimensions Not Tested

A number of lessons cannot be drawn directly from Desert Storm because systems were not stressed in ways that could be considered likely and operationally realistic for future conflict. For example: (1) with little or no Iraqi electronic countermeasures against U.S. munitions, airborne intelligence assets, or target identification and acquisition sensors, no data were obtained on how these systems would perform in the presence of such countermeasures; (2) with almost no Iraqi air-to-air opposition for most of the war, many U.S. aircraft were also not exposed to these threats; and (3) many U.S. weapons were not delivered within the low-altitude parameters for which they were designed, both platforms and munitions (thus, we do not know how they would perform if delivered lower).

However, precisely because of the advantages enjoyed by the coalition, the problems that were encountered should be especially noted. These include the substantial amounts of unguided and guided munitions that were used to achieve successful target outcomes and the severe effect that the weather had on target identification and designation sensors—some of which had earlier been described to the Congress as capable in "all weather," "adverse weather," or "poor weather." (See apps. II-IV.) These problems should be considered as warning signs about the effectiveness of various systems and technologies under more stressful circumstances in the future.

Conclusions

Operation Desert Storm was a highly successful and decisive military operation. The air campaign, which incurred minimal casualties while

---

[30]GWAPS, Highlights (briefing slides), p. 30.

B-260509

effecting the collapse of the Iraqis' ability to resist, helped liberate Kuwait and elicit Iraqi compliance with U.N. resolutions.

Our analysis of the air campaign against strategic targets revealed several air power issues that should be planned for in the next campaign. First, the effectiveness of air power in Desert Storm was inhibited by the aircraft sensors' inherent limitations in identifying and acquiring targets and by DOD's failure to gather intelligence on the existence or location of certain critical targets and its inability to collect and disseminate timely BDA. Pilots noted that IR, EO, and laser systems were all seriously degraded by clouds, rain, fog, smoke, and even high humidity, and the pilots reported being unable to discern whether a presumed target was a tank or a truck and whether it had already been destroyed. The failure of intelligence to identify certain targets precluded any opportunity for the coalition to fully accomplish some of its objectives. And the reduced accuracies from medium and high altitudes and absence of timely BDA led to higher costs, reduced effectiveness, and increased risks from making unnecessary restrikes.

Second, U.S. commanders were able to favor medium- to high-altitude strike tactics that maximized aircraft and pilot survivability, rather than weapon system effectiveness. This was because of early and complete air superiority, a limited enemy response, and terrain and climate conditions generally conducive to air strikes. Low-altitude munitions deliveries had been emphasized in prewar training, but they were abandoned early. The subsequent deliveries from medium and high altitudes resulted in the use of sensors and weapon systems at distances from targets that were not optimal for their identification, acquisition, or accuracy. Medium- and high-altitude tactics also increased the exposure of aircraft sensors to man-made and natural impediments to visibility.

Third, the success of the sustained air campaign resulted from the availability of a mix of strike and support assets. Its substantial weight of effort was made possible, in significant part, by the variety and number of air-to-ground aircraft types from high-payload bombers, such as the B-52, to PGM-capable platforms, such as the stealthy F-117, to high-sortie-rate attack aircraft, such as the A-10. A range of target types, threat conditions, and tactical and strategic objectives was best confronted with a mix of weapon systems and strike and support assets with a range of capabilities.

Fourth, despite often sharp contrasts in the unit cost of aircraft platforms, it is inappropriate, given aircraft use, performance, and effectiveness

B-260509

demonstrated in Desert Storm, to characterize higher cost aircraft as generally more capable than lower cost aircraft. In some cases, the higher cost systems had the greater operating limitations; in some other cases, the lower cost aircraft had the same general limitations but performed at least as well; and in still other cases, the data did not permit a differentiation. (See app. IV.)

Fifth, the air campaign data did not validate the purported efficiency or effectiveness of guided munitions, without qualification. "One-target, one-bomb" efficiency was not achieved. On average, more than 11 tons of guided and 44 tons of unguided munitions were delivered on targets assessed as successfully destroyed; still more tonnage of both was delivered against targets where objectives were not fully met. Large tonnages of munitions were used against targets not only because of inaccuracy from high altitudes but also because BDA data were lacking. Although the relative contribution of guided munitions in achieving target success is unknowable, they did account for the bulk of munitions costs. Only 8 percent of the delivered munitions tonnage was guided, but at a price that represented 84 percent of the total munitions cost. During Desert Storm, the ratio of guided-to-unguided munitions delivered did not vary, indicating that the relative preferences among these types of munitions did not change over the course of the campaign. More generally, Desert Storm demonstrated that many systems incorporating complex or advanced technologies require specific operating conditions to operate effectively. These conditions, however, were not consistently encountered in Desert Storm and cannot be assumed in future contingencies.

Four issues arise from these findings. First, DOD's future ability to conduct an efficient, effective, and comprehensive air campaign will depend partly on its ability to enhance sensor capabilities, particularly at medium altitudes and in adverse weather, in order to identify valid targets and collect, analyze, and disseminate timely BDA. Second, a key parameter in future weapon systems design, operational testing and evaluation, training, and doctrine will be pilot and aircraft survivability. Third, the scheduled retirement of strike and attack aircraft such as the A-6E, F-111F, and most A-10s will make Desert Storm's variety and number of aircraft unavailable by the year 2000. Fourth, the cost of guided munitions, their intelligence requirements, and the limitations on their effectiveness demonstrated in Desert Storm need to be considered by DOD and the services as they determine the optimal future mix of guided and unguided munitions.

B-260509

DOD and associated agencies have undertaken initiatives since the war to address many, but not all, of the limitations of the air campaign that we identified in our analysis, although we have not analyzed each of these initiatives in this report. First, DOD officials told us that to address the Desert Storm BDA analysis and dissemination shortcomings, they have

- created an organization to work out issues, consolidate national reporting, and provide leadership;
- developed DOD-wide doctrine, tactics, techniques, and procedures;
- established more rigorous and realistic BDA training and realistic exercises; and
- developed and deployed better means to disseminate BDA.

DOD officials acknowledge that additional problems remain with improving BDA timeliness and accuracy, developing nonlethal BDA functional damage indicators (particularly for new weapons that produce nontraditional effects), and cultivating intelligence sources to identify and validate strategic targets. Moreover, because timely and accurate BDA is crucial for the efficient employment of high-cost guided munitions (that is, for avoiding unnecessary restrikes), it is important that acquisition plans for guided munitions take fully into account actual BDA collection and dissemination capabilities before making a final determination of the quantity of such munitions to be acquired.

Second, DOD officials told us that the most sophisticated targeting sensors used in Desert Storm (which were available only in limited quantities) have now been deployed on many more fighter aircraft, thereby giving them a capability to deliver guided munitions. However, the same limitations exhibited by these advanced sensor and targeting systems in Desert Storm—limited fields of view, insufficient resolution for target discrimination at medium altitudes, vulnerabilities to adverse weather, limited traverse movement—remain today.

Third, DOD officials told us that survivability is now being emphasized in pilot training, service and joint doctrine, and weapon system development. Pilot training was modified immediately after the air campaign to meet challenges such as medium-altitude deliveries in a high AAA and IR SAM threat environment. Service and joint doctrine now reflects lessons learned in Desert Storm's asymmetrical conflict. Several fighter aircraft employment manuals specifically incorporate the tactics that emphasized survivability in the campaign. DOD and service procurement plans include new munitions with GPS guidance systems, justified in part by their

B-260509

abilities to minimize the medium-altitude shortcomings and adverse weather limitations of Desert Storm while maximizing pilot and aircraft survivability.

Fourth, DOD officials told us that although Desert Storm's successful aircraft mix will not be available for the next contingency, DOD and the services have made plans to maintain an inventory of aircraft that they believe will be more flexible and effective in the future. Flexibility will be anticipated partly from the modernization of existing multirole fighters to enable them to deliver guided munitions (the aircraft systems being retired are single-role platforms), and their effectiveness is expected to increase as new and more accurate guided munitions are put in the field. However, we believe that strike aircraft modernization and munition procurement plans that include increasing numbers and varieties of guided munitions and the numbers of platforms capable of delivering them require additional justification.[31]

Recommendations

Desert Storm established a paradigm for asymmetrical post-Cold War conflicts. The coalition possessed quantitative and qualitative superiority in aircraft, munitions, intelligence, personnel, support, and doctrine. It dictated when the conflict should start, where operations should be conducted, when the conflict should end, and how terms of the peace should read. This paradigm—conflict where the relative technological advantages for the U.S. forces are high and the acceptable level of risk or attrition for the U.S. forces is low—underlies the service modernization plans for strike aircraft and munitions. Actions on the following recommendations will help ensure that high-cost munitions can be employed more efficiently at lower risk to pilots and aircraft and that the future mix of guided and unguided munitions is appropriate and cost-effective given the threats, exigencies, and objectives of potential contingencies.

1. In light of the shortcomings of the sensors in Desert Storm, we recommend that the Secretary of Defense analyze and identify DOD's need

---

[31]In Desert Storm, 229 U.S. aircraft were capable of delivering laser-guided munitions; in 1996, the expanded installation of LANTIRN on F-15Es and block 40 F-16s will increase this capability within the Air Force to approximately 500 platforms. The services have bought or are investing over $58 billion to acquire 33 different types of guided munitions totaling over 300,000 units. (See Weapons Acquisition: Precision Guided Munitions in Inventory, Production, and Development (GAO/NSIAD-95-95, June 23, 1995.) Air Force plans reveal that nearly 62 percent of all interdiction target types in a major regional conflict in Iraq could be tasked to either guided or unguided munitions today (1995) but that will fall to approximately 40 percent in 2002. Concurrently, the percentage of targets to be tasked to only guided munitions will increase from 19 percent in 1995 to nearly 43 percent in 2002.

B-260509

to enhance the capabilities of existing and planned sensors to effectively locate, discriminate, and acquire targets in varying weather conditions and at different altitudes. Furthermore, the Secretary should ensure that any new sensors or enhancements of existing ones are tested under fully realistic operational conditions that are at least as stressful as the conditions that impeded capabilities in Desert Storm.

2. In light of the shortcomings in BDA exhibited during Desert Storm and BDA's importance to strike planning, the BDA problems that DOD officials acknowledge continue today despite DOD postwar initiatives need to be addressed. These problems include timeliness, accuracy, capacity, assessment of functional damage, and cultivation of intelligence sources to identify and validate strategic targets. We recommend that the Secretary of Defense expand DOD's current efforts to include such activities so that BDA problems can be fully resolved.

3. In light of the quantities and mix of guided and unguided munitions that proved successful in Desert Storm, the services' increasing reliance on guided munitions to conduct asymmetrical warfare may not be appropriate. The Secretary should reconsider DOD's proposed mix of guided and unguided munitions. A reevaluation is warranted based on Desert Storm experiences that demonstrated limitations to the effectiveness of guided munitions, survivability concerns of aircraft delivering these munitions, and circumstances where less complex, less constrained unguided munitions proved equally or more effective.

Agency Comments

The Department of Defense partially concurred with each of our three recommendations. In its response to a draft of this report, DOD did not dispute our conclusions; rather, it reported that several initiatives were underway that will rectify the shortcomings and limitations demonstrated in Desert Storm. Specifically, it cited (1) the acquisition of improved and new PGMs, (2) two studies in process—a Deep Attack/Weapons Mix Study (DAWMS) and a Precision Strike Architecture study, and (3) several proposed fiscal year 1997 Advanced Concept Technology Demonstrations (ACTD) as programs capable of correcting Desert Storm shortcomings. In addition, DOD emphasized the importance of providing funds to retain the operational test and evaluation function to ensure the rigorous testing of our weapons and weapon systems. (See app. XII for the full text of DOD's comments.)

B-260509

We agree that the actions DOD cited address the shortcomings in sensors, guided munitions, and battle damage assessment we report in our conclusions. However, the degree to which these initiatives are effective can be determined only after rigorous operational test and evaluation of both new and existing munitions and after the recommendations resulting from the Deep Attack/Weapons Mix and Precision Strike Architecture studies have been implemented and evaluated. Moreover, we concur with the continuing need for operational test and evaluation and underscore the role of this function in rectifying the shortcomings cited in this report.

DOD also supplied us with a list of recommended technical corrections. Where appropriate, we have addressed these comments in our report.

If you have any questions or would like additional information, please do not hesitate to call me at (202) 512-6153 or Kwai-Cheung Chan, Director of Program Evaluation in Physical Systems Areas, at (202) 512-3092. Other major contributors to this report are listed in appendix XIII.

Joseph F. Delfico
Acting Assistant Comptroller General

Appendix I
Scope and Methodology

The data we analyze in this report are the best information collected during the war. They were compiled for and used by the commanders who managed the air campaign. These data also provided the basis for postwar Department of Defense (DOD) and manufacturer assessments of aircraft and weapon system performance during Desert Storm. We balanced the limitations of the data, to the extent possible, against qualitative analyses of the system. For example, we compared claims made for system performance and contributions to what was supportable given all the available data, both quantitative and qualitative. In the subsequent appendixes, we use these data to describe and assess the use of aircraft and weapon systems in the performance of air-to-ground missions. And to the extent that the data permit, we assess the claims for and relative effectiveness of individual systems. Finally, we use these data to discuss the overall effectiveness of the air campaign in meeting its objectives.

Scope

In this report, we assess the effectiveness of various U.S. and allied air campaign aircraft and weapon systems in destroying ground targets, primarily those that fall into the category of "strategic" targets. In Operation Desert Storm, some targets were clearly strategic, such as Iraqi air force headquarters in Baghdad, while others, essentially the Iraqi ground forces in the Kuwaiti theater of operations, could be considered both strategic and tactical. For our purposes, we concentrated on the effects achieved by the air campaign before the start of the ground offensive, including successes against ground forces in Kuwait. Unlike most previous large-scale conflicts, the air campaign accounted for more than 90 percent of the entire conflict's duration. Therefore, what we have excluded from our analysis is the role of air power in supporting ground forces during the ground offensive ("close air support"), as well as such nonstrategic missions as search and rescue.

We evaluated the aircraft and munitions that were deemed to have had a major role in the execution of the Desert Storm air campaign by virtue of their satisfying at least one (in most cases, two) of the following criteria: the system (1) played a major role against strategic targets (broadly defined); (2) was the focus of congressional interest; (3) may be considered by DOD for future major procurement; (4) appeared likely to play a role in future conflict; or (5) even if not slated currently for major procurement, either was used by allied forces in a manner or role different from its U.S. use or used new technologies likely to be employed again in the future. These criteria led us to assess the A-6E, A-10, B-52, F-111F, F-117A, F-15E, F-16, F/A-18, and British Tornado (GR-1). We examined

Appendix I
Scope and Methodology

both guided and unguided munitions, including laser-guided bombs, Maverick missiles, Navy cruise missiles, and unguided "dumb" bombs. (We did not examine Air Force cruise missiles because so few were used.)

We focused our analysis on strategic targets in part because they received the best-documented bomb damage assessments (BDA), although there was very substantial variation from target to target and among target types in the quantity and quality of BDAs. Twelve categories of strategic targets in Desert Storm are listed in table I.1. With the exception of mobile Scud launchers and ground forces, each type of target was a fixed item at a known location on which battle damage assessments were possible.

Table I.1: Twelve Strategic Target Categories in the Desert Storm Air Campaign

Abbreviation	Target category
C^3	Command, control, and communication facilities
ELE	Electrical facilities
GOB	Ground order of battle (Iraqi ground forces in the Kuwait theater of operations, including the Republican Guard)[a]
GVC	Government centers
LOC	Lines of communication
MIB	Military industrial base facilities
NAV	Naval facilities
NBC	Nuclear, biological, and chemical facilities
OCA	Offensive counterair installations
OIL	Oil refining, storage, and distribution facilities
SAM	Surface-to-air missile installations
SCU	Scud missile facilities

[a]In our database, GOB targets are in the kill box target set.

Methodology

Data Needs and Sources

To examine how the different types of aircraft and munitions performed and were used to achieve the air campaign objectives, we required data on the aircraft missions flown and missiles launched against each type of target. To assess the effectiveness of the aircraft and munitions, we needed data on the outcome of each aircraft and missile tasked (what was dropped or launched and where it landed) as well as the physical and functional impact of the munitions on the targets. We had to review DOD

Appendix I
Scope and Methodology

and manufacturers' Desert Storm claims for selected weapon systems and seek out data to validate their assertions.

To assess the relative costs of the systems employed, we needed various cost measures of the systems and sufficient data on their effectiveness to be able to relate cost and performance. To examine operating conditions of the air campaign, we required data on the characteristics of the Iraqi threat, political and military operating conditions in the theater, and the environmental conditions in which combat occurred.

To determine the degree to which air campaign objectives were met with air power, we required, first, data that described the campaign objectives and the plans to achieve those objectives and, second, data that addressed the outcome of air campaign efforts in pursuit of air campaign objectives.

We obtained descriptive data on objectives and plans from a series of interviews and a review of the literature. We interviewed 108 Desert Storm veteran pilots, representing each type of aircraft evaluated, with the exception of British Tornados.[1] We also interviewed key Desert Storm planners and analysts from a wide spectrum of organizations, both within and outside DOD. (See table I.2.)

We also conducted an extensive literature search and reviewed hundreds of official and unofficial documents describing the planning for, conduct of, and performance by the various aircraft and munitions used in the campaign, and we searched for documents on Desert Storm operating conditions.

To examine the nature and magnitude of Desert Storm inputs employed against strategic target categories, as well as outcomes, we needed two types of databases. We needed the "Missions" database generated by the Gulf War Air Power Survey (GWAPS) to assess inputs. And we needed the Defense Intelligence Agency's (DIA) phase III battle damage assessment reports to assess Desert Storm outcomes.

---

[1]We did not select pilots randomly, given constraints on their availability, travel, and time. The only requirement was that a pilot had flown the relevant type of aircraft in a Desert Storm combat mission. In most cases, the pilots had flown numerous missions. The purpose of interviewing pilots was to receive as direct input as possible from the aircraft and munition user rather than views filtered through official reports. In Operation Desert Storm: Limits on the Role and Performance of B-52 Bombers in Conventional Conflicts (GAO/NSIAD-93-138, May 12, 1993), we assessed the B-52 role in detail. Where they were relevant, we incorporated the data and findings from that report into our comparisons. The British government denied our requests to interview British pilots who had flown in Desert Storm. However, we were able to obtain some official assessments of the British role in the air campaign, and we questioned U.S. pilots about their interactions with British pilots.

Appendix I
Scope and Methodology

Table I.2: Organizations We Contacted and Their Locations

Organization	Location
Air Combat Command	Langley Air Force Base, Va.
Center for Air Force History	Washington, D.C.
Center for Naval Analyses	Alexandria, Va.
Central Intelligence Agency	Langley, Va.
Defense Intelligence Agency	Washington, D.C.
Department of Air Force, Headquarters	Washington, D.C.
Embassy of the United Kingdom	Washington, D.C.
Foreign Science and Technology Center	Charlottesville, Va.
Grumman Corporation	Bethpage, N.Y.
Gulf War Air Power Survey (research site)	Arlington, Va.
Institute for Defense Analyses	Alexandria, Va.
Lockheed Advanced Development Corporation	Burbank, Calif.
McDonnell Douglas Corporation	St. Louis, Mo.
Naval A-6E Unit	Oceana Naval Air Station, Va.
Naval F/A-18 Unit	Cecil Naval Air Station, Fla.
Navy Operational Intelligence Center, Strike Projection Evaluation and Anti-Air Research (SPEAR) Department	Suitland, Md.
Office of the Chief of Naval Operations	Washington, D.C.
Office of the Secretary of Defense	Washington, D.C.
Rand Corporation	Santa Monica, Calif.
Securities and Exchange Commission	Washington, D.C.
Survivability/Vulnerability Information Analysis Center	Wright-Patterson Air Force Base, Ohio
Texas Instruments	Dallas, Tex.
U.N. Information Center	Washington, D.C.
U.S. Atlantic Fleet, Headquarters	Norfolk, Va.
U.S. Central Air Forces, Headquarters	Shaw Air Force Base, N.C.
U.S. Central Command, Headquarters	MacDill Air Force Base, Fla.
U.S. Space Command	Cheyenne Mountain Air Force Base, Colo.
4th Tactical Fighter Wing	Seymour Johnson Air Force Base, N.C.
48th Tactical Fighter Wing	RAF Lakenheath, U.K.
49th Fighter Wing	Holloman Air Force Base, N.Mex.
57th Test Group	Nellis Air Force Base, Nev.
363rd Fighter Wing	Shaw Air Force Base, S.C.
926th Fighter Wing (reserve)	New Orleans Naval Air Station, La.

Appendix I
Scope and Methodology

Missions Database

The Missions database represents a strike history of air-to-ground platforms and ordnance in the Persian Gulf War. GWAPS researchers compiled a very large computerized database on aerial operations in the Gulf War from existing records. It documents aircraft strikes on ground targets, number and type of ordnance, date, and time on target (TOT) information, target names and identifiers, desired mean point of impact (DMPI), and additional mission-related information. It contains strike history information across the duration of the air campaign for most of the air-to-ground platforms that participated. There are data on 862 numbered targets that together comprise more than 1 million pieces of strike information.

The Missions database also contains strike records across the duration of the air campaign for most of the air-to-ground platforms that participated in the Gulf War. This database includes platforms from the U.S. military services and some non-U.S. coalition partners. The Missions database was intended to provide information not on aircraft sortie counts but, rather, on aircraft strike counts and associated target attack information. Further, it was not intended to provide information on platform or munition effectiveness.

The selection criteria that guided our use of the database records required us to select targets that were designated by a unique basic encyclopedia (BE) number and an associated target priority code (target category designation) and that were records of identifiable U.S. aircraft strikes or strikes conducted by the British Tornado, GR-1 (interdiction variant).[2] We did not include records that did not meet these criteria.[3] Also, we did not include A-10 records because the majority of A-10 strike events as represented in the database are unclear.[4] Finally, we did not include strike events that were designated as ground aborted missions or headquarters cancellations. Unless indicated otherwise, the data we reviewed on strategic target categories, the nine platforms, and their munitions originate from this data set.

---

[2]Designating targets by a BE number is a method of identifying and categorizing target installations for target study and planning.

[3]In several instances in which records met all selection criteria except for a missing target category designation, we used all available target-identifying information and assigned the target to a target category based on automated intelligence file (AIF) target category designations.

[4]At least one-third of the A-10 strike data could not be accurately determined from the original records, and GWAPS researchers were not able to reconcile the inconsistencies.

Appendix I
Scope and Methodology

Targets were assigned to target categories based on the AIF functional target category designations. (See table I.3.)

The AIF target category designations indicate broad categories of strategic targets (for example, offensive counterair) as well as provide more specific examples of individual target types within the broad target categories (for example, hardened aircraft shelters). The AIF strategic target category referred to as ground order of battle (GOB) was expanded to include all "kill box" targets that had an assigned BE number, and it is subsequently identified in our database as the KBX category.[5]

Table I.3: AIF Target Categories and Target Types

Target category	Target type
Government control (GVC)	Government control centers
	Government bodies, general
	Government ministries and administrative bodies, nonmilitary, general
	Government detention facilities, general
	Unidentified control facility
	Trade, commerce, and government, general
	Civil defense facilities (in military use)
Electricity (ELE)	Electric power generating, transmission, and control facilities
Command, control, and communications (C³)	Offensive air command control headquarters and schools
	Air defense headquarters
	Telecommunications
	Electronic warfare
	Space systems
	Missile headquarters, surface-to-surface
	National, combined and joint commands
	Naval headquarters and staff activities
Surface-to-air missiles (SAM)	Missile support facilities, defensive, general
	SAM missile sites/complexes
	Tactical SAM sites/installations
	SAM support facilities

(continued)

[5]Kill boxes were areas where the Republican Guard (RG) and other Iraqi troops were dug in. According to GWAPS, the vast majority of kill box strikes were directed against GOB targets. However, GWAPS did not include the universe of BE-numbered kill boxes in the GOB target category. Therefore, we expanded the GOB target category to include all BE-numbered kill boxes and subsequently identified it as the KBX category. GWAPS indicates that approximately 8 percent of kill box strikes were conducted against targets other than GOB targets. Examination of the database indicates that these other target types include SAM sites, artillery pieces, and some bridges.

Appendix I
Scope and Methodology

Target category	Target type
Offensive counterair (OCA)	Airfields (air bases, reserve fields, helicopter bases)
	Noncommunications electronic installations (radar installations, radars collocated with SAM sites, ATC/Nav aids, meteorological radars)
	Air logistics, general (air depots)
	Air ammo depots (maintenance and repair bases, aircraft and component production and assembly)
Nuclear, biological, and chemical (NBC)	Atomic energy feed and moderator materials production
	Chemical and biological production and storage
	Atomic energy-associated facilities production and storage
	Basic and applied nuclear research and development, general
Military industrial base (MIB)	Basic processing and equipment production
	End products (chiefly civilian)
	Technical research, development and testing, nonnuclear
	Covered storage facilities, general
	Material (chiefly military)
	Industrial production centers
	Defense logistics agencies
Scuds (SCU)	Guided missile and space system production and assembly
	Fixed missile facility, general
	Fixed, surface-to-surface missile sites
	Offensive missile support facilities
	Medium-range surface-to-surface launch control facilities
	Fixed positions for mobile missile launchers
	Tactical missile troops field position
Naval (NAV)	Mineable areas
	Maritime port facilities
	Cruise missile support facilities, defensive
	Shipborne missile support facilities
	Cruise surface-to-surface missile launch positions
	Naval bases, installations, and supply depots
Petroleum, oil, and lubricants (POL)	POL and related products, pipelines, and storage facilities
Lines of communication (LOC)	Highway and railway transportation
	Inland water transportation

(continued)

Appendix I
Scope and Methodology

Target category	Target type
Ground order of battle (GOB)[a]	Military troop installations
	Ground force material and storage depots
	Fortifications and defense systems

[a]In our database, GOB targets are in the kill box target set.

While the Missions database contains an abundance of Desert Storm strike history information, it has its limits. Different reporting procedures adopted during Desert Storm and the use of different terminology and language, within and among services, have resulted in more or less detailed data for particular platforms. These limitations in the final form of the database transfer to all users of the database. For example, in some instances, database records documenting Air Force aircraft strikes may be more complete with fewer missing observations than the same data for other service platforms because services may have adopted different methods of tracking and identifying outcomes during the war. As stated previously, GWAPS indicates that A-10 data are difficult to summarize and interpret because of the way the data were initially recorded. Where relevant and necessary for this research, we consulted with the appropriate GWAPS staff regarding limitations and usage of the Missions database.

Studies using the database for different purposes should not be expected to generate identical data. For example, the number of strikes conducted by a particular platform against strategic targets may not be equivalent across studies because of the degree of specificity in the question being posed. One study may be concerned with strategic targets regardless of any other delimiting factors, while another may be concerned with strike counts against strategic targets, discounting those strikes where some mechanical failure of the aircraft was reported to have occurred over the target area. Therefore, differences among studies that rely on the use of the Missions database, in some form or another, should be interpreted considering differences in research questions, methodologies, and protocols.

We also used the Missions database to create the variables to measure air campaign inputs. These variables are used to measure either the weight of effort (WOE) or the type of effort (TOE) expended and are defined in table I.4.

Appendix I
Scope and Methodology

Table I.4: Definition of Composite Variables for WOE and TOE Measures

Measure	Variable
WOE	Quantity of BE numbers to which platforms were tasked
	Quantity of strikes that platforms conducted
	Quantity of bombs that platforms delivered
	Quantity of bomb tonnage that platforms delivered
TOE	Quantity of bombs that were guided bombs
	Quantity of bombs that were unguided bombs
	Quantity of bomb tonnage that was guided
	Quantity of bomb tonnage that was unguided
Other	Quantity of day and night strikes

The only variable in the list above that was directly accessible from the Missions database was the number of BEs to which aircraft were tasked. All other variables were derived by us from the raw data provided in the Missions database.

WOE Variables

Quantity of BE Numbers. BE numbers are a method of categorizing and identifying various types of target installations for target study and general planning. The number of BEs are only considered an approximation of the actual number of targets or desired mean points of impact (DMPI) that aircraft were assigned to and may have struck. The quantity of BE numbers can only be considered an approximation because a single BE number can encapsulate more than a single DMPI. For example, an entire airfield may be assigned a single BE number, yet there may exist multiple DMPIs on that airfield (hardened aircraft shelters) that could potentially inflate the actual number of targets.[6]

Quantity of Strikes. We used the GWAPS method of assessing strike counts based on Missions data. We excluded only those strike efforts that were most likely not to have expended some actual weight of effort against targets. For example, we included strike events from the database that were signified as weather-aborted or canceled, without reference to why or whether or not the cancellation occurred over the target or on the ground before takeoff. Aircraft that arrived at the target area, and then the strike events were canceled because of weather, still represented a part of the weight of effort that was expended on a target. This is because

---

[6]The lack of consistently detailed DMPI indicators in the database does not permit a reliable estimate of the actual number of targets represented by individual BE-numbered targets within all target categories. Because the database contains at least two fields to capture information on DMPIs, there could be at least two DMPIs per BE number. This would effectively double the number of targets. Therefore, at most, the 862 BE-numbered targets in our database may be the lower bound of the actual number of targets.

**Appendix I
Scope and Methodology**

numerous resources are required simply to get the aircraft safely to the target (for example, tankers, planning time and resources, airborne warning and control system (AWACS) resources, and possibly escort and SEAD aircraft). As concluded by GWAPS researchers, their database has inconsistent abbreviations and meanings attached to the codes for canceled missions.[7] This lack of consistency and clarity suggests that using mission cancellation codes as a filter for strike summary information is not reliable, and therefore, we did not use them.

Quantity of Bombs. The quantity of bombs was determined from those database fields that provided some information on the number of bombs that an aircraft delivered and the number of aircraft that delivered it. If the database fields listing the quantity of bombs were empty, bomb quantities for those strike events were not determined.[8] The quantity of bombs measure does not include clearly designated air-to-air ordnance, aircraft gun ordnance, decoys, or psyop delivery canisters.

Quantity of Bomb Tonnage. The quantity of bomb tonnage was determined by entering a new variable into the database representing the weight of air-to-ground bombs (in pounds), summing these weights, and then dividing the sum by 2,000 to determine the overall amount of bomb tonnage. The quantity of bomb tonnage could only be calculated for those entries in the database where a verifiable type and quantity of bomb actually appeared.[9]

TOE Variables

Quantity of Guided and Unguided Bombs. The quantity of guided and unguided bombs was calculated in the same manner as the quantity of bombs described previously; however, ordnance was categorized according to whether it was precision-guided or unguided.

The ability to determine guided and unguided bomb categorizations was dependent on the way that ordnance was designated in the database. If the type of bomb was clearly indicated in the Missions database, then the category to which it belonged—guided or unguided—could be determined. In many cases, if bomb types were unclear or missing (thus not permitting

---

[7]Gulf War Air Power Survey, vol. V, pt. I: Statistical Compendium and Chronology (Secret), pp. 425-26.

[8]Approximately 2 percent of the database records used in the analysis, and which provide designation of the primary type of aircraft ordnance, were blank.

[9]The quantity of bomb tonnage is obviously a function of information on the quantity of bombs. Thus, the baseline percentage of database records where information on bomb tonnage could not be calculated is 2 percent—as noted in the previous footnote.

Appendix I
Scope and Methodology

clear categorizations), those bombs would not have been categorized.[10] However, in those instances in which a bomb type was unclear but additional information permitted a categorization, bomb categorizations were done. For example, it was not unusual to see an entry like '27X' in the database field that was supposed to contain the primary type of aircraft ordnance. In many cases, examination of the type of aircraft that was associated with the ordnance would indicate what type of ordnance it was. Using the example above, aircraft ordnance entries like '27X' had other data indicating that the delivery platform was an F-117; thus, the bomb was assumed to be a GBU-27 and a guided categorization would have been provided.

<u>Quantity of Guided and Unguided Bomb Tonnage.</u> The method and restrictions for calculating guided and unguided bomb tonnage are the same as those described previously under the WOE Variables section.

Other Descriptive Variables

The time at which strikes occurred was determined from the time on target variable provided in the Missions database. TOTs, designated in Zulu time, were translated to an air tasking order (ATO) time to determine whether strike events were occurring during daylight or night hours. A key provided by GWAPS indicated the ATO hours associated with daylight and night hours.[11]

DIA Phase III BDA Reports

The Defense Intelligence Agency (DIA) generated battle damage assessments during Operation Desert Storm in support of U.S. Central Command (CENTCOM). The DIA's phase III reports detailed the extent of physical and functional damage on strategic targets based on multiple intelligence sources.[12] DIA prepared phase III BDA reports only for targets identified by CENTCOM. These targets were of special interest to CENTCOM and lent themselves to data collection from national sources. The phase III analyses reported the degree to which campaign objectives were met at a

---

[10]Estimates are approximately the same as noted previously—about 2 percent of the database records used in the analysis.

[11]GWAPS, vol. V, pt. I (Secret), p 558.

[12]Intelligence sources included imagery from national sources, human intelligence, signal intelligence or electronic intelligence, and tactical reconnaissance.

Appendix I
Scope and Methodology

BE-numbered target at a specific point in time.[13] These reports did not necessarily assess the impact of any one mission or strike package; rather, they assessed the effect of the cumulative efforts of the air campaign on the function and capability of a specific target. After assessing all sources of intelligence to determine the functional damage achieved at a target, DIA made a summary recommendation of whether a restrike was needed.

Phase III reports were written for 432 fixed strategic targets. The number of strategic targets assessed by DIA is only somewhat over half the number of strategic targets CENTCOM identified by the end of the war (772) and half the number of the BE-numbered targets identified in GWAPS' Missions database (862). In addition, these targets were not necessarily representative of the entire strategic target set.[14] However, they do represent the targets of greatest interest to CENTCOM planners. CENTCOM's level of interest is reflected in the repeated assessments requested for and conducted on some key targets; several of the targets were assessed over 10 times.

The phase III reports do not provide strike-by-strike functional BDA for each strategic target, but they represent the best cumulative all-source BDA available to planners during the course of the war.[15] Though a few agencies produced postwar BDA analyses on narrowly defined target sets, no other agency or organization prepared BDA reports comparable to DIA's, which drew upon multiple sources and assessed hundreds of diverse targets throughout the theater.[16]

---

[13]DIA also produced phase I and II reports during the war. Phase I reports identified whether a target was hit or missed on a specific mission. These reports contained the initial indications from the imagery and were transmitted orally to the theater. Phase II reports were more detailed than phase I reports, describing the extent of physical damage as well as functional impact based on imagery. Phase III reports also provided functional BDA to the theater but required more time because they were based on a fusion of all available intelligence sources rather than imagery alone.

[14]Our data sources did not provide us with some detailed target information such as number and characteristics of DMPIs, threat environment, campaign objectives, or Iraqi adaptations or countermeasures that would enable us to compare targets assessed by DIA and those that were not.

[15]Gulf War planners who were frustrated with the timeliness, coverage, and occasionally the conclusions of BDA based primarily on imagery increasingly relied on aircraft video to assess strike success. One blackhole planner stated that strike BDA was assessed in theater based on F-117, F-15E, and F-111F video (taken during the delivery of laser-guided bombs) and restrikes were postponed until phase III reports confirmed or refuted the cockpit video. Thus, during the campaign, for some targets, BDA and restrike determinations were supplemented by—but not wholly replaced by—cockpit video.

[16]See Central Intelligence Agency, Operation Desert Storm: A Snapshot of the Battlefield (Sept. 1993); Defense Intelligence Agency, Vulnerability of Hardened Aircraft Bunkers and Shelters to Precision Guided Munitions (Apr. 1994); Foreign Science and Technology Center, Desert Storm Armored Vehicle Survey/BDA (Charlottesville, Va.: Joint Intelligence Survey Team, Jan. 1992).

Appendix I
Scope and Methodology

Our Determinations of Target Success

We used phase III reports on fixed strategic targets to determine the extent to which the functional capabilities of the target had been eliminated.[17] Using the final BDA report prepared during the campaign on each target, we assessed whether the campaign against that target had been fully successful or not fully successful. We based our judgments on the phase III report's (1) physical damage summary, (2) cumulative summary of intelligence data on functional damage, and (3) restrike recommendation, if provided.

We rated the campaign against a target as <u>fully successful</u> (FS) if the phase III report stated following:

- The target was destroyed or so damaged as to be unusable or nonfunctional, and the diminished condition of the target was because of the physical damage of air strikes or indirectly attributable to the air campaign, such as the threat of strikes.
- The restrike recommendation was "no."[18]

We rated the campaign against the target as <u>not fully successful</u> (NFS) if the phase III report stated the following:

- The target was not destroyed or so damaged as to be unusable or nonfunctional.
- The facility had been struck and suffered only partial (or no) damage or degradation and remained on the target list.
- Insufficient data were available to confirm that the objective had been met, and the target therefore remained on the list.[19]
- The restrike recommendation was "yes."[20]

Table I.5 illustrates examples of the phase III BDA information reported by DIA and our FS or NFS determinations.

---

[17]DIA generated 986 phase III reports covering 432 separate targets. We used the final phase III report when more than one report was produced on a target.

[18]Additional strikes on a target were recommended by DIA to CENTCOM when the results of their BDA indicated that military activity or capability remained at the target site. Restrikes may or may not have occurred for a number of reasons (for example, changing or conflicting priorities in-theater, constraints imposed by the weather, or limited dissemination of BDA results).

[19]It was standard procedure during the air campaign to retain targets on the daily air tasking order and the Master Target List (MTL) and retask aircraft to the target if BDA was absent or inconclusive.

[20]By categorizing a target as NFS, we are not implying that the strikes (or other actions of the air campaign) did not have an adverse impact on the enemy at that location. In many instances, strikes resulted in the partial destruction of the targets and may have affected the tactics and level of enemy activity. An NFS rating implies only that the complete destruction of the target or the elimination of its function had not been achieved (or could not be confirmed) and additional strikes were necessary.

Appendix I
Scope and Methodology

Table I.5: Examples of Phase III BDA and Our FS or NFS Assessments

Target category	Target type	BDA summary	Our assessment
C³	Air defense radar	50 percent degraded; nonoperational; restrike: no	FS
	Air defense radar	Radar and command capability remain; restrike: yes	NFS
ELE	Power plant	Turbines not operating; restrike: no	FS
	Power plant	Installation 70 percent operational; switchyard must be destroyed	NFS
LOC	Highway bridge	Direct hit, bridge nonoperational; traffic rerouted	FS
	Highway bridge	Bridge still operable; no damage	NFS
NBC	Munitions storage	All bunkers out of operation; restrike: no	FS
	Chemical warfare production and storage	Laboratory intact; restrike: yes	NFS
OCA	Airfield	Limited operations possible; restrike: no—unless flight operations resume	FS
	Airfield	50 percent hardened aircraft shelters intact; airfield operational; restrike: yes	NFS

Data Limitations

Although DIA's phase III reports were by far the most comprehensive compilation of BDA for strategic, fixed targets produced during or after the campaign, there were several limitations to these data. These include

- Not all strategic targets were assessed. DIA issued phase III reports on 432 BE-numbered strategic targets, which was a total lower than either the final number of strategic targets identified by CENTCOM during the war or the number of BE-numbered targets in the Missions database, and which was a set of targets that were not necessarily representative of the universe of strategic targets.
- No effort was made after the campaign to update or verify the vast majority of the reports. The accuracy of some analyses without ground verification is very difficult to determine.
- Imagery limitations can hinder analysis. Imagery collection may at times have preceded strikes because combat missions were delayed or postponed. Imagery may not have been taken from the optimal side of a target or at an inappropriate angle for assessment purposes.
- According to DIA, the reliability of assessments grew over the course of the war with the increased experience of the analysts. Thus, the assessments later in the conflict may be more reliable than those made earlier because analysts learned more about the capabilities of the aircraft and munitions through the course of the war.

Appendix I
Scope and Methodology

Other Data

We obtained aircraft and munitions cost data from Air Force and Navy documents and costs as identified in DOD's periodic Selected Acquisition Reports to the Congress.

Analyses

To analyze the use of aircraft and munitions in achieving air campaign objectives, we used the Missions database to determine weight-of-effort and type-of-effort measures at two levels. First, we calculated WOE and TOE at the broad level of the target category for each of the 12 strategic target categories shown in table I.1. Second, we calculated WOE and TOE for each aircraft and TLAM across the 12 categories.

We used phase III reports on 432 fixed strategic targets to determine the extent to which the functional capabilities of the target had been eliminated. To correlate outcomes on targets with the input to them, we matched phase III data with data in the Missions database. For 357 strategic targets (where both BDA and WOE/TOE data existed), we sought to assess the relationship between the WOE and TOE data representing campaign inputs with phase III BDA representing campaign outcomes at the target level.[21]

We conducted our work between July 1992 and December 1995 in accordance with generally accepted government auditing standards.

Strengths and Limitations

This analysis of campaign, aircraft, and munitions use and effectiveness benefited from our use of the most comprehensive strike and BDA data produced from the Persian Gulf War; a previously untried methodology to match inputs and outputs on targets; additional qualitative and quantitative data obtained from Desert Storm veterans and after-action reports to corroborate information in the primary databases; and the results of other Desert Storm analyses, such as the Gulf War Air Power Survey.

This study is the first to match available Desert Storm strike and BDA data by target and to attempt to assess the effectiveness of the multiple weapon systems across target categories. Despite the data limitations discussed below, our methodology provided systematic information on how weapon systems were employed, what level and types of weapons were required to

---

[21]This methodology was discussed with DIA analysts who were familiar with both the Missions database and the phase III reports. They identified no reason why this methodology would not result in valid comparisons of inputs and outcomes. In addition, they believed that the use of WOE and TOE variables would alleviate data problems previously encountered by analysts conducting strike BDAs.

Appendix I
Scope and Methodology

achieve success, and what was the relative cost-effectiveness of multiple platforms. The reliability and validity of these findings are strengthened by our use of interviews, after-action reports, and other Desert Storm analyses to better understand platform performance variables and place the results of our effectiveness analyses in the appropriate context.

Our analyses of campaign inputs (from the Missions database) and outcomes (from the phase III reports) against ground targets have limitations of both scope and reliability imposed by constraints in the primary Desert Storm databases. Systematically correlating munition inputs against targets to outcomes was made highly problematic by the fact that the phase III BDA reports did not provide a comprehensive compilation of BDA for all strategic targets and could not differentiate the effects of one system from another on the same target.[22]

We sought to work around data limitations through a qualitative analysis of systems, based on diverse sources. Claims made for system performance were assessed in light of the most rigorous evaluation that could be made with the available data. We have explicitly noted data insufficiencies and uncertainties. Overall, data gaps and inconsistencies made an across-the-board cost-effectiveness evaluation difficult. However, there were sufficient data either to assess all the major claims made by DOD for the performance of the major systems studied or to indicate where the data are lacking to support certain claims.

---

[22]Such assessments, system by system, were not the goal of these reports. Since targets were generally assessed only episodically and, in most cases, after being hit by numerous diverse aircraft and munitions over a period of time, it was impossible to know which munition from which aircraft had caused what amount of damage.

Appendix II
The Use of Aircraft and Munitions in the Air Campaign

In this appendix, we respond to the requesters' questions about the use, performance, and contributions of individual weapon systems used in Desert Storm, particularly in regard to stealth technology and the F-117. We organize our discussion by four sets of subquestions, as follows.

- <u>Operating environment</u>: What predominant operating conditions prevailed during the air campaign? Specifically, we examine the time available to the coalition to plan the air campaign and deploy forces to the region; the desert environment, the weather, and environmental factors that affected air operations; and the quality of the Iraqi threat, including Iraqi air defense capabilities and countermeasures to coalition bombing efforts.
- <u>Weapon system capability and actual use</u>: Based on original design or previous performance, what were the expected capabilities of the U.S. air-to-ground aircraft and their munitions before the war? Did performance during Desert Storm differ from expectations and, if so, in what way? We assess patterns of aircraft and munition use during the war, such as the kind of targets to which aircraft were tasked; night versus day employment; the relative use of guided and unguided munitions; and the particular performance capabilities of the F-117. We also evaluate official statements made before and after the war about the capabilities of aircraft and their respective target sensors in locating and identifying targets in various weather and when operating at night.
- <u>Combat operations support requirements</u>: What was required to support the air-to-ground aircraft in the form of refueling tankers, sensors, and suppression of Iraqi defenses? We also address three controversies related to support for the F-117: Did the F-117s receive radar jamming or other types of support? What is the evidence that they were detectable by radar? Did they achieve tactical surprise?
- <u>Survivability</u>: Were the survival rates of the various air-to-ground aircraft similar, and what factors affected aircraft survivability? In particular, was the F-117 survival rate unique among these aircraft? And were the defenses faced by the F-117s uniquely severe or comparable to those encountered by other aircraft?

Operating Conditions: Time, Environment, and Enemy Capability

In this section, we review the operating conditions in Desert Storm with the object of distilling the lessons that can be learned for the future.

A 6-Month Planning and Deployment Period

Following the Iraqi seizure of Kuwait, U.S. forces had nearly 6 months to plan the air campaign and to deploy massive forces, many to existing

Appendix II
The Use of Aircraft and Munitions in the Air
Campaign

bases and facilities in Saudi Arabia and the other Persian Gulf states, supplied in part from prepositioned stores as the buildup proceeded.[1] The Iraqis chose not to interfere in any regard with this massive buildup, leaving their own troops in static positions as the coalition deployed increasingly large air, ground, and sea forces. The coalition had the luxury of time to deploy all the forces it needed, along with their supplies, while the enemy did little to obstruct the process. In considering future contingencies, and using Desert Storm as a baseline experience, it is important to remember that the United States was permitted an uncurtailed buildup of forces and military supplies to existing infrastructures on foreign, yet friendly, soil that directly bordered the hostilities.

The 6-month period also permitted identifying and studying important strategic targets in Iraq. Planners were able to extensively review and revise plans for the critical strikes that took place in the opening days of the air campaign. During this period, many of the units that saw some of the most activity in Desert Storm were able to practice flying in the desert environment, honing their skills under conditions for which some had not previously trained, given the expectation that large-scale combat would most likely take place in a European scenario. There were opportunities to accumulate intelligence on the nature of Iraqi defenses in part by intentionally tripping Iraqi radars and observing Iraqi reactions. In effect, the U.S. military services were able to plan their initial actions thoroughly and in great detail, including the complex interactions among dozens of U.S. and allied military units, and to build up large frontline forces and reserves without enemy interference.

The Desert Environment and Air Power

The vast, flat, open terrain of the KTO and Iraq was considerably more favorable the effective employment of air power than most other geographies around the globe. While camouflage, gullies, and revetments offered some possibilities for Iraqi concealment, almost all analyses of the conflict conclude that, overall, it was easier to find targets in the desert than in jungle or mountainous terrain. Moreover, until the ground campaign started after 40 days of air bombardment, many Iraqi ground forces remained entrenched in fixed positions, permitting repeated strikes against both personnel and equipment.

---

[1]See Operation Desert Storm: Transportation and Distribution of Equipment and Supplies in Southwest Asia (GAO/NSIAD-92-20, Dec. 26, 1991).

Appendix II
The Use of Aircraft and Munitions in the Air Campaign

Cloud cover and storms made for the worst weather in that region for at least 14 years, but conditions were no worse than what would probably be the best ones likely in other conflicts. At the same time, because many air strikes were carried out at night, and some under adverse weather conditions, the sensors used by aircraft and munitions to locate, identify, and track targets were used under a wide variety of environmental conditions.

Iraqi Air Defense Capabilities

On paper, Iraq's air defense system appeared to be formidable to many observers before the air campaign. Iraq had purchased what was widely described as a state-of-the-art integrated air defense system (IADS) from France, which linked 17 intercept operations centers (IOC) to four sector operations centers (SOC). The IOCs were linked to air bases with interceptor aircraft, as well as to dozens of surface-to-air missile and antiaircraft artillery sites. With multiple and redundant communication modes, the system could, in theory, rapidly detect attacking aircraft and direct antiaircraft defenses against them. (The IADS is described in app. VI.)

However, the Iraqi IADS had been designed to counter limited threats from either Israel, to its west, or Iran, to its east, not from the south and north, nor from a massive coalition force to which the United States alone contributed more than 1,000 combat aircraft. As the Navy's Strike Projection Evaluation and Anti-Air Research (SPEAR) department reported before the war:

"the command elements of the Iraqi air defense organization (the . . . interceptor force, the IADF [Iraqi Air Defense Force], as well as Army air defense) are unlikely to function well under the stress of a concerted air campaign."[2]

Similarly, on almost every performance dimension, the Iraqi IADS was remarkably vulnerable to massive and rapid degradation. Evidence from the Air Force, DIA, GWAPS, SPEAR, and other expert sources shows that the principal deficiencies of the Iraqi IADS were that (1) it could track only a limited number of threats, and it had very limited capabilities against aircraft with a small radar cross-section, such as the F-117; (2) its design was easy to disrupt, and the key IADS nodes were easy to target, [DELETED]; and (3) many of its SAMs were old or limited in capability, and the Iraqi air force played almost no role in the conflict, although it had been intended to be a major component of air defenses.

---

[2]Naval Intelligence Command, Navy Operational Intelligence Center, SPEAR Department, Iraqi Threat to U.S. Forces (Secret), December 1990, p. 3-14.

Appendix II
The Use of Aircraft and Munitions in the Air Campaign

In addition, the political context of the war permitted the development of a strong, cohesive, coalition force while Iraq had few allies, none of which were particularly strong or in a position to materially aid Iraq.

Iraqi Countermeasures

Our review of unit after-action reports, lessons-learned reports, and interviews with pilots suggests that Iraqi countermeasures to degrade or impede the effectiveness of coalition air attacks or communications were inconsistent and did not appear to have represented as much as could have been achieved.

[DELETED]

Finally, toward the end of the war, the Iraqis ignited hundreds of Kuwaiti oil wells, creating vast plumes of black oil-based smoke, which seriously degraded visual observation and air reconnaissance as well as the infrared (IR) and electro-optical (EO) weapon sensors and the laser designators on aircraft. The purpose of this action appears to have been more to punish Kuwait than to impede bombing efforts, although it ultimately did this.

It is difficult to assess the overall success of the Iraqi countermeasures employed against aircraft sensors since it is not readily known how many decoy targets were attacked or how many actual targets were not attacked because they were effectively camouflaged or hidden among their surroundings. At the same time, given the absence of attempted Iraqi jamming of satellite communications, little if any jamming against coalition aircraft radars, and the apparent absence of any discovery during or after the war that countermeasures were used on a massive or even broad scale, it would appear, on balance, that the use of countermeasures in Desert Storm was inconsistent, at best, and did not seriously stress or impede U.S. aircraft sensors, bombing efforts, or communications.

In sum, to answer our first subquestion, we found that a number of unique political, logistic, intelligence, and threat conditions characterized the environment in which Desert Storm took place. These conditions appear to have, at minimum, facilitated the overall planning and execution of the air campaign and, therefore, must be considered in assessments of Desert Storm outcomes and in generalizing the lessons learned from this campaign.

Appendix II
The Use of Aircraft and Munitions in the Air Campaign

Air-to-Ground Weapon Systems: Planned Versus Actual Use

The second major evaluation subquestion concerns the prewar capabilities of air-to-ground aircraft, munitions, and sensors; their stated prewar missions; and their actual use in Desert Storm.[3] In this section, we discuss (1) comparing prewar aircraft mission capabilities to actual mission use in Desert Storm, (2) examining specific performance issues for the F-117, and (3) comparing prewar target location and acquisition capabilities to capabilities observed in Desert Storm.

Pre-Desert Storm Aircraft Missions Versus Desert Storm Use

We compared official Air Force and Navy descriptions of the types of combat missions for which their respective air-to-ground aircraft were designed and produced to whether each aircraft actually performed such missions in Desert Storm.[4] (See table II.1.)

---

[3]A comparison of design and actual Desert Storm missions for aircraft under review has the potential to reveal findings about the attributes and limitations of the aircraft, the adequacy of pilot and crew training, and the nature of the conflict. For example, deviations found between design and actual missions might reveal (1) an inability of an aircraft to perform an expected mission, (2) an unanticipated mission, or (3) a unique tactical environment.

[4]We excluded two types of missions that are highly specialized—search and rescue and support of special operations forces.

Appendix II
The Use of Aircraft and Munitions in the Air Campaign

Table II.1: Air-to-Ground Combat Mission Categories Attributed to Selected Aircraft Before Desert Storm Versus Those Actually Performed[a]

Aircraft	AI[b] C	AI[b] DS	CAS[c] C	CAS[c] DS	SEAD[d] C	SEAD[d] DS	OCA[e] C	OCA[e] DS	DCA[f] C	DCA[f] DS	SCAP and JMO[g] C	SCAP and JMO[g] DS
F-117	X	X	N	N	X	X	X	X	N	N	X[h]	N
F-111F	X	X	N	N	X	X	X	X	N	N	X[i]	N
F-15E	X	X	N	N	X	X	X	X	X	N	X	N
A-6E	X	X	X	X	X	X	X	X	N	N[j]	X	X
F-16	X	X	X	X	X	X	X	X	X	N	X	X
F/A-18	X	X	X	X	X	X	X	X	X	X	X	X
A-10	X[k]	X	X	X	X	X	N	X	X	N	X[l]	N
B-52	X	X	X	N	X	X	X	X	N	N	X	N
GR-1(U.K.)	X	X	X	N	X	X	X	X	X	N	X	N

[a]An "X" in column C (capability) indicates that the platform was credited with the mission capability before Desert Storm (DS); an "N" indicates that it was not credited with the capability. An "X" in column DS indicates that records show that the platform conducted missions or strikes of this type in Desert Storm; an "N" indicates that available records do not show this.

[b]**Air interdiction (AI)**: These are missions to destroy, neutralize, or delay enemy ground or naval forces before they can operate against friendly forces. AI targets include transportation systems and vehicles, military personnel and supplies, communication facilities, tactical missiles, and infrastructure.

[c]**Close air support (CAS)**: These missions support ground operations by destroying enemy capability in close proximity to friendly ground forces.

[d]**Suppression of enemy air defenses**: These missions strive to increase the survival or effectiveness of friendly aircraft operations by destroying or neutralizing enemy air defenses.

[e]**Offensive counterair**: These missions seek out and neutralize or destroy enemy aerospace assets, such as airfields, aircraft in shelters, and radar sites.

[f]**Defensive counterair**: These are defensive air-to-air missions flown against airborne enemy aircraft.

[g]**Surface combat air patrol and joint maritime operations:** Surface combat air patrol are sorties of naval aircraft to protect surface ships from attack. Joint maritime operations include the use of Air Force aircraft to assist in the achievement of military objectives in the naval environment.

[h]The F-117's JMO capability to attack naval targets at sea is described as "minimal." It does, however, have the capability to attack ships and other naval targets in port.

[i]Note h applies to the F-111F also.

[j]The A-6E is not credited with capability in this mission category. Only four DCA sorties were flown in Desert Storm; for that reason, the cell has an "N."

[k]The A-10's AI capability was described as limited in MCM 3-1 vol. III.

[l]The A-10's JMO capability was described as limited.

Appendix II
The Use of Aircraft and Munitions in the Air Campaign

Sources: USAF TAC MCM 3-1 vols. III, V, VI, XIII, XVII, XIX (Secret), NAVAIR Tactical Manuals for the F-18 and A-6 (Confidential), official descriptions of the GR-1 from the Ministry of Defense of the United Kingdom, and GWAPS, vol. V, pt. I (Secret), pp. 336-404.

We note in the table where the Air Force or Navy declared a mission capability to be limited. If an aircraft performed a very small number of missions, such as fewer than five, we did not credit the aircraft with exhibiting that capability in Desert Storm. A very small sample of missions does not permit the reliable determination that the aircraft, successfully or unsuccessfully, demonstrated the capability.

Table II.1 shows that in the four mission categories that emphasize air-to-ground attack—AI, CAS, SEAD, and OCA—all the aircraft under review were used to a meaningful extent during Desert Storm to perform missions consonant with their stated capabilities. In only one case—that of A-10s carrying out OCA missions—was an aircraft used for a mission for which it had not been envisioned.[5]

The DCA mission category was one of two in which aircraft were <u>not</u> used for a mission for which they had an acknowledged pre-Desert Storm capability. Except for F/A-18s, none of the aircraft under review credited with a defensive air-to-air capability actually had an opportunity to use it in Desert Storm. Overall, nearly all of the Iraqi aircraft that were shot down were attacked by F-15Cs.

The relative paucity of air-to-air combat missions reflects the fact that, for the most part, comparatively few Iraqi aircraft attempted to attack either coalition aircraft or ground targets, despite the fact that Iraq had about 860 combat aircraft and attack helicopters combined. Overall, the Iraqi air force essentially chose not to challenge the coalition. Over 100 Iraqi combat aircraft were flown to Iran during the war.

In sum, the data on intended versus actual Desert Storm mission use indicate no substantial discrepancies between the anticipated capabilities of aircraft and the missions for which they were actually employed in Desert Storm. Where stated capabilities were not used, it was apparent that there was little need for them. (See app. VII.)

Patterns of Aircraft and Munitions Use

Our second evaluation subquestion further concerns whether the Desert Storm data revealed particular patterns of aircraft and munitions usage, on

---
[5]Although Navy aircraft performed SCAP and JMO missions, Air Force aircraft with this capability performed no significant number. This may have reflected a combination of sufficient Navy assets to deal with these targets and traditional service rivalries.

Appendix II
The Use of Aircraft and Munitions in the Air Campaign

the weight of effort and type of effort measures, across the 12 strategic target categories. (See app. I for a summary of the WOE and TOE analysis.)

Patterns in Aircraft Target Assignments

Many strategic targets were assigned basic encyclopedia numbers in the target planning and study process. Target assignment data that include the number and type of aircraft and munitions were available from the Missions database for 862 targets with BE numbers, including kill box targets assigned individual BE numbers.[6] Figure II.1 shows BE-numbered strategic targets in each of 12 categories that were tasked to different types of aircraft.[7] The data in figure II.1 can be analyzed in terms of the pattern (or lack thereof) in aircraft target assignments to BE-numbered targets across the target categories, thus suggesting which aircraft, if any, planners tended to prefer.

In less than half the strategic target categories—that is, GVC, NAV, NBC, SCU, and C³—did one or two types of aircraft strongly predominate. First, in the GVC category, F-117s were assigned to 27 (87 percent), F-16s to 8 (26 percent), and F-111Fs to 1 (3 percent) of the BE-numbered targets. Given that GVC targets were generally high-value, in heavily defended areas, and sometimes either deeply buried bunkers or heavily reinforced structures, the F-117's role here appears consistent with its intended mission and the capabilities of the specially designed warhead-penetrating I-2000 series LGBs with which it was equipped.

---

[6]KBX targets were mostly related to ground troops, for example, tanks, artillery, and trucks located in large geographic areas. (See app. I for a discussion of kill box targets.)

[7]This and similar analyses of the Missions database do not include the A-10. If the data on the over 8,000 A-10 sorties had been usable, it obviously would have comprised a major part of these analyses.

Appendix II
The Use of Aircraft and Munitions in the Air Campaign

Figure II.1: BE-Numbered Targets Assigned to Aircraft[a]

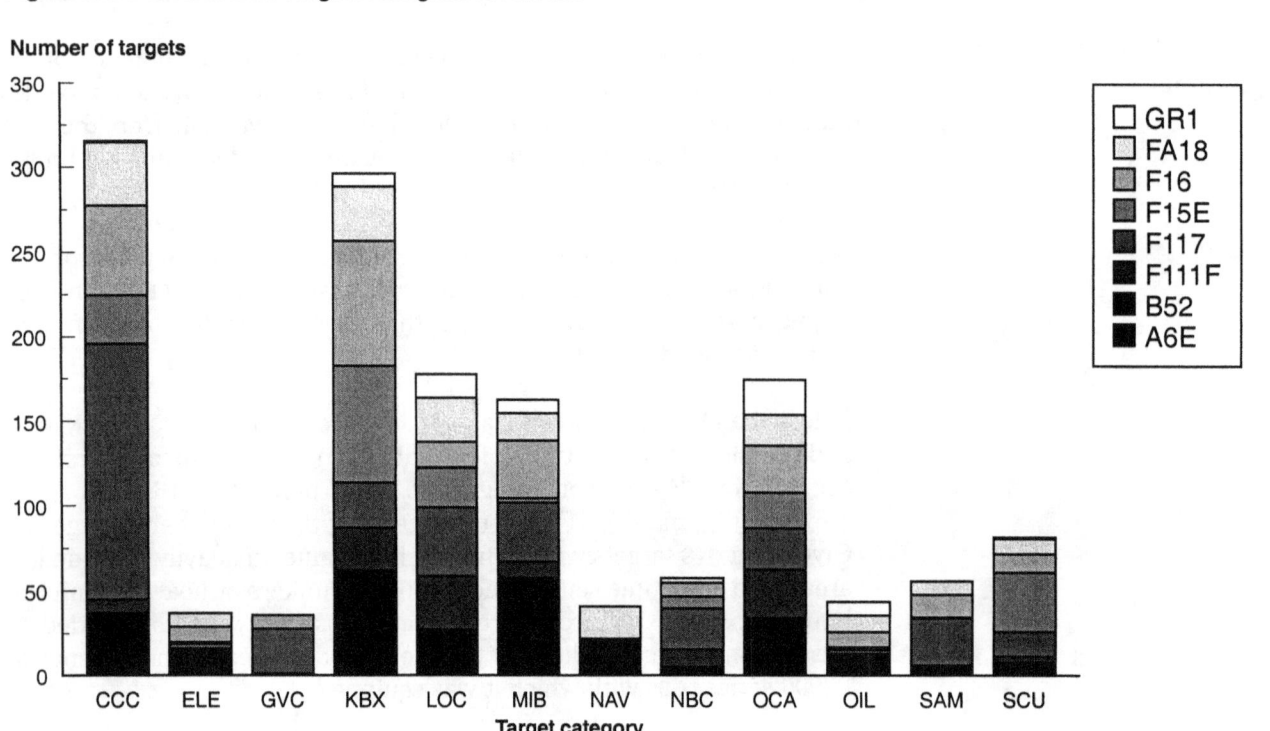

[a]The total BE-numbered targets depicted is greater than 862 because some BEs were assigned to more than 1 type of aircraft.

A preference pattern can also be found in F-117 assignments to NBC targets (25 of 29, or 86 percent) and C³ targets (151 of 229, or 66 percent). In none of these was any other aircraft assigned to even half the percentage accounted for by the F-117s. However, considerable redundancy among aircraft target assignments is apparent: while the F-117s were assigned to 86 percent of the NBC BEs, the seven other aircraft, in sum, were assigned to over 90 percent of these BEs.

Second, a strategic target category assignment preference was evident in the NAV category, where two types of Navy aircraft, A-6Es and F/A-18s,

Appendix II
The Use of Aircraft and Munitions in the Air Campaign

were respectively assigned to 83 and 79 percent of the 24 naval-related targets with BEs.[8]

Third, a pattern of preference can be found in the SCU category, where F-15Es were assigned to just over 68 percent of the 51 BE-numbered targets. In contrast, the next highest participant against these targets was the F-117, assigned to about 30 percent.

Finally, in half of the strategic target categories—ELE, KBX, LOC, MIB, OIL, OCA—no aircraft among those under review was alone assigned to more than 60 percent of the targets or was otherwise clearly predominant in terms of assigned BEs.[9] For example, in the OCA category, all eight aircraft were assigned to between 27 and 48 percent of the BE-numbered targets, indicating very substantial overlap among assigned aircraft and targets. The data show similar overlap in the five other categories (ELE, KBX, LOC, MIB, and OIL).

In sum, the F-15E, F-117, A-6E, and F/A-18 were preferred platforms against particular sets of strategic targets. However, the general patterns suggest that preferences, as revealed by patterns in target assignments, were the exception and that among the aircraft reviewed, most were assigned to multiple strategic targets across multiple target categories.

Patterns of Munitions Use

Contrary to the general public's impression about the use of guided munitions in Desert Storm, our analysis shows that approximately 95 percent of the total bombs delivered against strategic targets were unguided; 5 percent were guided. Unguided bombs accounted for over 90 percent of both total bombs and bomb tonnage. Approximately 92 percent of the total tonnage was unguided, compared to 8 percent guided. These percentages characterized not only the overall effort but also the proportion of guided and unguided tonnage delivered in each week of the air campaign.

Interviews with pilots and Desert Storm planners and a review of relevant DOD reports, such as tactical manuals on aircraft and munitions, identified reasons for this pattern. Among these were (1) poor weather and

---

[8]Clearly, 83 and 79 percent do not add to 100 percent. When the combined percentages of individual aircraft target assignments do not add to 100, it means that at least two or more aircraft were assigned to some of the same BE-numbered targets.

[9]The F-16 was assigned to 51 percent of the BE-numbered KBX targets. However, a large number of the targets in this category had no BEs assigned to them and are therefore not included in this analysis. Thus, the 51 percent for the F-16s may not most accurately characterize the percentage of KBX-related targets that were assigned to F-16s.

Appendix II
The Use of Aircraft and Munitions in the Air Campaign

conflict-induced environmental conditions such as smoke from bombing, which degraded or blocked the targeting sensors required for the delivery of guided ordnance; (2) the comparatively high cost of guided bombs and resulting smaller inventories (pilots were frequently told to conserve guided bomb deliveries); and related to inventory, (3) the fact that many strategic targets were large and therefore generally appropriate for the use of unguided ordnance.

The F-111F and the F-117 accounted for the majority of the guided bomb tonnage delivered against strategic targets compared to the other platforms reviewed. Together, the 42 F-117s and 64 F-111Fs in theater delivered at least 7.3 million pounds of guided bombs against Desert Storm strategic targets over the course of the 43-day air campaign. Overall, more guided bomb tonnage was delivered against OCA targets than against the other types of strategic targets, and the F-111F accounted for the bulk of this delivery. OCA targets included hardened aircraft shelters and bunkers, which were considered important and were targeted consistently, not least because they housed much of Iraq's air force. The achievement and retention of air supremacy was critical to the successful, safe continuation of the air campaign; thus, OCA targets were important.

In at least one case—that of the Navy's night-capable A-6E—it appears that capability to deliver LGBs was used only sparingly, despite the fact that the 115 A-6Es deployed constituted almost 51 percent of all U.S. LGB-capable aircraft on the first day of Desert Storm. A-6Es delivered fewer than 600 LGBs, or approximately 1.1 million pounds of bombs; these constituted about 7 percent of all the LGBs used in the war.

Summing across all target categories, the data show that, excluding the A-10, F-16s and B-52s accounted for the preponderance (70 percent) of all unguided bomb tonnage delivered. B-52s delivered at least 25,000 tons (37 percent of total tonnage), and F-16s delivered at least 21,000 tons of unguided ordnance against strategic targets (31 percent).[10]

Night Strikes

Most strikes against strategic targets, including nearly all from U.S. LGB-capable aircraft, were conducted at night. Five of the eight air-to-ground aircraft under review carried out at least two thirds of their strikes against strategic targets at night: F-117 (100 percent), F-111F

---

[10]The tonnage delivered by A-10s is unknown but may have been substantial given its sizable payload and more than 8,000 sorties during the air campaign.

Appendix II
The Use of Aircraft and Munitions in the Air Campaign

(99.6 percent), F-15E (94.2 percent), A-6E (72 percent), and B-52 (67 percent). Figure II.2 compares the percentage of day and night strikes.

Figure II.2: Percent of Day and Night Strikes for Selected Aircraft

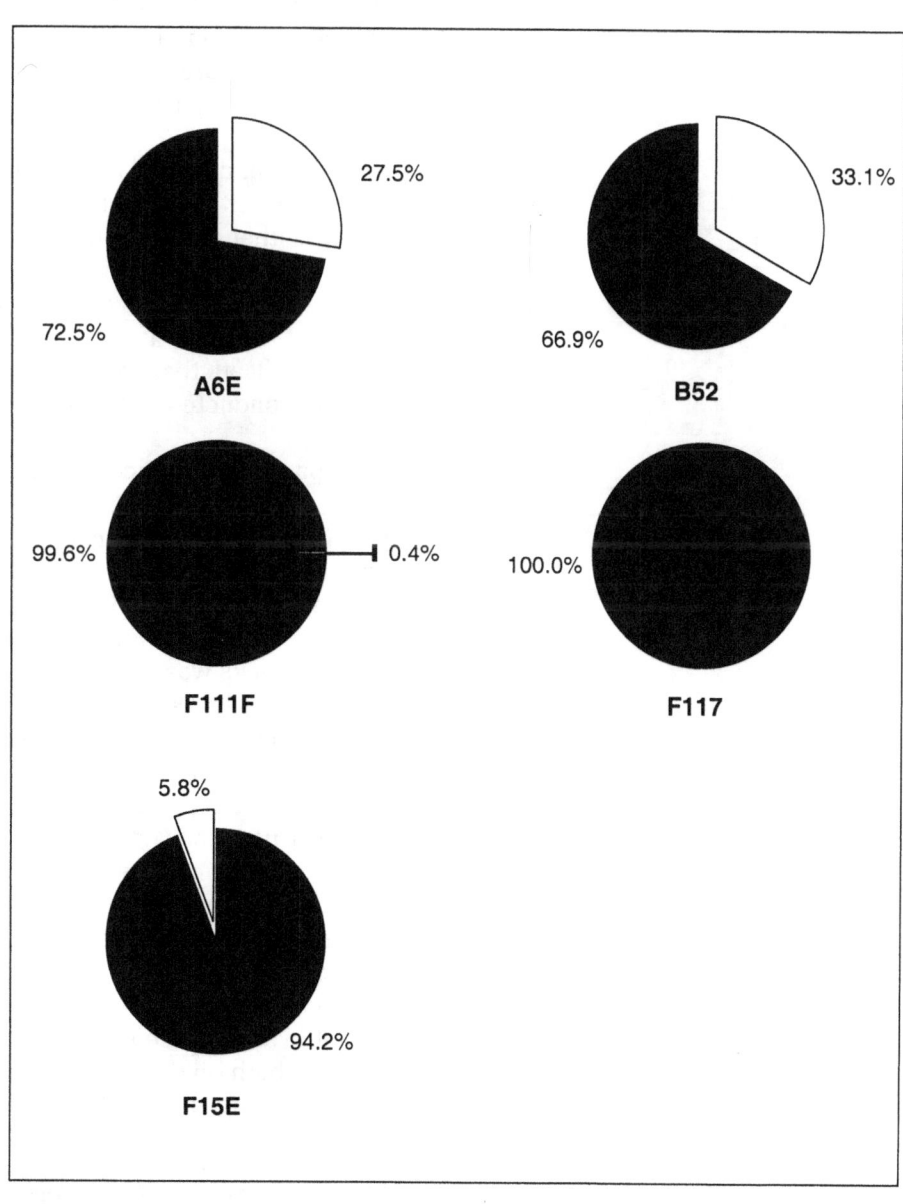

Appendix II
The Use of Aircraft and Munitions in the Air Campaign

The use of the F-117 and F-111F nearly exclusively at night reflects pre-Desert Storm expectations regarding mission capability. Although the F-111F can operate during the day, it has a designated emphasis on night operations. The F-117 can <u>technically</u> also operate during the day. But it was designed for night employment: it is not stealthy in day or low-light conditions, being readily visible to the human eye. Some of the design and performance characteristics that make the F-117 low-observable to radar [DELETED] compared to other aircraft.

The F-15E conducted 94.2 percent of its strikes at night, reflecting a preference for this operational context since its stated mission capability includes either day or night operations. B-52s and A-6Es also showed a preference for night operations, with more than two thirds of their strikes against strategic targets conducted at night. Finally, the British Tornado was about evenly split on its percentage of day and night strikes. Overall, the data indicate that among the air-to-ground platforms reviewed, more than half conducted two thirds or more of their operations at night.

The apparent preference for nighttime operations seems most likely related to maximizing aircraft survivability. As discussed later in this appendix, in Desert Storm, optically guided Iraqi IR SAMs and AAA were responsible for the largest number of aircraft casualties (losses and damage). Therefore, nighttime operations appear to have enhanced aircraft survivability. Further, in the desert environment, the effectiveness of night attacks was improved for aircraft with infrared targeting systems because operations at night provide optimal heat contrast for some targets as the sand cools faster than many objects in it.

F-117 Performance

The F-117 has received highly favorable press for its achievements in the Gulf War. The Air Force has officially stated that the F-117 contributed much more to the Desert Storm strategic air campaign than would have been expected given its limited numbers. In its September 1991 white paper on Desert Storm, the Air Force stated that although the F-117s made up only 2.5 percent of the aircraft in theater on the first night of the war, they hit over 31 percent of the strategic targets, and this pattern was exhibited both on the first night of the campaign, when Iraqi air defenses were the strongest, and throughout the remainder of the war.[11]

---

[11]As recently as the February 1995 Annual Report to the President and the Congress, the report of the Secretary of the Air Force stated that "the F-117 destroyed 40 percent of all strategic targets while flying only 2 percent of all strategic sorties during Desert Storm." (See p. 300) While the portion of the coalition air forces represented by the F-117 is addressed in this section, the accuracy and effectiveness of the F-117 are addressed in appendix III.

Appendix II
The Use of Aircraft and Munitions in the Air Campaign

Similarly, Lockheed, the primary contractor for the F-117, reported that over the course of the war, F-117s represented only 2 percent of total tactical assets yet accounted for 40 percent of all strategic targets attacked. The contribution of the F-117s was also highlighted in DOD's title V report as the only aircraft to strike targets in all 12 strategic categories.

Clearly, the question of the relative contribution of the F-117, in combination with claims about its accuracy (see app. III) and stealth characteristics, has important implications for future force structure and procurement decisions. In particular, we sought to determine if the F-117 had been appropriately compared to aircraft with similar missions and whether the data supported the claims made for F-117 performance.

The Appropriateness of Aircraft Comparisons

The 2.5 percent DOD cited as representing the percentage of F-117s in the "shooter" force is derived from data that include many types of aircraft that cannot bomb ground targets—the only mission of the F-117. Shooters are defined as aircraft that can deliver any kind of munitions from bullets to bombs. Table II.2 lists Desert Storm combat aircraft classified as "shooters."

Not all shooter aircraft, however, can perform the same missions. Shooter aircraft include those that have solely air-to-air capabilities as well as those that have air-to-ground capability. Since air-to-air shooters cannot hit ground targets but were included in the shooter totals, the claim about the percentage of the total shooter force that F-117s represented in Desert Storm is not accurate.[12] Although they may have attacked 31 percent of the strategic targets, they did not comprise only 2.5 percent of the relevant shooters in the theater—that is, those that could deliver munitions against ground targets.

We sought to determine what percentage of the relevant aircraft they did comprise. On the first day of Desert Storm, 229 aircraft were capable of both designating targets with lasers and autonomously delivering LGBs.[13]

---

[12]The shooters total used to calculate the 2.5 percent figure included not only air-to-air aircraft but also over 500 non-U.S. aircraft that never entered Iraq during Desert Storm. Neither French nor coalition Arab aircraft attacked targets in Iraq, although some were used against Iraqi forces in Kuwait. Thus, these coalition aircraft did not represent aircraft that performed the same type of mission as the F-117 (that is, attacking ground targets in Iraq).

[13]Four types of LGB-capable aircraft and their respective percentages in theater were 36 F-117 (15.7), 115 A-6E (50.2), 66 F-111F (28.8), and 12 F-15E (5.2). Although the interdiction variant of the Panavia Tornado, which the United Kingdom, Saudi Arabia, and Italy had in theater, did deliver LGBs in a few instances, these aircraft could not or did not autonomously operate with LGBs. Therefore, they are not included here. Similarly, only the 12 F-15Es that could autonomously deliver LGBs are included.

Appendix II
The Use of Aircraft and Munitions in the Air Campaign

The 36 F-117s in theater at the start of the campaign were 15.7 percent of these 229 aircraft. Thus, of all the aircraft that had the potential to deliver some kind of LGB, the stealth force represented not 2.5 percent of the assets but 15.7 percent. Moreover, because the I-2000 series LGBs were only in the Air Force's inventory, the F-117s actually constituted 32 percent of all coalition aircraft that could deliver such bombs.

Appendix II
The Use of Aircraft and Munitions in the Air Campaign

Table II.2: Number and Percent of Coalition "Shooter" Aircraft

Aircraft type	Number	Percent
F-117	42	2.2
A-6E	115	6.2
A-7E	24	1.3
A-10	132	7.0
AC-130	8	0.4
AV-8B	62	3.3
B-52	66	3.5
EA-6B	39	2.1
F-4G	60	3.2
F-111E	18	1.0
F-111F	66	3.5
F-14	100	5.3
F-15C	124	6.6
F-15E	48	2.6
F-16	247	13.2
F/A-18	169	9.0
A-4 (Kuwait)	19	1.0
CF-18 (Canada)	24	1.3
F-15 (Saudi Arabia)	81	4.3
F-16C/D (Bahrain)	12	0.6
F-5 (Bahrain)	12	0.6
F-5E/F (Saudi Arabia)	84	4.5
Hawks (Saudi Arabia)	30	1.6
Jaguar (France)	24	1.3
Jaguar (United Kingdom)	12	0.6
Mirage (United Arab Emirates)	64	3.4
Mirage 2000 (France)	12	0.6
Mirage F-1 (France)	12	0.6
Mirage F-1 (Qatar)	12	0.6
Mirage F-1 (Kuwait)	15	0.8
Strikemaster (Saudi Arabia)	32	1.7
Tornado F3 (United Kingdom)	53	2.8
Tornado ADV (Italy)	9	0.5
Tornado ADV (Saudi Arabia)	48	2.6
Total	**1,875**	**100.0**

Source: DOD title V report, 1991.

Appendix II
The Use of Aircraft and Munitions in the Air Campaign

Comparisons of Target Assignments

Contrary to DOD claims, the F-117 represented approximately 16 percent of the Desert Storm LGB assets on day one and 32 percent of LGB-capable aircraft that could deliver the penetrating I-2000 series LGBs, particularly useful against hardened, reinforced, and buried hardened targets. Given this, it is not altogether surprising that the F-117 seems to have been a preferred platform against GVC and NBC targets. The F-117 attacked approximately 78 percent of the targets receiving LGBs on day one and attacked about one-third of all the first-day targets, but it attacked less than 10 percent of all the strategic targets that had been identified at the start of the air campaign.

During the first day of Desert Storm, F-117s performed 61 strikes, which accounted for 57 percent of all first day LGB strikes against strategic targets.[14] Three of the four LGB-capable carriers actually delivered LGBs—the A-6Es, the F-111Fs, and the F-117s; F-15Es delivered unguided munitions exclusively. However, the F-117s and F-111Fs accounted for all but about 7 percent of the strikes with LGBs. Fifty-nine BE-numbered targets received 108 strikes with LGBs. F-117 strikes represented 57 percent of these strikes (which were against 46 of the 59 targets, or 78 percent); F-111F strikes were 36 percent of the total.

Comparison of Target Assignments Throughout the War

One of the prominent claims the Air Force made for the F-117 in comparing it to other bombers was that it, alone, attacked targets in all 12 strategic target categories. We found this claim to be accurate; however, we also found that in three of the target categories—naval, oil, and electricity—the F-117s attacked only one, two, and three BE-numbered targets, respectively. Further, we found that F-16s, F/A-18s, and A-6Es each attacked targets in 11 of the 12 strategic target categories; F-15Es attacked targets in 10 categories; and B-52s and F-111Fs attacked targets in 9 categories. As table II.3 shows, each of the other U.S. air-to-ground aircraft in Desert Storm attacked targets in no less than three-fourths of the target categories.

---

[14]The first "day" was actually the first 29 hours in the Missions database, from 1800 Zulu on January 16, 1991, to 2300 Zulu on January 17, 1991.

Appendix II
The Use of Aircraft and Munitions in the Air Campaign

Table II.3: Coverage of Strategic Target Categories, by Aircraft Type

Aircraft	C³	ELE	GVC	KBX	LOC	MIB	NAV	NBC	OCA	OIL	SAM	SCU	Total	Percent
F-15E	X	X	a	X	X	X	a	X	X	X	X	X	10	83
F-117	X	X	X	X	X	X	X	X	X	X	X	X	12	100
F-16	X	X	X	X	X	X	a	X	X	X	X	X	11	92
F-111F	X	a	X	X	X	X	a	X	X	a	X	X	9	75
F/A-18	X	X	a	X	X	X	X	X	X	X	X	X	11	92
A-6E	X	X	a	X	X	X	X	X	X	X	X	X	11	92
B-52	X	X	a	X	X	X	a	X	X	X	a	X	9	75
GR-1	X	a	a	X	X	X	a	a	X	X	a	X	7	58

ᵃNo targets in this category were attacked, by aircraft type.

Although the F-117s attacked at least one target in each of the 12 categories, their taskings were concentrated on a narrow range of target types within target categories. These types of targets were typically fixed, small, and greatly reinforced, being deeply buried or protected by concrete. F-117s conducted relatively few strikes in categories where the targets were area or mobile (for example, MIB or KBX targets). Characteristic F-117 targets had known locations and did not require searching.

The relative contribution of the F-117 can also be assessed by examining the number of targets assigned exclusively to it. Table II.4 shows that the F-117 was assigned exclusive responsibility for more targets than any other aircraft among the 862 BE-numbered targets for which there are data. These targets were primarily in C³, GVC, NBC, and SAM—categories that include known, fixed, often hardened targets.

Appendix II
The Use of Aircraft and Munitions in the Air Campaign

Table II.4: BE-Numbered Targets Assigned Exclusively to One Type of Aircraft

Aircraft	Target category												Exclusive targets	
	C³	ELE	GVC	LOC	MIB	NAV	NBC	OCA	OIL	SAM	SCU	Unknown	Total	Percent[a]
A-6	8	3	0	2	4	4	0	2	1	3	0	0	27	14.6
B-52	3	4	0	0	8	0	0	2	2	0	0	0	19	11.7
FA-18	4	3	0	1	0	4	0	1	2	2	1	2	20	10.1
F-111F	0	0	0	6	0	0	1	6	0	1	1	1	16	13.6
F-117	94	3	13	7	7	0	8	4	2	27	3	7	175	46.3
F-15E	12	0	0	7	1	0	0	0	0	0	21	1	42	22.6
F-16	25	4	2	6	3	0	1	2	4	8	1	1	57	16.9
GR-1	1	0	0	7	1	0	0	1	7	0	0	12	29	46.0
TLAM	1	9	2	0	0	0	0	0	0	0	0	0	12	31.6

[a]Percent of all target assignments that were exclusive.

Prewar Target Acquisition Capabilities Versus Desert Storm Capabilities

Here we address how the claimed prewar aircraft target acquisition capabilities compared to those experienced in Desert Storm. The capabilities of aircraft to locate targets and then deliver munitions accurately against them is intimately connected to sensors that aid the pilots in carrying out these tasks.

A series of steps must be performed to successfully attack a ground target from the air, especially when precision munitions are being used. For fixed targets that have been previously identified and located, the delivery aircraft must navigate to the geographic coordinates of the target and then pick it out from other possibilities, such as neighboring buildings or other objects. For mobile targets, the aircraft may have to search a broad area to find and identify the right candidates for attack. For either type of target, the pilot may need to determine that the target is a valid one—for example, the extent of previous damage, if any; for vehicles, what kind; whether the object is a decoy; and so forth.

Target Sensor Systems Deployed in Desert Storm

Various sensor systems were used in Desert Storm to search for, detect, and identify valid targets and to overcome impediments to normal human vision, such as distance, light level (night versus day), weather, clouds, fog, smoke, and dust. These sensor systems can be grouped into three technology categories: infrared, radar, and electro-optical. (See app. IX.) Each of these different sensor technologies has been described to the

Appendix II
The Use of Aircraft and Munitions in the Air Campaign

Congress and to the public as enhancing capability in poor visibility conditions, such as in the day; at night; and in "poor," "adverse," or "all" weather conditions. Table II.5 shows the prewar official descriptions of the capabilities of the sensors as well as their Desert Storm demonstrated capability.[15]

Table II.5: Official Public Descriptions of the Prewar and Desert Storm Capabilities of Air-to-Ground Aircraft Sensors

Aircraft	Target search and detection sensor	Prewar description of target-sensing capability	Our findings on Desert Storm actual capability
F-117	Infrared (FLIR and DLIR)[a]	Night only;[b] weather is "a constraint not imposed by technology limitations"[c]	Clear weather only; flew exclusively at night
F-15E	Infrared (LANTIRN) radar	Day and night; "adverse weather"	All weather only with unguided bombs; clear weather only for guided munitions; flew almost only at night
F-111F	Infrared (Pave Tack) radar	Day and night; "poor weather"	All weather only with unguided bombs; clear weather only for guided munitions; flew almost only at night
A-6E	Infrared (TRAM)[d] radar	Day and night; "all weather"	All weather only with unguided bombs; clear weather only for guided munitions; flew day and night
F-16	Infrared, electro-optical (LANTIRN) and IR and EO (Maverick),[e] and radar	Day and night; "under the weather" (LANTIRN); "adverse weather" (Maverick)	Clear weather only (Maverick); all weather only with unguided bombs; flew day and night
F/A-18[f]	Infrared (FLIR) radar; electro-optical (Walleye)	Day and night and adverse weather capability not prominently stated	All weather only with unguided bombs; clear weather only for Walleye and FLIR pod; flew day and night
A-10	Infrared and electro-optical (Maverick)	Day and night capable; "adverse weather" (Maverick)	Clear weather only for guided (Maverick) and unguided munitions; flew day and night
B-52	Radar	Day and night and weather capability not prominently stated	All weather only with unguided bombs; flew day and night

[a]Forward- and downward-looking infrared.

[b]Based on a postwar Air Force description; unofficial prewar descriptions available to us did not make clear the night-only limitation.

[c]Prewar unclassified descriptions were unclear about the F-117's weather capability, so this is a postwar statement.

[d]Target recognition and attack multisensor.

[e]Some F-16s were equipped with LANTIRN navigation pods but no targeting pods.

[f]See Naval Aviation: The Navy Is Taking Actions to Improve the Combat Capabilities of Its Tactical Aircraft (GAO/NSIAD-93-204, July 7, 1993).

[15]Equipment and capabilities beyond those specifically described and directly related to target sensing functions are not addressed. For example, separate navigation and air-to-air combat equipment and capabilities are not assessed.

Appendix II
The Use of Aircraft and Munitions in the Air
Campaign

Effect of Operating Conditions on Target Sensor Performance

Although desert environments are widely believed to exhibit relatively nonhazy, dry weather providing uninhibited visibility, there was actually great variation on this dimension in Desert Storm. Moreover, winter weather in the gulf region during Desert Storm was the worst in 14 years. Records show that there was at least 25-percent cloud cover on 31 of the war's 43 days, more than 50-percent cloud cover on 21 days, and more than 75 percent on 9 days. Also, there were occasionally violent winds and heavy rains. As a result, the adverse-weather capabilities of the target-sensing systems were frequently tested in the air campaign. While the frequency and severity of cloud cover and poor weather were not comparable to more adverse weather conditions normal for other climates, they were not nearly as benign as had been expected.

IR, EO, and laser sensor systems demonstrated [DELETED] degradation from adverse weather, such as clouds, rain, fog, and even haze and humidity, [DELETED]. Sensors were also impeded by conflict-induced conditions, such as dust and smoke from bombing. In effect, these systems were simply [DELETED] systems as characterized by DOD. In contrast, air-to-ground radar systems were not impeded by the weather in Desert Storm. This permitted their use for delivery of unguided munitions, although usually with low target resolution.

Similarly, night weapon delivery capabilities were tested, since as noted previously, a large percentage of aircraft strikes were conducted at night, including essentially all F-117 and F-111F strikes and most F-15E strikes. Of the more than 28,000 U.S. combat strikes and British Tornado strikes, about 13,000 (46 percent) were flown at night.

At the same time, a number of conditions during the air campaign aided the effectiveness of target-sensing systems. The flat, open, terrain in the KTO, without significant foliage or sharp ground contours, exposed targets to sensors and made all but the smallest targets hard to conceal completely.[16] The desert climate provided a strong heat contrast for targets on the desert floor, especially at night. The flat, monochrome nature of much of the terrain presented a good optical contrast during much of the day for EO systems, by making objects or their shadows—when camouflaged—salient. The Iraqi practice of deploying tanks in predictable patterns facilitated their identification. Similarly, because many Iraqi frontline ground units remained in fixed positions for nearly 6 weeks of the air campaign—essentially until the coalition ground

---

[16]For example, there is evidence that the Iraqis took advantage of areas where there was greater terrain variation to hide mobile Scud launchers under bridges.

Appendix II
The Use of Aircraft and Munitions in the Air Campaign

offensive began—they were easy to find and not difficult to distinguish from friendly forces.

[DELETED]

Performance of Infrared Sensors

Pilots generally reported that certain target sensors and bombing systems gave them an effective capability to operate at night that they otherwise would not have had. These assessments were particularly relevant to the IR sensing systems, such as LANTIRN, IR Maverick, TRAM, Pave Tack, and FLIR/DLIR.

[DELETED] F-15E pilots stated that they were "exponentially more effective" with LANTIRN than without. The A-10 was able to operate at night in significant numbers [DELETED].

IR sensors proved important for effective night attack; however, pilots of virtually every aircraft type also told us about a variety of limitations.

Effects of High-Altitude Releases on IR Sensor Resolution. During the air campaign, the majority of bombs were released from aircraft flying above 12,000 to 15,000 feet because Brig. Gen. John M. Glosson ordered that restriction enforced after aircraft losses early in the air campaign during low-altitude munition deliveries.[17] Higher altitudes provided a relative sanctuary from most air defenses but resulted in a major compromise in terms of bomb accuracy and, ultimately, effectiveness.[18] For example, some F/A-18 pilots reported that bombing from high altitude sometimes meant a total slant range to the target of 7 miles. At this range, even large targets, like aircraft hangars, were "tiny" and hard to recognize. [DELETED]

Several methods were used to help overcome poor target image resolution. [DELETED]

Other Hindrances to IR Sensors. Pilots reported that a variety of environmental conditions, some natural and some conflict-induced, impeded the capabilities of their IR sensor systems. [DELETED]

---

[17]Brig. Gen. Glosson was Deputy Commander, Joint Task Force Middle East, and Director of Campaign Plans for the air campaign.

[18]In general, the higher an aircraft flew, the less vulnerable it was to AAA, IR SAMs, and small arms fire.

Appendix II
The Use of Aircraft and Munitions in the Air Campaign

Field of View and Other Design Problems

Field of View Issue

[DELETED]

Electro-Optical Systems

EO sensors depended on both light and optical contrast for target searching and identification. This obviated their use at night and in any significantly adverse weather or visual conditions where the line of sight to a target was obscured. The requirement for visual contrast between the target and its immediate surroundings imposed an additional problem: for Walleye delivery, F/A-18 pilots reported that a target was sometimes indistinguishable from its own shadow. This made it difficult to reliably designate the actual target, rather than its shadow, for a true weapon hit. They also said that the low-light conditions at dawn and dusk often provided insufficient light for the required degree of optical contrast.

F/A-18 pilots told us that a "haze penetrator" version of Walleye used low-light optics to see through daytime haze and at dawn and dusk, permitting use in some of the conditions in which other optical systems were limited. That notwithstanding, EO systems proved at least as vulnerable to degradation as other sensors and lacked full-time night capability.

Radar Systems

[DELETED]

Despite the target discrimination limitations of most radar systems, they had the advantage of not being impeded by adverse weather. However, even with this advantage, only comparatively inaccurate unguided bombs could be delivered in poor weather since all the guided munitions used in Desert Storm basically required clear weather to enable their various IR, EO, and laser sensors and designator systems to deliver munitions.

Combat Operations Support

A realistic evaluation of the performance of combat aircraft in Desert Storm involves acknowledgment of the nature and magnitude of their support. Here we address our third evaluation subquestion: What was required in Desert Storm to support various air-to-ground aircraft?

Targeting activity and the success of strike aircraft are inextricably linked to the performance and availability of external support assets. In many

Appendix II
The Use of Aircraft and Munitions in the Air Campaign

instances, aircraft relied on a number of support assets to conduct missions: for example, refueling tankers; airborne control platforms like AWACS; airborne platforms that permit battlefield command and control capability like JSTARS (Joint Surveillance Target Attack Radar System); platforms that provide fighter escort for strike aircraft (such as F-15Cs); airborne platforms that conduct electronic warfare (such as F-4Gs, EA-6Bs, and EF-111s); and airborne reconnaissance platforms that collect intelligence and information used for BDA and those that detect and monitor threats.

Approximately 1,011 U.S. fixed-wing combat aircraft were deployed to Desert Storm, compared to 577 support aircraft, or a ratio of 1.75 to 1.[19] While combat aircraft outnumbered support aircraft in Desert Storm, the latter flew more sorties—a fact that is important to consider for future military contingencies. Nearly 50,000 sorties were conducted in support of approximately 40,000 combat air-to-ground sorties, for a ratio of about 1.25 to 1. Support aircraft were relied upon for air-to-ground and air-to-air missions in Desert Storm, both of which were conducted around the clock. To support the efforts of combat aircraft, the smaller number of combat-support platforms would have had to fly more sorties.

Desert Storm as a Tanker-Dependent War

In-Flight Aircraft Refueling

One of the combat-support platforms that was perhaps most critical to the execution of the air campaign was the aerial refueling tanker. Most Desert Storm combat missions required refueling because of around-the-clock operations and the great distances from many coalition aircraft bases and U.S. aircraft carriers in the Red Sea to targets in Iraq.[20] Virtually every type of strike and direct combat support aircraft required air refueling. At least 339 U.S. in-flight refueling tankers off-loaded more than 800 million pounds of fuel. For Air Force tankers alone, there were approximately 60,184 recorded refueling events. On average, over the 43-day air campaign, there were 1,399 refueling events per day, or approximately 58 per hour.

---

[19]See GWAPS, vol. V, pt. I (Secret), pp. 31-32. Fixed-wing Air Force, Navy, and Marine Corps aircraft as of February 1, 1991, are the only aircraft included in the 1,011 total. Aircraft identified as "Special Operations" are not included. Combat aircraft include fighters, long-range bombers, attack aircraft, and gunships. Combat-support aircraft include tankers, airlift, reconnaissance, surveillance, and electronic combat aircraft.

[20]DOD's title V report (Secret), p. 115.

Appendix II
The Use of Aircraft and Munitions in the Air Campaign

Table II.6 shows the percentages of total known refueling events accounted for by some of the U.S. platforms reviewed here (data on the F-117 were "not releasable").[21] Among all the known, recorded, Desert Storm refueling events from U.S. Air Force tankers, the F-16 and F-15 account for the highest percentages among the selected platforms.[22]

Table II.6: Percent of Total Known Refueling Events for Selected Air-to-Ground Platforms

Platform	Percent[a]
F-16	23.0
F-15	20.0
F/A-18	9.5
A-10	6.0
F-111	4.3
B-52	3.5
A-6	3.4
F-117	[b]

[a]Percentages of the total known number of Desert Storm refueling events from U.S. Air Force tankers only.

[b]Data were not available.

To put the percentage of aircraft refueling events in context, we examined the extent to which the number of known refueling events was related to the number of strikes that platforms conducted. We found that the statistical correlation between the number of refueling events and the number of strikes was large, indicating that among all aircraft considered, there was a positive relationship.[23] In effect, as the number of strikes conducted by all the included aircraft increased, generally, so did the number of refuelings required by those aircraft. This is clearly illustrated by the F-16s, which accounted for both the largest percentage of known aircraft refueling events and the largest number of strikes among the platforms reviewed.

---

[21]Although the number of F-117 refueling events was not available, we developed an approximation measure in order to estimate a lower bound of their number. Based on the reported number of F-117 Desert Storm sorties (1,299) and the minimum number of reported refueling events per sortie (2), we estimate the lower bound of F-117 refueling events to be 2,598, or 4.1 percent of a total of 62,782 from U.S. Air Force tankers only.

[22]Not only U.S. Air Force platforms received fuel from U.S. Air Force tankers. Air Force tankers provided fuel for some non-Air Force aircraft, including some Navy and Marine Corps aircraft. Therefore, the percentages reported in table II.6 are percentages based on total number of refueling events for Air Force aircraft only.

[23]Pearson correlation coefficient, $r = 0.69$. Strikes conducted against strategic targets as reported in our WOE/TOE analysis, which does not include F-117 data.

Appendix II
The Use of Aircraft and Munitions in the Air Campaign

In-Flight Refueling Complications

In-flight refueling is a normal, routine part of air operations and not one for which aircrew or tanker crew were unprepared. However, a number of factors in the Desert Storm environment caused this routine process to become highly complex and sometimes quite dangerous for tankers as well as other airborne platforms and, in instances, resulted in restrictions or limitations in air operations.

The use of large strike packages as well as constant, around-the-clock air strikes resulted in heavily congested air space during most of the air campaign. The number of airborne aircraft was sometimes constrained by the number of tankers that had to be present to meet refueling needs. Aircraft strikes on targets were sometimes canceled or aborted because aircraft were unable to get to a tanker.

To preserve tactical surprise as well as to keep tankers, which have no self-protection capability, out of the range of Iraqi SAMs, nearly all tanker tracks or orbits occurred in the limited airspace over northern Saudi Arabia, south of the Iraqi border.[24] The heavily saturated airspace alone increased the probability of near midair collisions (NMAC). Nighttime operations and operations in bad weather only exacerbated an already complex, precarious, operational environment.[25]

The Air Force Inspection and Safety Center reported 37 Desert Storm NMACs, believing, however, that these were only a fraction of the actual number. In one reported NMAC, a KC-135 tanker crew saw two fighter aircraft approaching from the rear, appearing to be rejoining on the tanker. It became apparent to the tanker crew that the fighters had not seen the tanker. The tanker crew accelerated to create spacing, avoiding an NMAC, but the reported distance between the fighters and the tanker was only between 50 and 100 feet before evasive action was taken.

Airborne Sensor Aircraft Support

The U.S. air order of battle (AOB) during the third week of the air campaign indicates that over 200 airborne sensor aircraft, providing a range of combat-support duties, were in the Persian Gulf theater. These included a variety of reconnaissance, surveillance, electronic combat, and battlefield

---

[24]We were told by several Desert Storm pilots, from different units, that there were instances in which tankers had to cross over into Iraq to refuel aircraft that would not have made it back to the tanker before running out of fuel.

[25]We made several recommendations for enhancing the efficiency of aerial refueling operations based on Desert Storm. See Operation Desert Storm: An Assessment of Aerial Refueling Operational Efficiency (GAO/NSIAD-94-68, Nov. 15, 1993).

Appendix II
The Use of Aircraft and Munitions in the Air Campaign

command and control platforms. A discussion of the roles of each of these can be found in appendix X.

Strike Support-Related Missions

Combat air patrol (CAP), escort missions, and SEAD are types of combat-support missions that, in Desert Storm, were frequently tied directly to aircraft strike missions or were conducted in areas near where strikes were occurring and, therefore, also benefited strike aircraft.

CAP missions protect air or ground forces from enemy air attack within an essentially fixed geographic area. In Desert Storm, these included coalition ships, aircraft striking targets, and high-value air assets such as AWACS and tankers. Escort missions were normally conducted by air-to-air fighter aircraft and were used to protect strike aircraft from attack by enemy air forces en route to and returning from missions. In contrast to CAP, escorts do not remain in a relatively fixed area but, rather, stay with the strike package. Fighter escort also served as force protection, when needed, for airborne assets such as AWACS and tankers that have limited or no self-protection capability. Finally, jamming and SEAD support aircraft like EF-111s, EA-6Bs, and F-4Gs provided direct support to strike packages or target area support that benefited nearby strike aircraft.

Figure II.3 compares the number of CAP, SEAD, and escort strike support missions conducted during each week of the Desert Storm air campaign. Overall, the total number of CAP missions was somewhat greater than SEAD missions and substantially greater than escort missions, and there were no significant fluctuations in this number during the 6-week air campaign. That CAPs were often necessary for combat-support aircraft (such as tankers and AWACS) as well as strike aircraft may explain the greater number of CAP missions relative to SEAD and escort missions. In figure II.3, we also observe that the only type of combat support-related activity that actually showed some gradual decline over time was escort missions. This is logical given that the threat from enemy aircraft was significantly diminished, if not eliminated, by the second week of the air campaign.

Appendix II
The Use of Aircraft and Munitions in the Air Campaign

Figure II.3: Strike Support Missions by Week

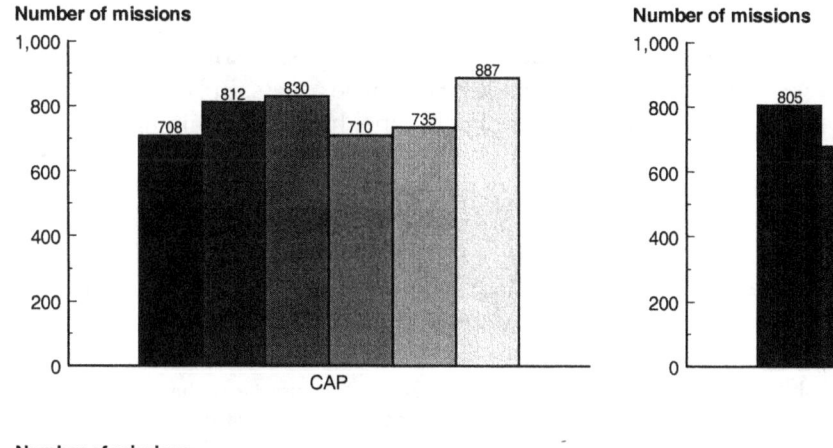
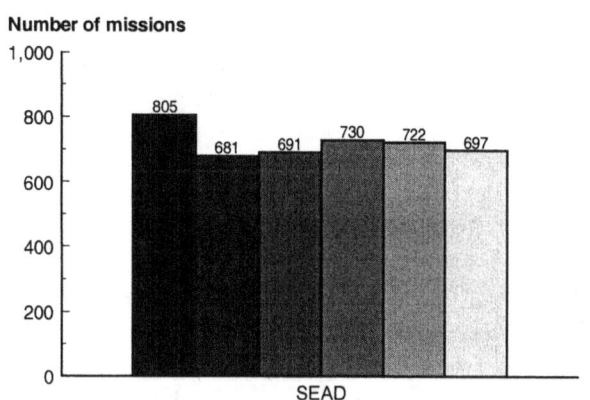
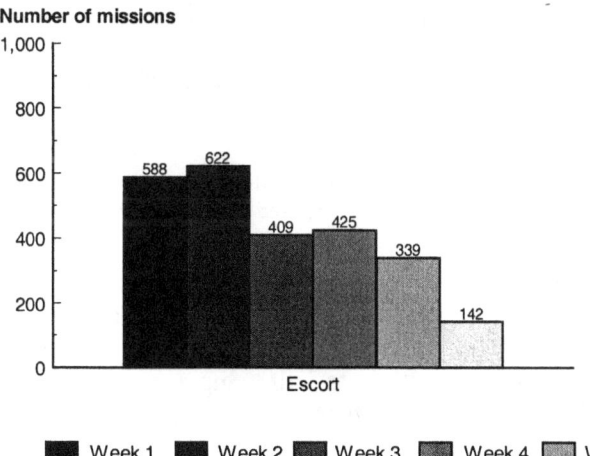

The only notable drop in SEAD missions was after the first week of the air campaign. However, the number remained rather static during the following 5 weeks. This may reflect the fact that although the Iraqi IADS had been disrupted early in the air campaign, numerous SAM and AAA sites remained a threat, with autonomous radars, until the end of the war. The fact that there was not a consistent decline in SEAD missions, over time, suggests that simply destroying the integrated capabilities of the air

Appendix II
The Use of Aircraft and Munitions in the Air Campaign

defense system did not, unfortunately, eliminate its many component parts. (This is discussed further in app. VI.)

Aircraft Maintenance Personnel

The range of combat-related support encompasses some understanding of the personnel required to maintain airborne assets. In Desert Storm, approximately 17,000 Air Force personnel had force maintenance responsibilities. This figure accounts for approximately 31 percent of the total Air Force population in the area of responsibility.

Support Provided for the F-117 Was Understated

Shortly after Desert Storm, Air Force Gen. John M. Loh told the Congress that

"Stealth . . . restores the critically important element of surprise to the conduct of all our air missions" and " . . . stealth allows us to use our available force structure more efficiently because it allows us to attack more targets with fewer fighters and support aircraft."[26]

In describing the performance of the F-117 in Desert Storm, another Air Force general testified that

"Stealth enabled us to gain surprise each and every day of the war. . . . Stealth allows operations without the full range of support assets required by non-stealthy aircraft."[27]

In contrast, as discussed previously, conventional aircraft in Desert Storm were routinely supported by SEAD, CAP, and escort aircraft. Because F-117s could attack with much less support than conventional bombers, they were credited with being "force multipliers," allowing a more efficient use of conventional attack and support assets.[28]

For example, in their April 1991 post-Desert Storm testimony to the Congress, Gens. Horner and Glosson testified that 8 F-117s, needing the

---

[26]Testimony by Gen. Loh (then USAF, Commander, Tactical Air Command). <u>Department of Defense Appropriations for 1992</u>, Hearings before the Subcommittee on the Department of Defense, House Committee on Appropriations, Apr. 30, 1991, p. 510.

[27]Testimony by Lt. Gen. Charles A. Horner, then commander of 9th Air Force and Central Command U.S. Air Forces, before the House Appropriations Subcommittee on Defense, Apr. 30, 1991, pp. 468-69.

[28]Information that would definitively address the extent to which the F-117s were detected by the Iraqis and the extent to which the F-117s were supported by other airborne assets in Desert Storm is classified. We requested but were not granted access to information that would have enabled us to fully understand the detectability of the F-117 during Desert Storm. Although that information could not have been presented in this report, our review of it would have given us greater confidence that the information contained in the report was reliable and valid. The information presented in this section was the best we could obtain given our limited access to records.

Appendix II
The Use of Aircraft and Munitions in the Air Campaign

support of only 2 tankers, could achieve the same results as a package of 16 LGB-capable, nonstealth bombers that required 39 support aircraft or 32 non-LGB capable, nonstealth bombers that required 43 support aircraft.[29] The Air Force depicted this comparison in its congressional testimony with the graphic reproduced as figure II.4.[30]

Figure II.4: "The Value of Stealth"

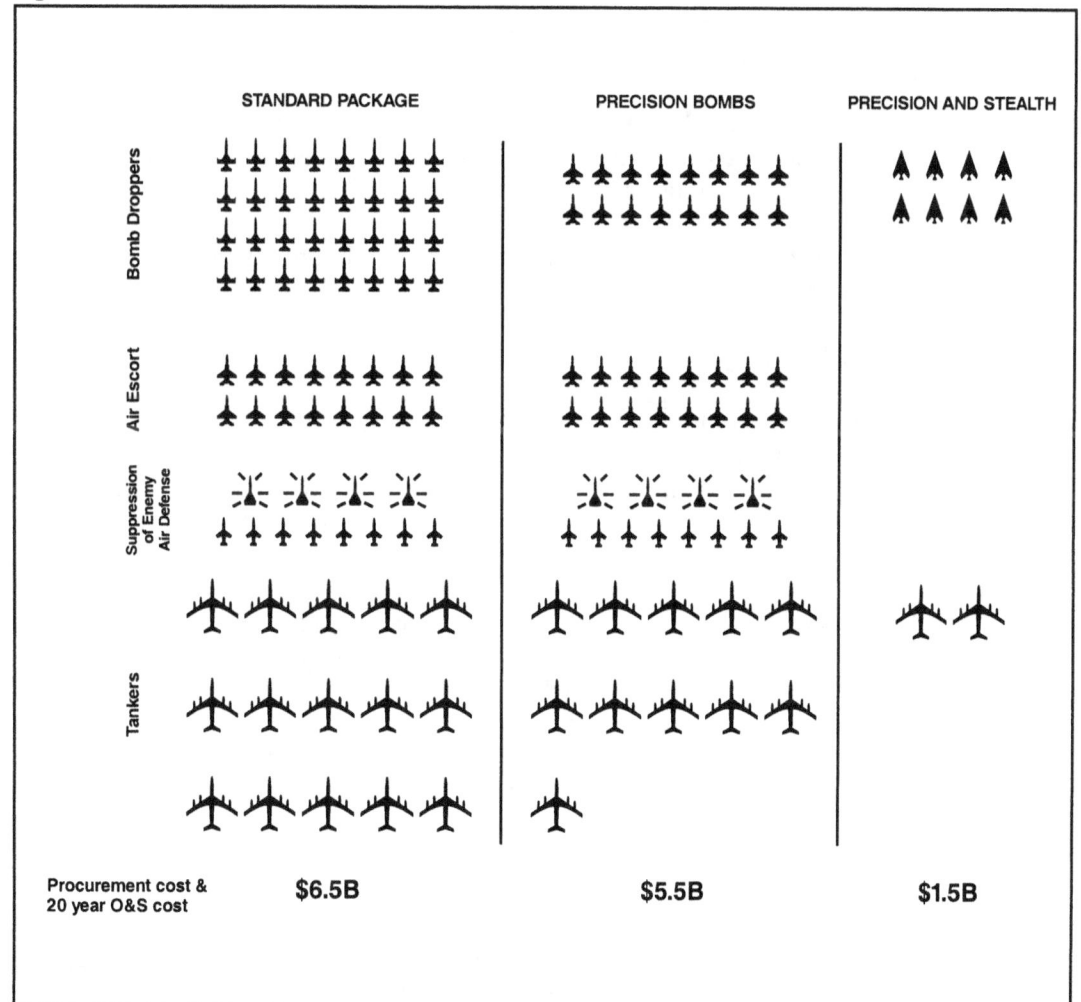

Source: House Appropriations Subcommittee on Defense (Apr. 30, 1991), p. 472.

[29]House Appropriations Subcommittee on Defense (Apr. 30, 1991), p. 472.

[30]Figure II.4 depicts two actual strike packages employed against the Baghdad Nuclear Research Facility. Appendix XI addresses the effectiveness of the conventional (F-16) and the stealth (F-117) strike packages against this target.

Appendix II
The Use of Aircraft and Munitions in the Air
Campaign

In figure II.4, the use of the stealthy F-117 in Desert Storm is depicted as having several positive effects: it reduces the number of aircraft employed on a mission, thereby reducing overall costs; it reduces the number of aircraft and pilots at risk; and it increases the number of missions that can be tasked without increasing the number of aircraft.[31] However, following our review of after-action reports and interviews with F-117 pilots and planners, we found that this depiction does not adequately convey the (1) specific operating procedures required by the F-117, (2) modifications in tactics during the campaign to better achieve surprise, and (3) support, in addition to tanking, that it received.

F-117 Detectability and Operating Procedures

In addition to its low observable features, the F-117 achieves stealthy flight through the avoidance of daylight, active sensors or communications, and enemy air defense radars.

[DELETED] Every F-117 strike mission in Desert Storm was carried out at night.

[DELETED]

Stealth Requires Extensive Mission Planning. Each pilot has an individual mission plan tailored to the assigned target and the threats that surround the target. Because F-117s are not "invisible" to radar but, rather, as the Air Force points out, are "low observable," a computerized mission planning system [DELETED]. [DELETED][32]

Stealth and Tactical Surprise in Desert Storm

A significant claim made by the Air Force is that because of stealth, F-117s were able to achieve tactical surprise each night of the campaign, including the first night when F-117s attacked the key Iraqi air defense nodes and, in so doing, opened the way for attacks by nonstealth aircraft, thereby greatly reducing potential losses. However, we found the following Desert Storm information to be inconsistent with the Air Force claim.

---

[31]The "value of stealth" depicted in figure II.4 is essentially anecdotal—it depicts two missions flown during the first week of the campaign. The Air Force does not cite evidence that this represents the typical, or average, use of support aircraft by conventional and stealth aircraft in Desert Storm. For example, because the standard package illustrated for the conventional fighters was substantially downsized by the end of the first week of the air campaign, as the threat level was reduced, the claimed life-cycle cost for each of these packages is not necessarily an appropriate measure for comparison. As discussed here, the depiction does not properly credit other (nontanker) support assets that helped the F-117s attain their Desert Storm achievements.

[32]The F-117s were deployed to King Khalid Air Base near Khamis Mushait in the southwestern corner of Saudi Arabia. Mission times averaged over 5 hours.

Appendix II
The Use of Aircraft and Munitions in the Air Campaign

AAA Before and After F-117 Bomb Impacts. A number of Air Force officials told us that because AAA did not start until after the first F-117 bombs had exploded, this was evidence that F-117s had achieved tactical surprise. However, we found that the absence of AAA prior to bomb impact was neither consistent for all F-117 missions nor unique to F-117s.

An Air Force after-action report stated that in the case of the A-10, AAA began after the first bomb detonation, not just sometimes but "in most cases" and in "the majority of first passes."[33] Similarly, pilots of other aircraft, including F-16s and F-15Es, also reported the same phenomenon. They encountered no AAA until after their bombs exploded, and like the F-117s, they were subject to AAA primarily during egress from the target. Moreover, F-117 pilots told us that, on occasion, AAA in a target area would erupt "spontaneously"—before they had released their bombs or the bombs had exploded. In response to this threat, the F-117 Tactical Employment manual states (on pp. 3-11, 3-29, and 3-31) that F-117 refueling and jamming support procedures were altered during Desert Storm to delay "spontaneous" AAA in the target area.

[DELETED]

In sum, the claim that the F-117s consistently achieved tactical surprise is not fully consistent with the information we obtained. The absence of AAA prior to F-117 bomb impact was not universally observed and was not unique to the F-117. [DELETED]

F-117s Benefit From Support Aircraft

In contrast to the Air Force illustration to the Congress that F-117s require only tanker support in combat (see fig. II.4), Desert Storm reports and participants stated explicitly that the F-117s did, in fact, receive more than just tanker support in Desert Storm.

At the end of 1991, after press accounts stated that the Air Force had exaggerated the degree to which F-117s operated without defense suppression and jamming support, Air Force officials then concurred that standoff jamming from EF-111s had been employed from time to time in conjunction with F-117 strikes.[34] This position—that the F-117 did, in fact, benefit from jamming on occasion—is more consistent with the title V

---

[33] 57th Fighter Weapons Wing, Tactical Analysis Bulletin, Nellis Air Force Base 92-2 (Secret), pp. 6-7 and 6-8.

[34] Bruce B. Auster, "The Myth of the Lone Gunslinger," U.S. News and World Report, November 18, 1991, p. 52, and Davis A. Fulghhum, "F-117 Pilots, Generals Tell Congress About Stealth's Value in Gulf War," Aviation Week and Space Technology, May 6, 1991, pp. 66-67, as reported in GWAPS, vol. II, pt. II (Secret), p. 354.

Appendix II
The Use of Aircraft and Munitions in the Air Campaign

report than with the Air Force's testimony in April 1991 that failed to note nontanking combat support having been provided to F-117s in Desert Storm. As discussed previously, the 37th Tactical Fighter Wing (TFW) lessons-learned report unambiguously describes how jamming assets were incorporated in F-117 tactics and operations. Pilot interviews and portions of the lessons-learned report also suggest that F-117s, occasionally, benefited from fighter support aircraft.

[DELETED]

In terms of air-to-air fighter support, the Air Force states that there was typically little or none provided for the F-117s. The Desert Storm "Lessons Learned" section of the F-117 Tactical Employment manual is unclear on this issue, stating (on p. 3-29) that

"Unit coordination with the F-15s occurred each day. While we never had any F-15s tied to us, we had to make sure they understood our general plan for the night."

In addition, several pilots we interviewed believed that air-to-air, F-15 aircraft were in a position to challenge any Iraqi interceptors that would have posed a threat to the F-117s.

Aircraft Survivability

The percentage of aircraft lost and damaged in Desert Storm was very low—compared both to planners' expectations and to historic experience. The attrition rates of the Israeli air force in the 1967 and 1973 Arab-Israeli wars were about 10 times those of Desert Storm.

Coalition combat aircraft conducted approximately 65,000 combat sorties in Desert Storm. A total of 38 aircraft was lost to Iraqi action, and 48 other aircraft were damaged in combat, making a total of 86 combat casualties. However, of these casualties, only 55 involved any of the 8 air-to-ground U.S. aircraft under review, of which just 16 were losses, with the remaining 39 being damage incidents. All coalition aircraft casualties and the known causes are shown in table II.7, with the aircraft

Appendix II
The Use of Aircraft and Munitions in the Air Campaign

under review listed first; for comparison, TLAM en route losses are also shown.[35]

---

[35]By aircraft "casualties," we mean both aircraft that were lost and aircraft that were damaged. While some, but not all, damaged aircraft were returned to service after repairs of varying extent and while there can be important differences between an aircraft that is lost and one that is damaged, we include damaged aircraft in our analysis for the following reasons: (1) air defense systems that incur only damage nonetheless often achieve their aim of forcing the damaged aircraft to return to base before the target is reached or weapons are released; (2) DOD reports and statements made about various aircraft refer not just to lost aircraft but also to hits from air defense systems; and (3) including damaged aircraft is more analytically conservative—that is, in assessing air defense systems and aircraft survivability, it is impossible to predict for the purposes of deriving "lessons learned" whether a hit will result in a loss or merely damage.

Appendix II
The Use of Aircraft and Munitions in the Air Campaign

Table II.7: Type of Coalition Aircraft Lost or Damaged and Attributed Cause

Aircraft	Radar SAM	IR SAM	AAA	Other	Total
F-117 lost	0	0	0	0	0
F-117 damaged	0	0	0	0	0
F-111F lost	0	0	0	0	0
F-111F damaged	0	0	3	0	3
F-15E lost	1	0	1	0	2
F-15E damaged	0	0	0	0	0
A-6E lost	1	0	2	0	3
A-6E damaged	0	0	3	2	5
O/A-10 lost	0	6	0	0	6
O/A-10 damaged	0	3	11	0	14
F-16 lost	2	0	1	0	3
F-16 damaged	1	2	0	1	4
F/A-18 lost	0	0	0	2[a]	2
F/A-18 damaged	0	7	1	0	8
B-52 lost	0	0	0	0	0
B-52 damaged	2	1	2	0	5
GR-1 lost[b]	4	1	2	2	9
GR-1 damaged[b]	1	0	0	0	1
Other lost[c]	2	6	3	2	13
Other damaged[c]	0	2	4	2	8
Total lost	**10**	**13**	**9**	**6**	**38**
Total damaged	**4**	**15**	**24**	**5**	**48**
Total casualties	**14**	**28**	**33**	**11**	**86**
TLAM lost[d]	0	0	0	[DELETED]	**[DELETED]**

[a]One loss was attributed by GWAPS to a MIG-25; the second was stated as unknown.

[b]GR-1 data in this table include aircraft from the United Kingdom, Italy, and Saudi Arabia.

[c]These rows include AC-130, EF-111, F-4G, F-14, F-15C, AV-8B, OV-10, A-4, F-5A, and Jaguar casualties. While these aircraft are not part of the focus of this report, they are included in this table as part of our discussion of the effectiveness of the Iraqi air defenses.

[d]TLAM losses are based on a study by Center for Naval Analyses (CNA) and DIA that found that of the 230 TLAM Cs and D-Is, an estimated [DELETED] did not arrive at their target areas. An additional 30 TLAM Cs with airburst mode warheads and 22 D-IIs could not be assessed. If the hit rate for these 52 TLAMS is assumed to be the same as for the 230 assessable TLAM Cs and D-Is, then an additional [DELETED] TLAMS did not arrive at their targets. Thus, an estimate for the total losses, using this assumption, would be a minimum of [DELETED] and a maximum of [DELETED].

Source: GWAPS, vol. V, pt. I (Secret), pp. 670-81.

Appendix II
The Use of Aircraft and Munitions in the Air Campaign

Relative Effectiveness of Iraqi Threat Systems

The system perceived before Desert Storm as most threatening—radar SAMs—actually accounted for less than one-fifth the number of casualties caused by AAA and IR SAMs. Moreover, the system generally considered to be a lesser threat, AAA, proved throughout the war to be quite lethal.

The data in table II.7 show that small, portable, shoulder-launched SAMs with IR guidance systems were the leading cause of Desert Storm aircraft kills, responsible for 13 of 38 (34 percent), followed by 10 (26 percent) attributed to radar SAMs and 9 (24 percent) to AAA. In contrast, AAA was the leading cause of damage to aircraft, accounting for 24 of 48 cases (50 percent of total damaged). IR SAMs were the next leading cause of damage, with 15 cases (31 percent), and radar SAMs were last, with 4 cases (8 percent).

If we sum the losses and damage by cause, portable IR SAMs accounted for 31 percent of the total casualties, and AAA accounted for 38 percent—both more than twice the 16 percent of total casualties from radar SAMs. In effect, the data show that the antiair threat assessed by many both before and during the war as the "high" threat system—radar SAMs—was responsible for just 16 percent of the coalition's total casualties. Conversely, the expected "low threat" AAA and man-portable IR SAMs, such as the 1970's vintage SA-7, which made up the majority of the Iraqi IR SAM force, accounted for 71 percent of total casualties (58 percent of total kills and 81 percent of total damage cases).

There are a number of possible explanations for this overall inversion of the perceived high and low threats to combat aircraft. First, radar SAM sites proved vulnerable to attack and destruction from U.S. high-speed antiradiation missiles (HARM) and other SEAD systems that were able to detect and thus locate radar systems and directly attack them.[36] Every time a SAM radar was turned on, it provided a beacon for the weapons that could attack it—as occurred frequently, according to pilots.

Second, and directly related, when the Iraqis operating the SAM sites chose not to turn on their radars, to avoid being detected and attacked, and then launched the SAMs ballistically—that is, without radar guidance—the SAMs could not track a moving aircraft. Therefore, these SAMs had little, if any, chance of damaging aircraft, which could easily evade them by maneuvering out of their path.

---

[36]Aircraft with HARMs or those that engaged in SEAD included the A-10, F/A-18, F-16, F-15E, F-117, F-111F, B-52, GR-1, F-4G, A-6E, EA-6B, and EF-111.

**Appendix II
The Use of Aircraft and Munitions in the Air Campaign**

In effect, the radar that was critical to ensuring SAM lethality made every SAM site vulnerable to destruction by U.S. SEAD aircraft. Further, coordination among SAM sites was essentially precluded by the fact that, as explained above, the Iraqi IADS proved vulnerable to disruption and degradation very early in the air campaign.[37] As a result, coalition aircraft were generally not threatened by a well-integrated air defense system, with coordinated multiple defense layers, but rather by hundreds of autonomously operating SAM and AAA sites with individual radar(s), and by thousands of inherently mobile, portable, shoulder-launched IR SAMs and thousands of AAA guns without radars.

Figure II.5 shows the day-by-day coalition aircraft casualties from radar-guided SAMs for the 43 days of the war. After day 5, aircraft casualties from radar-guided SAMs dropped off sharply: there were nine casualties over the first 5 days but only five more from radar-guided SAMs during the remaining 38 days of the war.

In sharp contrast to the readily detectable and locatable radar-guided SAMs (of which there were hundreds), neither IR SAMs nor optically aimed AAA emit any signal during their search and acquisition phase. Moreover, there were thousands of AAA sites throughout Iraq and the KTO and thousands of portable IR SAMs in the KTO. Except for the small number of fixed AAA sites that had, and actually used, radar, all IR SAMs and most AAA were very hard to find before they were actually used. As a result, even at the end of the war, pilots reported little if any diminution of AAA, and aircraft casualties from AAA and IR SAMs continued up to February 27—at the end of the war. As the Desert Storm "Lessons Learned" section of the F-117 <u>Tactical Employment</u> manual reported (on p. 3-29), "The threats [to aircraft] were never attrited . . . AAA tended to be the highest threat."

---

[37]See the "Operating Conditions" section above and appendix VI. See also Joint Electronic Warfare Center (JEWC), <u>Proud Flame Predictive Analysis for Iraq</u> (Secret), San Antonio, September 1990, p. 28.

Figure II.5: Combat Aircraft Casualties From Radar SAMs

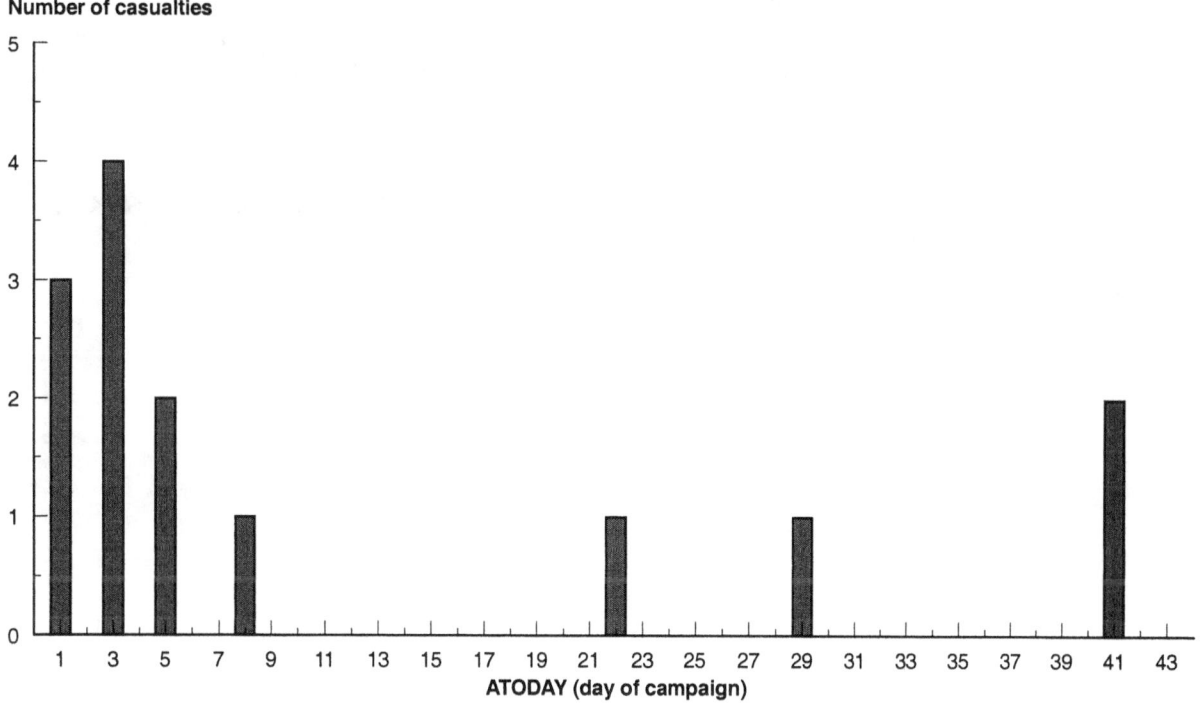

Note: Air tasking order day (ATODAY).

Figure II.6 shows clearly that 17 aircraft casualties occurred within the first 24 hours, or nearly 20 percent of the war's entire aircraft casualties (during less than 2.5 percent of its total length). It was during this time that Iraqi defenses were at their strongest and were first attacked and that coalition pilots were at their lowest levels of Desert Storm combat experience. Similarly, there was a significantly higher overall daily casualty rate in the first 5 days of the war, during which 31 aircraft casualties occurred (36 percent of the total and an average of 6.2 per day), compared to the following 38 days, with a total of 55 more casualties (an average of 1.45 per day).

Appendix II
The Use of Aircraft and Munitions in the Air Campaign

This diminution in aircraft casualty rates may partly be explained by the fact that losses to radar-guided SAMs fell to nearly 0 after day 5, having accounted for 29 percent (9 out of 31) of total casualties by then. They accounted for just 9 percent (5 out of 55) of all aircraft casualties in the remainder of the war. It is apparent, therefore, that by the end of day 5 of the air campaign, radar SAMs had been virtually eliminated as an effective threat to coalition aircraft.

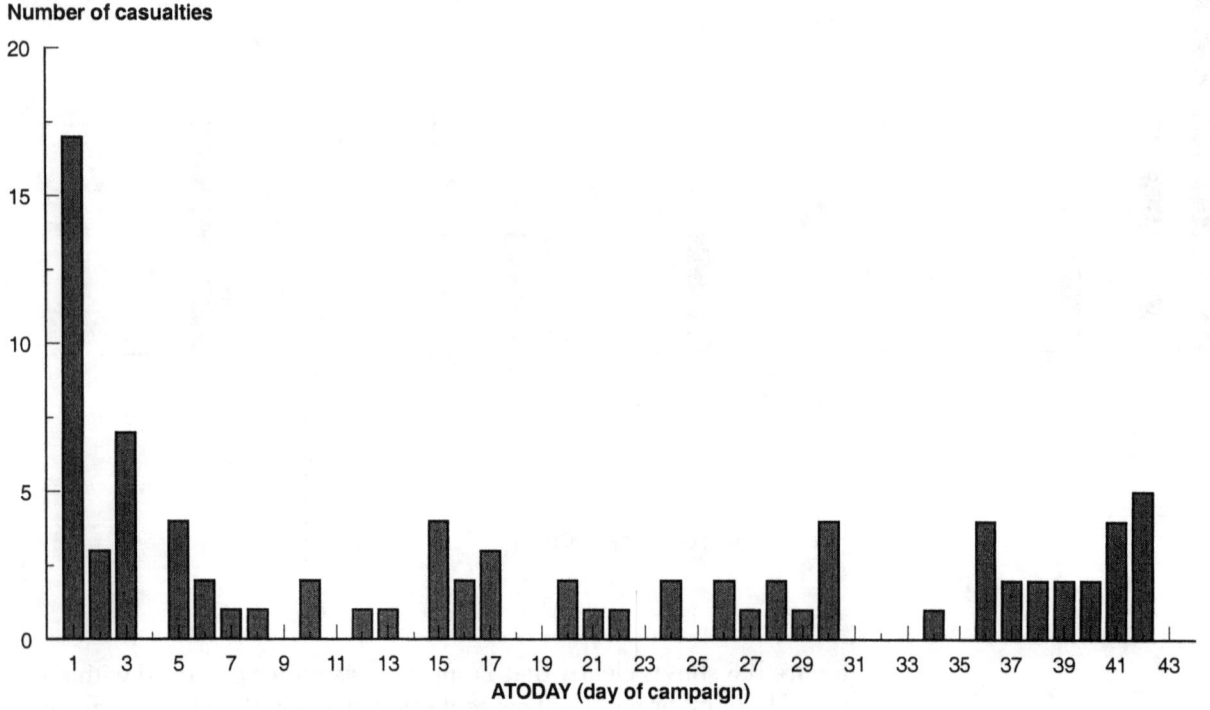

Figure II.6: Daytime Combat Aircraft Casualties From All Threats

Moreover, in the first 3 days of the war, some aircraft (B-52s, A-6Es, GR-1s, and F-111Fs) attacked at very low altitude, where they found they were vulnerable to low-altitude defenses—AAA and IR SAMs. As a result, on day two, Brig. Gen. Glosson ordered that all coalition aircraft observe a

**Appendix II
The Use of Aircraft and Munitions in the Air Campaign**

minimum attack level of about 12,000 feet. While probably improving overall survivability, this tactic also resulted in much less accuracy with unguided weapons (see discussion in app. III). In effect, Brig. Gen. Glosson's order served to manage the attrition rate of the air campaign, taking into account the view, as one general stated, that no Iraqi target was so important as to justify the loss of a pilot's life.

Since the effects of having degraded the Iraqi IADS cannot be easily separated out from the effects of also consistently flying only at higher altitudes, the extent to which the latter decreased vulnerability cannot be quantitatively specified. However, there are data on the altitude at which 32 U.S. Air Force aircraft casualties occurred (data were not available for other aircraft). Of these 32 cases, 21, or about two-thirds, were hit at or below 12,000 feet.[38] This suggests that the altitude floor did serve to save lives.[39]

Figure II.6 also shows that after the first week, aircraft casualties occurred sporadically, but there were 17 hits during the last week of the war. Since only two of these were attributed to a radar-guided SAM, it is apparent that AAA and IR SAMs remained potential threats to the end. The casualty data therefore confirm the statements of numerous pilots who told us that, unlike radar SAMs, AAA and IR SAMs were never effectively suppressed, thereby continuing as lethal threats throughout the war.

Aircraft Casualty Rates

Aircraft casualty rates can be calculated by dividing casualties by total sorties or total strikes. Table II.8 shows aircraft casualty rates per strike for the aircraft under review.

The overall aircraft casualty rate was 0.0017 per strike, or in other words, about 0.0017 aircraft were lost or damaged per strike in Desert Storm. The F-117 was the only aircraft under review that reported no losses or damage. However, using an analysis performed in DOD but not publicly

---

[38]Of those 21, 12 were A-10 casualties. A-10s were permitted to operate below 12,000 feet to as low as 4,000 to 7,000 feet on January 31 and thereafter. After January 31 is when 10 of the 12 medium- to low-altitude casualties occurred.

[39]Additional evidence that low-altitude deliveries were more lethal than higher ones can be found in the pattern of A-6E and British Tornado losses. Of the seven British Tornados that were lost, four were shot down during the first week of the campaign at very low altitude while conducting strikes against airfields. In an analysis, DIA concluded that the basic cause was delivering ordnance at very low altitude in the face of very heavy defenses, rather than being the function of a defect in the aircraft. After the change to medium-altitude deliveries, only three more British Tornados were lost in the remaining 5 weeks of the air campaign. A-6E pilots told us that their casualty rate dropped significantly after units using low-altitude tactics switched to high altitudes.

Appendix II
The Use of Aircraft and Munitions in the Air Campaign

reported, we calculated the likelihood of a nonstealthy aircraft being hit if it flew the same number of strikes as the F-117 (that is, 1,788), with a general probability of hit equal to 0.0017.[40] This calculation showed that 0 hits would be the most likely outcome for a nonstealthy aircraft conducting 1,788 strikes. This indicates that although there were no F-117 casualties in Desert Storm, the difference between its survivability and other aircraft may arise from its smaller number of strikes as much as other factors.

Table II.8: Desert Storm Aircraft Casualty Rates

Aircraft	Total casualties	Total strikes	Aircraft casualty rate per strike
F-117	0	1,788	0
F-111F	3	2,802	0.0011
F-15E	2	2,124	0.0009
A-6E	8	2,617	0.0031
O/A-10	20	8,640[a]	0.0023
F-16	7	11,698	0.0006
F/A-18	10	4,551	0.0022
B-52	5	1,706	0.0029
GR-1	10	1,317	0.0076
Total	**65[b]**	**37,243**	**0.0017**

[a]Precise A-10 strike data were not available. GWAPS recorded 8,640 A-10 sorties. Given the definition of a strike, the number of A-10 strikes may have been larger than the number of bombing sorties. If the number of A-10 strikes is larger than 8,640, then its per-strike aircraft casualty rate would be lower.

[b]Totals do not conform to the total shown for all coalition aircraft in this table because only the air-to-ground aircraft under review are included.

Aircraft Casualties During Night Attacks

Other ways to compare Desert Storm aircraft casualty rates put the F-117's survival rate in a clearer perspective. Since the F-117s attacked only at night, we examined the casualties for other aircraft during night missions, in effect controlling for daylight (when optically aimed antiaircraft weapons can be used most effectively). Data on whether aircraft casualties occurred in day or at night were provided for 61 of the 86 coalition aircraft casualties. Twenty-five (29 percent) were not identified as either day or night and were presumably unknown or unrecorded. Of the 61, 44 (72 percent) of the casualties with a known time occurred in

---

[40]This analysis considers only the number of strikes flown. Factors known to be related to aircraft survivability—for example, the severity of defenses and the time of day when strikes were conducted—were not factored into the analysis.

Appendix II
The Use of Aircraft and Munitions in the Air Campaign

daytime; 17 (28 percent) occurred at night. (See table II.9.) These and other data strongly suggest that flying combat operations at night was safer than flying during the day.

Table II.9: Aircraft Casualties in Day and Night

Aircraft	Day casualties (44)		Night casualties (17)	
	Lost	Damaged	Lost	Damaged
F-117	a	a	a	a
F-111F	a	a	a	3
F-15E	a	a	2	a
A-6E	2	1	1	a
O/A-10	6	12	a	a
F-16	3	3	a	a
B-52	a	2	a	1
F/A-18	1	a	1	a
GR-1	3	a	4	a
Other	11	a	4	1
Total	**26**	**18**	**12**	**5**

[a]No casualties or no day or night data on casualties.

Five types of aircraft—F-111Fs, F-15Es, A-6Es, A-10s, and F-16s—flew at least as many night strikes as the F-117. As shown in table II.9, of these aircraft, F-111Fs, A-10s, and F-16s also incurred no losses at night, and the A-6Es, A-10s, and F-16s received no damage at night. In this context, it is notable that the aircraft that incurred the highest absolute number of casualties, but not the highest attrition rate, the A-10, incurred neither losses nor damage at night, although it conducted approximately the same number of night sorties as the F-117. These data suggest that, in Desert Storm, flying at night was much safer than during the day, regardless of size of radar cross-section or other aircraft-specific characteristics.

The casualty data also show that after the first few days of the war, the number of night casualties fell off considerably. Of the 17 identifiable nighttime casualties, all but 3 occurred during the first 6 days of the war. There are two plausible, complementary explanations for this. First, by day five, the IADS and radar SAMs, which were unaffected by time of day, had been rendered ineffective through a combination of actual destruction to radar facilities and deterrence in turning radars on, achieved through bombing. Second, after day three, most low-altitude attacks, and their lower survival rates, were terminated. Thus, by the end of the first week,

Appendix II
The Use of Aircraft and Munitions in the Air Campaign

the only air defense weapon that was not impeded at night—radar SAMs—had been suppressed and the optically aimed AAA and IR SAMs that were impeded by night were reduced in effectiveness by the coalition's use of high-altitude tactics.

In effect, the data indicate that most Desert Storm aircraft casualties occurred during the day. Therefore, it is simply less likely that any aircraft, including the F-117, which operated only at night, would have been hit or lost, especially after radar SAMs were suppressed and low-altitude attacks were discontinued.

Air Defense Concentrations

Because no F-117s were lost or damaged in Desert Storm, they have been thought of as uniquely survivable, compared to other aircraft. Indeed, the Air Force contended in its September 1991 Desert Storm white paper that "the F-117 was the only airplane that planners dared risk over downtown Baghdad" where air defenses are claimed to have been uniquely dense or severe.[41]

Downtown Threats

More radar-guided SAM systems were deployed to the Baghdad area than any other area in Iraq, and diagrams of SAM coverage confirm that the greatest concentration of defenses were in that area. (Table II.10 presents the number and location of Iraqi SAM batteries.)

Table II.10: Number and Location of Iraqi SAM Batteries

Location	SA-2	SA-3	SA-6	SA-8	Roland	Total
Mosul/Kirkuk	1	12	0	1	2	16
H-2/H-3	1	0	6	0	6	13
Talil/Jalibah	1	0	0	0	2	3
Basrah	2	0	8	0	5	15
Baghdad	10	16	8	15	9	58

Source: USAF, History of the Air Campaign, p. 254.

However, it is relevant to note that the defense systems located in the Baghdad area did not necessarily protect downtown Baghdad at a higher threat level than the rest of the overall metropolitan area. This would be logical, since likely targets for any of Iraq's adversaries were not only downtown, but were dispersed—along with radar SAM sites—throughout the Baghdad area. The distribution of radar SAMs deployed to the overall

[41]USAF, Reaching Globally, Reaching Powerfully: The United States Air Force in the Gulf War (Sept. 1991), p. 56.

**Appendix II
The Use of Aircraft and Munitions in the Air Campaign**

Baghdad region is shown in figure II.7. These include SA-2, SA-3, SA-6, SA-8, and Roland missiles.

Figure II.7: Radar-Guided SAM Locations in the Baghdad Area

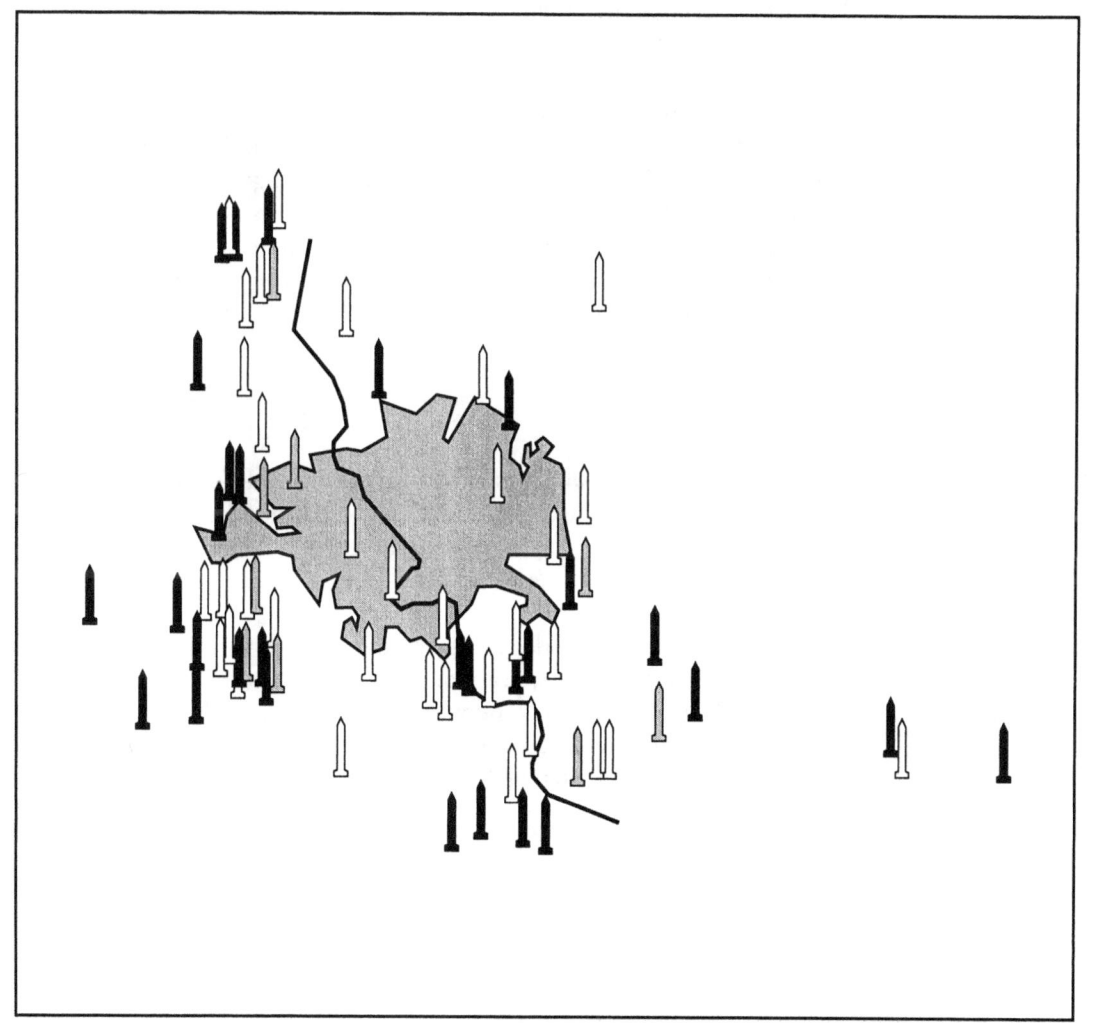

Source: 52nd Fighter Wing Desert Storm, A success story, Briefing, GWAPS Files, GWAP, vol. IV, pt. I: Weapons, Tactics, and Training Report (unclassified), p. 12.

**Appendix II
The Use of Aircraft and Munitions in the Air Campaign**

The greatest concentrations of radar SAMs were clearly not in the center of the city but, rather, in its outlying regions. The lethal range of these systems was described by Air Force intelligence experts as extending over the general Baghdad area, as far as 60 miles outside the city.

Moreover, because the engagement range of the five different types of SAMs varied, and because they were dispersed throughout the Baghdad area, it appears unlikely that they somehow converged over the downtown area to make it the most dangerous locus of all. The maximum engagement ranges of the systems varied from 3.5 miles for the Roland to 27 miles for the SA-2.[42] Only the Vietnam-era vintage SA-2s would have had sufficient range to cover most of the area shown in figure II.7 and to converge over the center of the city.[43] For the others, with ranges varying from 3.5 to 13 miles, the deployment pattern shows that the densest concentrations of overlapping radar SAM defenses were outside downtown Baghdad.

[DELETED]

With regard to the two other principal antiaircraft defenses, IR SAMs and AAA, there were clearly more AAA sites in the Baghdad area than elsewhere in Iraq, but IR SAMs were deployed only to army field units, mostly in the KTO and not at all in Baghdad. (See fig. II.8.)

However, AAA sites, like radar SAMs, were deployed throughout the greater metropolitan Baghdad area, not just downtown. Therefore, while AAA in the Baghdad region may have been more severe than elsewhere, it is also the case that it endangered not just the F-117s but all other coalition aircraft that conducted strikes in the general metropolitan area.

---

[42]According to USAF intelligence data, the maximum ranges were SA-2, 27 miles; [DELETED]; Roland, 3.5 miles.

[43]Also, the SA-6, with the next greatest assessed range of these systems, is at least 20 years old and [DELETED].

Appendix II
The Use of Aircraft and Munitions in the Air Campaign

Figure II.8: AAA Deployment in Iraq[a]

[FIGURE DELETED]

[a]Does not include IR SAMs and AAA deployed to Iraqi army and Republican Guard forces in the field.

Source: GWAPS, vol. II, pt. I: Operations Report (Secret), p. 82.

Aircraft Risked Over Downtown

Given the distribution of defenses throughout the Baghdad region, the survivability of the F-117 is more appropriately compared to that of other aircraft that were tasked to targets in the region, not just to those tasked to downtown targets.[44] In this context, we found that five other types of aircraft made repeated strikes in the Baghdad region—F-16s, F/A-18s, F-111Fs, F-15Es, and B-52s. Large packages of F-16s were explicitly tasked to "downtown" targets in the first week of the air campaign, but these taskings were stopped after two F-16s were lost to radar SAMs over the Baghdad area during daytime. Available data report no casualties over the Baghdad area, except for one F/A-18, one GR-1, and the two F-16s cited above.[45]

Assertions that the F-117 was uniquely survivable because it alone was tasked to uniquely severe defenses over downtown Baghdad are therefore not supported by the data. F-117s never faced the defenses that proved to be the most lethal in Desert Storm—daytime AAA and IR SAMs. Whereas, the defenses around metropolitan Baghdad were among the most potent in Iraq, the defenses over downtown were not more severe than those over the metropolitan area. Other aircraft were tasked to equally heavily defended targets. Moreover, some aircraft that flew at night also conducted strikes without casualties.

---

[44]Other aircraft that were tasked to Baghdad and attacked during the day would have faced more severe defenses than did the F-117s at night: during the day optically aimed AAA would be able to operate at its most effective level.

[45]GWAPS and other reports did not specify the locations of all aircraft casualties. Therefore, it is possible that some of these aircraft were damaged or lost over the Baghdad metropolitan area, but the data available do not specify locations.

Appendix II
The Use of Aircraft and Munitions in the Air
Campaign

In sum, the factor most strongly associated with survivability in Desert Storm appears to have been the combination of flying high and flying at night—an environment that the F-117s operated in exclusively.

Other Factors in Aircraft Survivability

Two additional factors are notable about aircraft survivability from available data.

Size of Strike Packages

One early tactic in the air war that may have had the effect of causing some aircraft losses to Iraqi defenses was to send large numbers of aircraft over a target one after another. While the first aircraft over the target frequently encountered no defenses, its bomb detonations would alert the Iraqis, resulting in AAA and SAMs being directed against the aircraft that followed. [DELETED]

Attempt to Change Aircraft Camouflage

The fact that the optically aimed AAA and IR SAMs remained lethal throughout the air campaign put a premium on the extent to which aircraft operating during the day could be made less visible through camouflage. A-10 pilots told us that the aircraft's dark green paint scheme—intended for low-level operations in northern Europe (including for concealment from aircraft from above)—made them stand out in the desert against both sand and sky. Consequently, some A-10 units began to paint their aircraft the same light grey color scheme of most other Air Force aircraft. However, the units that repainted their A-10s were subsequently ordered by Air Force Component, Central Command (CENTAF) to change them back to dark green.

A total of 20 A-10s was hit during the war—nearly 25 percent of all aircraft casualties. Some A-10 pilots we spoke to believed—and one participating unit's after-action report stated—that the dark green paint was unacceptable and may have been responsible for some of the casualties. A postwar Air Force study on survivability stated that the concerns over the A-10's paint scheme were "valid" and recommended that, in the future, "Paint schemes must be adaptive to the environment in which the aircraft operate."[46] It is noteworthy that no A-10s were shot down, or even damaged, at night, when the dark paint scheme very probably assisted them or, at minimum, did not make them stand out.

---

[46]USAF Air Warfare Center, U.S. Air Force Surface-to-Air Engagements During Operation Desert Storm (Secret), Eglin Air Force Base: January 1992, p. 12.

Appendix II
The Use of Aircraft and Munitions in the Air Campaign

Summary

In this appendix, we addressed questions concerning pre-Desert Storm claims made for air-to-ground aircraft, munitions, and target sensor systems versus how they were actually used in Desert Storm. In addition, we examined trends in aircraft and munition use, with particular emphasis on the F-117, and aircraft survivability, including the factors suggested by Desert Storm data that are most likely to account for aircraft casualties.

We first examined the operating environment of Desert Storm to provide the relevant context. The coalition faced a well-understood threat and had considerable lead time to prepare and actually practice for the eventual conflict. This provided coalition forces with an edge that should not be discounted in evaluations of the outcomes of the Persian Gulf War. The coalition had 6 months to plan for the war, deploy the necessary assets to the theater, practice strikes and deceptions, gather intelligence on targets, and become highly familiar with the operating environment. The fact that the coalition knew which IADS nodes to hit to inflict the most damage, the most quickly, was critical to its rapid degradation, and to the achievement of a form of air supremacy—elimination of an integrated, coordinated air defense. Without this supremacy, the air campaign might have proceeded at a much slower pace and perhaps with more losses. Further, the United States had the advantage of facing a highly isolated adversary, essentially unable to be reinforced by air, sea, or ground. The unique and often cooperative conditions of Desert Storm also severely limit the lessons of the war that can be reasonably applied to potential future contingencies.

We next compared planned aircraft and munitions use to actual Desert Storm use, along with patterns of aircraft and munition weight of effort against sets of strategic targets. While there were few notable discrepancies between original aircraft or munitions design and actual use of either in the conflict, two that are related did stand out: the survivability decision to bar munitions deliveries from below 12,000 feet after day 2 and the corresponding fact that most unguided munitions tactics, before the war, planned for low-altitude deliveries. The switch to medium- to high-altitude deliveries meant that the accuracy of unguided munitions was greatly reduced. This trade-off was feasible in Desert Storm as a way to reduce attrition—in fact, to almost eliminate it. But since 95 percent of the bombs and 92 percent of the total tonnage were unguided, there may have been a severe reduction in the accuracy of that ordnance.

In less than half of the strategic target categories, there was a clear preference for a particular type of air-to-ground platform. Preferences were evidenced for F-117s, F-15Es, A-6Es, and F/A-18s against C^3, GVC, NBC

**Appendix II
The Use of Aircraft and Munitions in the Air
Campaign**

(F-117), NAV (A-6E and F/A-18), and SCU (F-15E) targets. Nonetheless, considering all target categories and selected platforms, most aircraft were assigned to multiple targets across multiple target categories.

The combination of the ban on low-altitude tactics after day two, the degradation of radar SAMs and the IADS in the early days of the war, and the fact that a high proportion of strikes were flown at night—which constituted another form of aircraft sanctuary—almost certainly was responsible for a coalition aircraft attrition rate well below what planners expected and below historical precedent in the Middle East.

The Desert Storm air campaign was not accomplished by the efforts of strike aircraft alone. Aerial refueling tankers, airborne intelligence-gathering aircraft, reconnaissance aircraft, and strike support aircraft like F-4Gs, F-15Cs, and EF-111s were vital ingredients in the successful execution of the air campaign.

While many factors about the operating environment in Desert Storm were highly favorable to the coalition's air effort, aircraft targeting capabilities and precision munitions were put to the test by some periods of adverse weather as well as adverse conditions like smoke from oil fires or dust from bombing. Even mild weather conditions, including humidity, rendered precision bombing sensors (such as IR target detection systems and laser target designation systems) either degraded or unable to work at all. Moreover, even in clear weather, pilots sometimes found it difficult to locate or identify valid targets from medium and high altitudes. In sum, our research and analysis found that official DOD descriptions of aircraft targeting capabilities were overstated based on the Desert Storm experience.

Finally, we addressed the role of the F-117 in the Desert Storm air campaign and examined some of the significant controversies about its use and contribution. Contrary to their "Lone Ranger" image, F-117s certainly required tanking as well as radar jamming support, while support from air-to-air fighter aircraft is less clear. The claim that F-117s—often, but not always—achieved tactical surprise, as defined by the absence of AAA until bombs made impact, was matched by the experience of other aircraft. The gains provided by stealthiness also required substantial trade-offs in terms of capabilities and flexibility, including [DELETED]. No F-117s were reported lost or damaged in Desert Storm, but they operated exclusively at night and at medium altitudes. This operational context was clearly less likely to result in aircraft casualties than low-level attacks or

Appendix II
The Use of Aircraft and Munitions in the Air
Campaign

attacks at any level in daylight. Moreover, like the F-117s, some other nonstealth attack aircraft experienced no losses operating in the high-threat areas of Baghdad and operating at night at medium altitude.

Appendix III
Aircraft and Munition Effectiveness in Desert Storm

In this appendix, we respond to requester questions concerning the effectiveness of the different types of aircraft and munitions, the validity of manufacturer claims about weapon system performance, and the extent to which the air campaign objectives for Desert Storm were achieved. We address aircraft and munition effectiveness by answering nine questions, the first of which focuses on the quality and scope of the weapon system performance data from the Gulf War. Questions 2 through 7 address the effectiveness of individual weapon systems, and questions 8 and 9 address the combined effectiveness of the air campaign in achieving various objectives. The specific questions are as follows.

1. Effectiveness Data Availability: What data are available to compare the effectiveness of the weapon systems used, and what are the limitations of the data?

2. Associations Between Weapon Systems and Outcomes: Did outcomes achieved among strategic targets vary by type of aircraft and munition used to attack targets?

3. Target Accuracy and Effectiveness as a Function of Aircraft and Munition Type: Did accuracy in hitting targets with LGBs vary by type of delivery platform? Similarly, did outcomes achieved among strategic targets vary by platforms delivering unguided munitions?

4. LGB Accuracy: Did laser-guided bombs achieve the accuracy claimed to permit using only one per target?

5. F-117 Effectiveness Claims: Did the F-117s actually achieve an unprecedented 80-percent bomb hit rate? Were the F-117s highly effective against strategic air defense targets on the first night of the campaign, thereby opening the way for more vulnerable nonstealthy aircraft to attack?

6. TLAM Effectiveness Claims: Do the data support claims for the effectiveness of Tomahawk land-attack (cruise) missiles?

7. Weapon System Manufacturers' Claims: What are the claims that have been made by defense contractors for the effectiveness of the weapons they produced, and do the data support these claims?

Appendix III
Aircraft and Munition Effectiveness in
Desert Storm

8. <u>Air Campaign Effectiveness Against Mobile Targets</u>: What was the effectiveness of the air campaign against small ground targets—tanks, armored personnel carriers, and artillery?

9. <u>Air Campaign Effectiveness in Achieving Strategic Objectives</u>: To what extent were the overall military and political objectives of Desert Storm met, and what was the contribution of air power?

Effectiveness Data Availability

Our first subquestion is concerned with the reliability of the data available to assess and compare the effects of the weapon systems used in Desert Storm. Under the best of circumstances, there would be sufficient data on the use of aircraft, missiles, and munitions, and on the damage inflicted on each target, to compare inputs and outcomes comprehensively. This would permit analysis, for example, of whether or not an aircraft with unguided bombs is as effective as one with LGBs or how different kinds of aircraft and munitions performed against various targets under a range of threat and strike conditions.

However, Desert Storm was not planned, executed, or documented to satisfy the information needs of operations analysts or program evaluators.[1] As a result, there are sometimes significant gaps in the data on weapon system performance and effectiveness, the latter as a result of insufficient BDA, in particular. For example, because multiple aircraft of different types delivered multiple bombs, often on the same aimpoint, and damage was often not assessed until <u>after</u> multiple strikes, for most targets, it is not possible to determine what target effects, if any, can be attributed to a <u>particular</u> aircraft or <u>particular</u> munition.

Making use of the best available data on both inputs and outcomes, we compared the effectiveness of several air campaign systems both quantitatively and qualitatively and also examined the extent to which campaign goals were achieved. Because specific aircraft and munitions could not, for the most part, be identified with specific damage to targets, we developed alternative measures of effectiveness. In particular, the Desert Storm data permitted us to determine (1) the aircraft, munitions, and missiles that were expended against the set of targets in each strategic category and (2) the levels of damage achieved for many of the targets in most target categories. BDA reports indicating that restrikes were needed provided a measure of inputs that had not fully achieved the required

---

[1]While some may see this as solely a problem for postwar evaluations, the frequent lack of timely data, such as BDA, was repeatedly cited by Desert Storm pilots and planners as a problem <u>during</u> the war.

Appendix III
Aircraft and Munition Effectiveness in
Desert Storm

results. And when BDA reports indicated success, this was taken as an upper-bound measure of what it took to achieve a successful outcome.

The total input measure can be compared with the prewar probability of destruction (PD) estimates of the effectiveness of a given munition, missile, or aircraft against a specific target type. Observed differences can potentially be explained by various factors such as the effect of tactics on effectiveness, the uniqueness of conditions encountered in Desert Storm, or the uncertainties and risks to be considered when tasking aircraft and missiles against specific target types.

Our assumption is that under wartime conditions with imperfect field information, delays in reporting BDA, communications breakdowns, and other sources of friction, the inputs used on a target or class of targets are likely to be the more accurate measure of future inputs than PD calculations derived from less than fully realistic field tests or earlier conflicts.[2] For example, the latter may indicate that, under certain conditions, a 2,000-pound LGB has a 0.9 PD of destroying a room inside a building with 2-feet-thick concrete walls. However, it may be more useful to know that, in an actual contingency, six LGBs were used against such targets, because the costs and risks of tasking additional pilots, aircraft, and munitions against a target were less than the risk that the target objectives had not been met.

Associations Between Weapon Systems and Outcomes

Our second subquestion is concerned with whether the degree to which target objectives were met varied by type of aircraft or munition used. The available data reveal associations of greater and lesser success against targets between types of aircraft and munitions over the course of the campaign and with respect to individual target categories. However, data limitations inhibit direct comparisons between weapon systems or generalizations about the effectiveness of individual weapon systems.

Target Outcomes by Type of Aircraft and Munition

Data on the number of munitions, aircraft, and TLAMs used against certain strategic targets were available, as were damage assessment reports for 432 strategic targets with BE numbers that were attacked. By matching inputs to the targets for which damage assessments were made, we examined whether any patterns could be ascertained between the types of inputs and the outcomes.

[2]Delivery accuracy data in the Joint Munitions Effectiveness Manual are based in part on visual, manual system accuracies achieved in prior combat dating as far back as World War II. (JMEM, ch. 1, p. 1-24, change 4.)

Appendix III
Aircraft and Munition Effectiveness in Desert Storm

Using specific criteria, we rated outcomes on the strategic targets with BE numbers for which there were sufficient phase III BDA data to reach a judgment about whether attacks on a target had been either "fully successful" or "not fully successful."[3] Out of 432 targets with BDA reports, 357 could be matched with BE-numbered targets for which campaign input data were also available.[4] For both the TLAMs and eight air-to-ground aircraft reviewed here that delivered ordnance against strategic targets, table III.1 shows a frequency count, by platform, of the number of targets that we rated as damaged to an FS or NFS level and the ratio of FS to NFS targets.

Table III.1: Number of Targets Assessed as Fully Successful and Not Fully Successful by Platform

Platform	FS	NFS	FS:NFS ratio
A-6E	37	34	1.1:1
A-10	a	a	a
B-52	25	35	0.7:1
F-111F	41	13	3.2:1
F-117	122	87	1.4:1
F-15E	28	29	1.0:1
F-16	67	45	1.5:1
F/A-18	36	47	0.8:1
GR-1	21	17	1.2:1
TLAM	18	16	1.1:1
Total[b]	**190**	**167**	**1.1:1**

[a]No data available.

[b]Individual platform data do not sum to the total because individual targets were often attacked by multiple platforms.

Table III.1 shows that, overall, there were more FS than NFS target assessments and that, except for the B-52, F-15E, and F/A-18, all platforms participated in more FS than NFS target outcomes. The ratio of FS to NFS target assessments was greatest for the F-111F, indicating that it participated in proportionally more FS than NFS target outcomes. In

---

[3]An FS assessment means that the target objective had been met sufficiently to preclude the need for a restrike. An NFS assessment does not equate with failure—rather, it means that despite the damage that may have been inflicted at the time of the BDA, the target objective had not been fully achieved and, in the opinion of the BDA analysts, a restrike was necessary to fully achieve the target objective. For a more complete explanation of the strengths and limitations of our methodology for assessing target outcomes, see appendix I.

[4]The Missions database contained input data on 862 BE-numbered targets.

Appendix III
Aircraft and Munition Effectiveness in
Desert Storm

addition, the ratios of FS to NFS outcomes for the F-117 and F-16 were similar in magnitude.

Another way in which to compare and contrast success rates among platforms is to look at the number of FS and NFS targets with which each delivery platform was associated across target categories. These comparisons are shown in table III.2.

Table III.2 illustrates associations between individual types of aircraft and outcomes (that is, number of FS and NFS assessments) in various strategic target categories. Two types of comparisons evident in the data include the success of individual platforms against individual target categories compared with (1) the success of all platforms against individual target categories and (2) a platform's success against all campaign targets.

Table III.2: Number of FS and NFS Targets by Platform and Target Type

Platform	C³ FS	C³ NFS	ELE FS	ELE NFS	GVC FS	GVC NFS	LOC FS	LOC NFS	MIB FS	MIB NFS
A-6E	9	6	4	0	a	a	9	1	3	7
B-52	0	4	3	3	a	a	0	2	8	18
F-111F	4	0	a	a	0	0	11	3	5	3
F-117	49	36	0	1	9	11	21	4	9	17
F-15E	3	6	1	0	a	a	8	1	0	2
F-16	19	10	4	2	3	3	3	1	10	16
F/A-18	6	9	3	0	a	a	7	5	3	8
GR-1	0	0	a	a	a	a	7	3	2	3
TLAM	6	1	2	6	7	3	0	0	1	0
All[b]	63	43	11	10	12	11	28	12	17	33

Appendix III
Aircraft and Munition Effectiveness in
Desert Storm

Platform	NAV FS	NAV NFS	NBC FS	NBC NFS	OCA FS	OCA NFS	OIL FS	OIL NFS	SAM FS	SAM NFS	SCU FS	SCU NFS
A-6E	3	9	1	1	7	4	0	2	1	0	0	4
B-52	a	a	1	1	10	2	2	3	a	a	1	2
F-111F	a	a	5	1	15	6	a	a	0	0	1	0
F-117	0	1	14	5	13	6	0	1	5	4	2	1
F-15E	a	a	1	0	12	6	0	1	0	1	3	12
F-16	a	a	4	2	16	5	2	1	3	0	3	5
F/A-18	1	9	1	1	10	6	1	4	3	0	1	5
GR-1	0	0	a	a	10	6	1	5	a	a	1	0
TLAM	0	0	0	3	1	1	1	2	0	0	0	0
All[b]	3	10	15	5	22	12	4	12	10	4	5	15

[a]No records of platform tasked against target type in Missions database.

[b]Individual platform data do not sum to category total because individual targets were often attacked by multiple platforms.

Success rates for individual platforms against individual categories did not necessarily mirror the overall campaign's rate of success against individual categories. For example, while the overall ratio of FS to NFS C^3 targets showed more FS relative to NFS assessments (63:43), the ratios for the B-52, F-15E, and F/A-18 (0:4, 3:6, and 6:9, respectively) indicate that these platforms were less successful against these types of targets than the campaign as a whole. However, some platforms are associated with higher rates of success against individual categories than were achieved by the overall campaign. For example, the number of FS:NFS LOC targets associated with the A-6E (9:1), F-111F (11:3), F-117 (21:4), and F-15E (8:1) indicate higher rates of success than were achieved by the campaign in the aggregate (28:12).

While most platforms participated in more FS than NFS outcomes during the campaign as a whole, some platforms participated against selected target categories in more NFS than FS outcomes. For example, TLAMs participated in strikes against more NFS than FS targets in the ELE and NBC categories, while F-117s and F-16s participated in more NFS than FS outcomes in the MIB targets. In contrast, while the B-52s and the F/A-18s had more NFS relative to FS overall against OCA targets, both platforms participated in more FS than NFS outcomes. In addition, the F/A-18s participated in more FS than NFS outcomes against ELE, LOC, and SAM targets.

Appendix III
Aircraft and Munition Effectiveness in
Desert Storm

The success rates for individual platforms over the course of the campaign did not necessarily mirror the pattern of success achieved by a platform against targets in specific categories. For example, while the ratio of FS:NFS for targets struck by the F-15E during the campaign was 28:29, its association with success in the LOC and OCA categories was proportionately far better (8:1 and 12:6, respectively), yet its association with success in the SCU category was worse (3:12). In another example, the ratio of FS to NFS for targets struck by B-52s over the course of the campaign was relatively unfavorable (25:35); its association with success in the OCA category was much better (10:2).

In sum, while these data do not allow direct effectiveness comparisons between aircraft types, they do indicate that effectiveness did vary by type of aircraft and by type of target category attacked. Subsequent subquestions address more direct aircraft effectiveness comparisons where the data permit.

Munition Types and Outcomes

Another way in which the Desert Storm databases permit comparison of inputs and outcomes is by type of munition used in each target category. Table III.3 shows the average amount, in tons, of guided and unguided munitions used per BE, by target category, for both FS and NFS targets and the ratio of unguided-to-guided bomb tonnage used.

Table III.3 shows that, on average, FS targets received more guided munition tonnage (11.2 tons versus 9.4) and less unguided munition tonnage (44.1 tons versus 53.7) per BE than NFS targets. However, this pattern did not hold across all target categories. For example, the opposite pattern occurred in the ELE, NAV, NBC, and SAM target categories, where NFS targets generally received more guided munition tonnage than targets rated FS, and the ratio of unguided to guided munition tonnage was lower than for targets rated FS, as well.

Appendix III
Aircraft and Munition Effectiveness in
Desert Storm

Table III.3: Average Guided and Unguided Tonnage Per BE by Outcome by Category

| | Fully successful | | | Not fully successful | | |
| | Average tons | | Unguided- | Average tons | | Unguided- |
Target	Unguided	Guided	to-guided	Unguided	Guided	to-guided
C³	7.2	3.9	1.9:1	14.7	4.0	3.6:1
ELE	49.8	5.4	9.2:1	36.8	7.5	4.9:1
GVC	6.7	11.2	0.6:1	4.4	9.5	0.5:1
LOC	8.5	7.6	1.1:1	18.4	6.1	3.0:1
MIB	120.2	10.0	12.0:1	119.8	5.2	23.1:1
NAV	17.5	1.2	14.2:1	29.0	5.2	5.6:1
NBC	41.1	19.3	2.1:1	125.7	73.7	1.7:1
OCA	152.6	43.9	3.5:1	106.7	36.0	3.0:1
OIL	110.8	2.3	49.3:1	45.6	1.5	31.4:1
SAM	7.2	0.8	8.8:1	1.1	4.8	0.2:1
SCU	94.2	7.1	13.3:1	66.3	5.0	13.3:1
Total	**44.1**	**11.2**	**3.9:1**	**53.7**	**9.4**	**5.7:1**

Bomb Tonnage, Munition Type, and Outcomes

A widespread image from Desert Storm was that of a single target being destroyed by a single munition. However, the data show that an average of 55.3 tons (110,600 pounds) of bombs were expended against each BE rated FS. The average for BEs rated NFS was 63 tons of bombs (126,000 pounds).[5] If the tonnage in each case was composed solely of 2,000-pound bombs, this would have meant using, at a minimum, nearly 56 bombs against every BE rated FS and about 63 on every NFS target. If the mix of munitions included smaller sizes as well, more than 56 munitions would have been dropped on each FS target. While some of this tonnage almost surely reflects the fact that many BE-numbered targets had more than one DMPI (or aimpoint), the fact remains that the amount of tonnage used per BE (whether FS or NFS), as well as the number of bombs that were dropped, was substantial.

Since the exact number of DMPIs per BE is not known, we are unable to determine whether the differences between the average tonnages dropped on FS versus NFS targets are meaningful. The fact that NFS targets received more tonnage, on average, than FS targets, may simply reflect restrikes directed at targets insufficiently damaged by initial attacks.

---

[5]These data represent the total weight of bombs dropped on targets according to the Missions database. The database does not consistently provide information on whether the bombs actually hit the intended aimpoints. Nor do these data include munitions dropped by coalition members other than the United States and the United Kingdom.

Appendix III
Aircraft and Munition Effectiveness in
Desert Storm

The data also show that FS targets received, on average, more tonnage per BE of guided munitions than NFS targets (11.2 tons versus 9.4) and less unguided tonnage per BE (approximately 44 versus 54 tons). Since most of the LGBs weighed from 500 to 2,000 pounds, the average difference of 3,600 pounds of munitions is equivalent to about one 2,000-pound LGB and three 500-pound LGBs or to about seven 500-pound LGBs.

Target Accuracy and Effectiveness as a Function of Aircraft and Munition Type

Although the Desert Storm input and BDA data do not permit a comprehensive aircraft-by-aircraft or munition-by-munition comparison of effectiveness, it is possible to compare and examine the effects of selected types of munitions and aircraft where they were used in similar ways. This is because the data on some systems—such as the F-117 and F-111F—are more complete, better documented, and more reliable than data collected on other systems. Thus, our third subquestion addresses the relationship between the (1) type of delivery platform and target accuracy using LGBs and (2) type of delivery platform and bombing effectiveness using unguided munitions.

A major issue raised during and after Desert Storm concerns the bomb delivery accuracy of stealthy versus conventional aircraft. The Air Force states that the F-117 was more accurate than any other LGB-capable platform because its stealthiness negated the necessity to engage in evasive defensive maneuvers in the target area, making it easier to hold the laser spot on the target and reducing the distance between the target and the aircraft. In contrast, nonstealthy aircraft are more likely to engage in defensive maneuvers after the bombs are released—increasing the chance of losing the laser spot, as the aircraft seeks to avoid air defense threats and speeds away from the target. Therefore, in LGB delivery against fixed targets, it was argued that the type of platform did make a difference in accuracy.

Of all the Desert Storm strike aircraft, there were sufficient data to compare only the F-117 to the F-111F on this dimension.[6] We compared the reported target hit rates of the F-117 and F-111F against 49 Desert

---

[6]The 48th TFW operations summary reported the outcome of each F-111F strike mission as a hit ("Yes") or miss ("No"). The F-111Fs dropped from one to four bombs per target, per mission. A hit was reported when at least one bomb struck the target. It was not possible to determine from the database the number of bombs that impacted on a target reported as hit. The F-117 database, in contrast, reported outcome data for each bomb dropped.

Appendix III
Aircraft and Munition Effectiveness in
Desert Storm

Storm targets struck by both aircraft.[7] The 49 targets comprised primarily airfields; bridges; large military industrial bases; and nuclear, biological, and chemical facilities. Table III.4 shows summary LGB strike data on the 49 targets for the F-117 and F-111F.

Table III.4: F-117 and F-111F Strike Results on 49 Common Targets[a]

Aircraft	Laser-guided bombs dropped	Number of strikes	Total dropped	Average bombs dropped per strike	Strikes where target was reported hit	
					Number	Percent
F-111F	GBU-10 GBU-12 GBU-15 GBU-24A/B GBU-28	422	93	2.1	357	85
F-117	GBU-10 GBU-12 GBU-27	456	517	1.1	363	80

[a]For this table, a strike is defined as one aircraft attacking one target where one or more bombs were dropped. More than one bomb can be delivered on the same target. More than one strike can occur on the same sortie, which is one flight by one aircraft.

The F-111Fs and the F-117s flew comparable numbers of bombing strikes against the same 49 targets—422 and 456, respectively. However, the F-111Fs dropped more bombs than the F-117s (893 versus 517); thus, the F-117s averaged only slightly more than 1 bomb per strike while the F-111Fs averaged over 2 bombs. For the F-111F, the reported target hit rate was 85 percent, for the F-117s, 80 percent. Thus, despite the advantages of stealth in LGB-deliveries—for the 49 common targets for which we have data—the reported target hit rate for the nonstealthy F-111F was greater than for the stealthy F-117.

As noted above, the total number of F-111F bomb hits on a given target was not recorded; a "hit" was counted if at least one bomb of four released hit the target. Therefore, it cannot be determined from these data whether perhaps (1) the F-111Fs achieved a higher reported target hit rate because they could drop more bombs on a target than the F-117s, and therefore, the F-111Fs had a greater number of chances of hitting the target with at

---

[7]Even though there are some data and methodological limitations to this comparison (that is, aimpoints may differ; over time, the intensity of the defenses could vary), the results on these 49 targets compare LGB results on the same targets, albeit with limitations to the conclusions that can be drawn.

Appendix III
Aircraft and Munition Effectiveness in
Desert Storm

least one bomb, or (2) the F-111Fs achieved more bomb hits per target than the F-117s, causing more damage per strike than the F-117s.[8]

F-117 Versus F-111F Target Hit Rates With Same Type of LGB

We compared the F-117 and F-111F target hit rates when using precisely the same munitions on the same targets by analyzing only strikes for which the same types of munitions were dropped (that is, GBU-10 or GBU-12).[9] Table III.5 shows the number and percent of strikes by F-117s and F-111Fs on 22 targets where only GBU-10 and GBU-12 LGBs were dropped.

Table III.5: F-117 and F-111F Strike Results on 22 Common Targets With GBU-10 and GBU-12 LGBs

Aircraft	Laser-guided bombs dropped	Number of strikes	Total dropped	Average bombs dropped per strike	Strikes where target reported hit	
					Number	Percent
F-111F	GBU-10 GBU-12	130	285	2.2	123	95
F-117	GBU-10 GBU-12	212	271	1.3	167	79

The F-117s flew almost twice as many strikes with GBU-10s and GBU-12s as the F-111F; however, the total number of GBU-10s and GBU-12s dropped was almost identical. Thus, the F-111Fs dropped more bombs per strike (2.2) than the F-117s (1.3). As with the set of 49 common targets, the percentage of strikes where the target was reported hit was higher for the F-111F than for the F-117, and the differential in target accuracy was greater.

Effectiveness by Aircraft Type With Unguided Bombs

To examine whether the type of aircraft used was related to the effectiveness of unguided bombs, we compared damage to targets attacked with only a single type of unguided bomb. Sixty-eight strategic targets were attacked with the 2,000-pound MK-84 unguided bomb and no other munition. The available data indicate that the platform of delivery may affect the effectiveness of the munition. Table III.6 shows the number

---

[8]In Desert Storm, the F-111F typically carried four LGBs per mission; the F-117 can carry a maximum of only two.

[9]Reliability and generalizability constraints on this comparison include the fact that the F-111F target hit data could not be verified; a significant portion of the reported F-117 hits lacked corroborating support or was inconsistent with other available data; and the calculated target hit rates per mission do not necessarily equate with bomb hit rate. Moreover, the results apply only to targets struck by both types of aircraft and thereby do not address other target types where one aircraft may have performed better than the other, such as F-111F conducting "tank-plinking" or F-117s striking hardened bunkers in Baghdad.

Appendix III
Aircraft and Munition Effectiveness in
Desert Storm

of targets attacked by aircraft type and the number and percent that were assessed as successfully destroyed.

Table III.6: Outcomes for Targets Attacked With Only MK-84 Unguided Bombs

Aircraft	Targets attacked	Targets successfully destroyed		Categories struck
		Number	Percent	
F-111E	1	0	0	MIB
F-15E	3	1	33	C^3, LOC
F-16	34	18	53	C^3, ELE, GVC, LOC, MIB, NBC, OIL, SCU
F/A-18	7	3	43	C^3, LOC, MIB, OIL
A-6E	1	1	100	ELE

The two types of aircraft with the highest representation were the F-16 and the F/A-18.[10] Of the 34 targets attacked by the F-16, 53 percent were successfully destroyed. Forty-three percent of the seven targets struck by the F/A-18 were fully destroyed. However, the differences in percentage of targets where the objectives were successfully achieved were not statistically significant.[11]

The number of target categories struck by the F-16 with MK-84s was considerably larger than those struck by the F/A-18. To eliminate any bias from the range of categories struck, table III.7 presents F-16 and F/A-18 strike results only for targets in categories common to both.

Table III.7: Outcomes for Targets Attacked With Only MK-84s Delivered by F-16s and F/A-18s

Aircraft	Targets attacked	Targets successfully destroyed		Categories struck
		Number	Percent	
F-16	23	12	52	C^3, LOC, MIB, OIL
F/A-18	7	3	43	C^3, LOC, MIB, OIL

[10]With only 2 exceptions, each of the 44 targets was attacked exclusively by a single type of aircraft. One target was struck by both the F-16s and F/A-18s, and a second target was struck by both the F-16s and F-111Es.

[11]We tested the direct comparisons between the F/A-18 and the F-16 statistically using the chi-square procedure, and we found them not to be significant at the 0.05 level.

Appendix III
Aircraft and Munition Effectiveness in Desert Storm

Table III.7 reveals that the F-16s appear to have been somewhat more effective than the F/A-18s.[12] As in table III.6, the difference in success rates was not statistically significant. However, the ratios of FS to NFS targets for each aircraft (12:11 for the F-16s; 3:4 for the F/A-18s) are consistent with the ratios of FS to NFS targets associated with these aircraft in the campaign. (See table III.1.) In each case, the FS to NFS ratio for the F-16s is greater than 1:1; the ratio for the F/A-18s is less than 1:1.

LGB Accuracy

Videotapes of LGBs precisely traveling down ventilator shafts and destroying targets with one strike, like those televised during and after Desert Storm, can easily create impressions about the effect of a single LGB on a single target, which was summed up by an LGB manufacturer's claim for effectiveness: "one target, one bomb."[13] The implicit assumption in this claim is that a target is sufficiently damaged or destroyed to avoid needing to hit it again with a second bomb, thus obviating the need to risk pilots or aircraft in restrikes. However, evidence from our analysis and from DIA's does not support the claim for LGB effectiveness summarized by "one target, one bomb."

To examine the validity of the claim, we used data from attacks on bridges, aircraft shelters, radar sites, and bunkers of various types with the most advanced LGBs used in Desert Storm, those with the "Paveway III" guidance system.[14] (See table III.8.)

---

[12]As noted in the discussion of table III.6, several data limitations limit the reliability of conclusions. These limitations include the fact that data on Air Force aircraft in the Missions database are more reliable than on Navy aircraft; some phase III reports on targets may have been produced before the final strikes occurred (with the result that damage that came after the last BDA report would not be credited); and not all of the 68 common targets were assessed by DIA.

[13]This phraseology has been used by Texas Instruments, a manufacturer of LGBs, in its public advertising.

[14]LGBs have three component parts: a guidance and control mechanism, a warhead or bomb body, and airfoil or wings. Three generations of Paveway LGB technology exist, each successive generation representing a change or modification in the guidance mechanism.

Appendix III
Aircraft and Munition Effectiveness in
Desert Storm

Table III.8: List of DMPIs and Identifying Information

Number	Target name	DMPI 1	ATODAY[a]
1	North Taji command bunker	Fac 2	3
2	Karbala depot, ammo storage	E bnkr (1) N.	17
3	Samarra CW facility	Bnk 1	20
4	Samarra CW facility	Bnk 4	20
5	Tallil airfield	Bnk 38 D116	23
6	Iraqi AF hdq, Baghdad	Bnk 5 OSP4	33
7	Iraqi intel hdq, Ku bks	Entrance	36
8	Al Fahud	Bridge	38
9	Suq Ash Shuyukh	Bridge	38
10	Pontoon bridge	None indicated	42
11	Taji bunker	Bunker	42
12	Highway bridge	32 08 90 N	2
13	Al Amarah	Command bunker	3
14	6 Corp Army hdq	Command bunker	14
15	Al Taqaddum	Shelter #2	8
16	Kuwait City	Radar Site	29
17	Al Qaim Mine	Mine entrance	32
18	Az Zubayr Radcom	Antenna	33
19	Al Qaim phosphate plant	Earth covered bnkr	33
20	Ar Rumaylah Afld	Bridge S. end	36

[a]ATODAY is the air tasking order day, the day of the war on which the strike occurred.

Source: Missions database, January 1993.

Each of these targets had a single, identifiable DMPI. If the "one-target, one-bomb" claim is accurate, there should have been a one-to-one relationship between the number of targets and the number of LGBs delivered to those targets. Our data did not allow us to determine whether one bomb typically caused sufficient damage to preclude a restrike, and campaign managers evidently did not assume this was the case, for the average number of LGBs dropped per target was four. Figure III.1 depicts the number of Paveway III LGBs that were delivered against 20 DMPIs.

Appendix III
Aircraft and Munition Effectiveness in
Desert Storm

Figure III.1: Paveway III LGBs Delivered Against Selected Point Targets

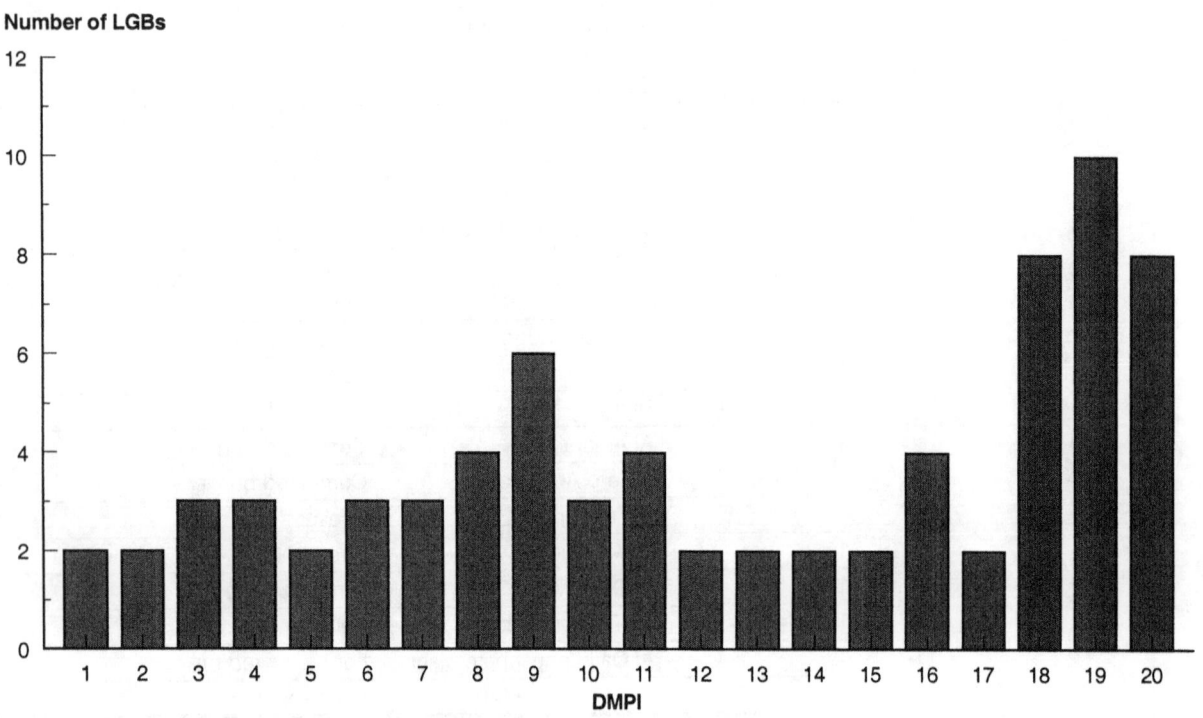

Figure III.1 shows that the "one-target, one-bomb" claim for Paveway III LGBs was not validated in a single case in this sample from Desert Storm. No fewer than two LGBs were dropped on each target; six or more were dropped on 20 percent of the targets; eight or more were dropped on 15 percent of the targets. The average dropped was four LGBs per target.[15]

Similarly, a DIA analysis of the effectiveness of 2,000-pound BLU-109/B (I-2000) LGBs dropped by F-117s and F-111Fs on Iraqi hardened aircraft shelters and bunkers found that many shelters were hit by more than one

---

[15]DOD commented that the types of targets in table III.8 are primarily hardened shelters and bunkers or bridges where probabilities of kill typically, require more than one bomb—even with a direct hit. We concur. A single advanced 2,000-pound LGB was often insufficient to achieve the desired level of damage against high-value single-DMPI targets. Thus, "one target, one bomb" was not routinely achieved.

Appendix III
Aircraft and Munition Effectiveness in Desert Storm

LGB, often as a result of insufficient BDA data prior to restrike.[16] At Tallil airfield, for example, many bunkers "were targeted with two or more weapons." (DIA, p. 28.) One bunker was hit by at least seven LGBs, although aircraft video showed that the required damage had been inflicted by the third and fourth bombs. As DIA noted, this meant that "two unnecessary restrikes using three more weapons were apparently conducted because complete information was not available, utilized, or properly understood/relayed." (DIA, p. 49.) The DIA analysis also shows that one bomb was insufficient; four bombs were required to achieve the necessary damage.

The DIA analysis noted that the "penetration capability of a warhead is determined by many factors: impact velocity, impact angle, angle of attack, target materials, and weapon design." (DIA, p. 7.) The DIA data are consistent with our finding that targets were hit by more than one LGB in part because more than one LGB was needed to reach the desired damage level. They also demonstrate that insufficient BDA sometimes prevented knowing at what point a target had been destroyed, thereby putting pilots and aircraft at risk in conducting additional strikes. Moreover, planners were apparently ordering the delivery of multiple bombs because either BDA revealed that one bomb did not achieve target objectives or they did not believe the presumption that "one target, one bomb" was being achieved.

F-117 Effectiveness Claims

The Air Force has written that

"The Gulf War illustrated that the precision of modern air attack revolutionized warfare. . . . In particular, the natural partnership of smart weapons and stealth working together gives the attacker unprecedented military leverage."[17]

According to a former Secretary of the Air Force, "In World War II it could take 9,000 bombs to hit a target the size of an aircraft shelter. In Vietnam, 300. Today [May 1991] we can do it with one laser-guided munition from an F-117."[18]

---

[16]DIA, Vulnerability of Hardened Aircraft Bunkers and Shelters to Precision-Guided Munitions (Secret), April 1994.

[17]USAF, Reaching Globally, Reaching Powerfully: The United States Air Force in the Gulf War (Sept. 1991), p. 55.

[18]Statement contained in a summary of public quotes and comments about performance of the F-117A Stealth Fighter in Operation Desert Storm provided to us by Lockheed Corporation on March 19, 1993.

Appendix III
Aircraft and Munition Effectiveness in Desert Storm

According to DOD's title V report, the F-117 proved to be a highly accurate bomber with a bomb hit rate of 80 percent against its targets—accuracy characterized by its primary contractor, Lockheed, as "unprecedented."[19] In addition, DOD emphasized in post-Desert Storm assessments that the F-117's stealth attributes and capability to deliver LGBs were instrumental on the first night of the war when the aircraft struck over 30 percent of all strategic targets, including components of the Iraqi IADS, thereby opening major gaps in Iraqi air defenses for conventional nonstealthy aircraft. The Air Force also contends that no other aircraft struck IADS and other targets in downtown Baghdad on the first night of the campaign and throughout the war because of the intensity of air defenses.

It may well be that the F-117 was the most accurate platform in Desert Storm. However, the Desert Storm data do not fully support claims for the F-117's accuracy against IADS-related targets, targets on the first night of the campaign, or targets throughout the war. As discussed in detail below, we estimate that the bomb hit rate for the F-117 was between 55 and 80 percent, the rate of weapon release was 75 percent. Thus, Desert Storm demonstrated that even in an environment with historically favorable weather conditions, the bomb release rate for the F-117 may be lower than for other aircraft.[20] Finally, the F-117 was not the only aircraft tasked to targets in downtown Baghdad, but after the third day, planners concluded that for the types of targets and defenses found in Baghdad, the F-117 was more effective.[21]

The F-117 Bomb Hit Rate

Various components of DOD and GWAPS reported similar bomb hit rates based on slightly different numbers of bomb drops and hits. DOD's title V report to the Congress stated that F-117s dropped 2,040 bombs during the campaign, of which 1,634 "hit the target," achieving a bomb hit rate of 80 percent. (DOD, p. T-85.) The Air Force Studies and Analysis Group reported that the F-117s achieved an 80-percent hit rate based on 1,659 hits. The Air Force Office of History reported that "Statistically, the 37th

---

[19]In a briefing to us in September 1993, Lockheed also concluded about the F-117 in Desert Storm "stealth, combined with precision weapons, demonstrated a change in aerial warfare . . . one bomb = one kill."

[20]For example, historically over Baghdad, the average percentage of time that the cloud ceiling is less than or equal to 3,000 feet is only 9 percent; comparable percentages over Beirut, Lebanon; Osan AB, Korea; and St. Petersburg, Russia; are 17, 33, and 64, respectively. Thus, while the weather over Iraq was less favorable than average for that location, the conditions encountered in Desert Storm may well have been better than likely conditions in other likely contingency locations.

[21]As discussed in appendix II, we also found that based on Air Force intelligence analysis and other data, the defenses of the greater Baghdad metropolitan area were as intense as those of "downtown" Baghdad. Multiple aircraft types were tasked to the large area without experiencing casualties.

Appendix III
Aircraft and Munition Effectiveness in
Desert Storm

Tactical Fighter Wing compiled a record that is unparalleled in the chronicles of air warfare: the Nighthawks [F-117s] achieved a 75 percent hit rate on pinpoint targets . . . recording 1,669 direct hits . . . ."[22]

The GWAPS report stated that "They [F-117s] scored 1,664 direct hits . . . ." and achieved a bomb hit rate of 80 percent.[23] We sought to verify the data supporting these statements.

Data Underlying Claimed F-117 Hits

During the war, mission videos of F-117 bomb releases were reviewed after each night's strikes by analysts at the 37th TFW (and often by planners in the Black Hole) to determine hits and misses and the need for restrikes. The analysts at the 37th TFW were able to determine whether a bomb hit its intended target, or if the bomb missed, why and by what distance. This information was recorded on the 37th TFW Desert Storm database, which summarized the disposition of each F-117 strike mission. Our review of the database and interviews with F-117 pilots and the analysts who compiled the database show that some reported hits (1) were accompanied by data indicating the "miss distance" between the DMPI and point of bomb impact, (2) were not based on mission video, (3) were credited when the available video failed to record bomb impact, and (4) were accompanied by conflicting remarks. Our finding is that approximately one-third of the bomb drops assessed to be hits either lacked corroborating video documentation or were in conflict with other information in the database. (See table III.9.)

---

[22]Office of History, Headquarters 37th Fighter Wing, Special Study: 37FW/HO-91-1 (Jan. 9, 1992).

[23]GWAPS, vol. IV, pt. I (Secret), p. 44; vol. II, pt. II (Secret), p. 392.

Appendix III
Aircraft and Munition Effectiveness in
Desert Storm

Table III.9: Reported F-117 Hits Lacking Corroborating Support or in Conflict With Other Available Data

F-117 hits	Number	Percent
Total reported	1,677	100.0
Hits with miss distance data	360	21.5
Hits with no video record	96	5.7
Hits with video tape recorder problems or impact not recorded	69	4.1
Hits with conflicting remarks	49	2.9
Total reports of hits lacking corroborating support or in conflict with other available data	574	
Reported F-117 hits without corroborating video or in conflict with other available data	535[a]	31.9
Reported F-117 hits with corroborating video	1,142	68.1

[a]This total is less than the sum of the first four rows because, in several instances, a reported hit was accompanied by more than one piece of missing or incompatible data.

Reported Hits With Miss Distance Data

The distance by which the bomb missed the aimpoint was recorded in the TFW database. For 360 of the 1,677 hits reported, the miss distances ranged from 1.6 meters (approximately 5 feet) up to 164.5 meters (approximately 540 feet). This range was comparable to the range of miss distances recorded for the 70 reported misses, which ranged from 3.2 to 178.1 meters.[24] However, while the ranges of miss distances for hits and misses were equivalent, the distribution of miss distances was clearly skewed toward larger values for reported misses. The mean miss distance for the hits was 13.1 meters (43 feet), while the mean miss distance for the misses was 69.2 meters (226.9 feet)—five times the mean for hits.[25]

Reported Hits Without Documenting Video

In 96 instances, hits were credited despite the absence of a video record of the mission and in contrast to 37th TFW peacetime training policy and the policies of other LGB-capable aircraft in Desert Storm. In peacetime training, bomb drops by F-117s without video documentation are considered misses. In Desert Storm, the 37th TFW credited hits solely on the basis of pilot accounts; in contrast, pilot reports were substantially discounted by Air Force analysts of air campaign hits or kills by other types of air-to-ground aircraft employing guided munitions but with inconclusive video. For example, for every three tanks claimed as kills by A-10 pilots, only one was credited, for a 33-percent kill rate; F-111F pilots

---

[24]Paradoxically, the database contains more miss distances for reported hits (360) than for reported misses (70). This may be because miss distances for misses occurring outside the field of view of the F-117 DLIR could not be determined.

[25]The median miss distance for the hits was 4.98 meters (16.33 feet), while the median miss distance for the misses was 66.75 meters (218.94 feet)—13 times the average for hits.

Appendix III
Aircraft and Munition Effectiveness in
Desert Storm

were credited with a 50-percent tank kill rate for pilot-only claims. The 37th TFW justified crediting hits based solely on pilot reports on the grounds that the F-117 demonstrated superior accuracy in Desert Storm.

Reported Hits With Video Problems or Where Bomb Impacts Were Not Recorded

In 69 instances, the video recorded during a mission—from which hits and misses are determined—was of poor quality or failed to record bomb impact. Poor quality video and video that did not record bomb impact within its field-of-view pose unique BDA problems for the F-117s. F-117s are unique in that all missions are flown at night. A lone pilot must concentrate on the cockpit display to aim the laser designator on the aimpoint until bomb impact, and the impact typically occurs directly beneath the aircraft as it passes over the target. The aircraft's video records the image seen by the pilot during the mission. There is no other means for the pilot or BDA analysts to view bomb impacts. The intelligence chief for the 37th TFW during Desert Storm told us that while to claim hits when miss distances were small could be justified, hit claims made when available video did not record bomb impact could not be justified. Table III.10 illustrates examples of remarks indicating nonsupporting video.

Table III.10: Examples of Remarks Indicating Nonsupporting Video

Day	BE	Reported hits	Remarks
022	A	2	No release on tape
006	B	2	No impact seen, bad tape
001	C	1	Gimbal, no impact seen
034	D	1	Tape bad . . . , can't see impact
019	E	1	Not on tape

Source: 37th TFW Desert Storm database.

Reported Hits With Conflicting Remarks

In 49 cases, credited hits were accompanied by remarks indicating that the bombs missed the aimpoint or malfunctioned. There was no standing requirement that remarks be entered in the database, but the analysts who reviewed mission video entered explanatory or clarifying comments at their discretion. Examples of remarks that are in conflict with reported hits include references to dud bombs, bombs that struck objects other than the DMPI, and bombs that did not guide. Table III.11 illustrates examples of remarks indicating nonsupporting video.

Appendix III
Aircraft and Munition Effectiveness in
Desert Storm

Table III.11: Examples of Remarks in Conflict With Reported Hits

Day	Target	Reported hits	Remarks
025	F	2	2nd bomb hit short and left
011	G	1	Dud wpn
040	H	2	One bomb no guide
023	I	1	Hit on wrong bunker
004	J	1	Bomb long

Source: 37th TFW Desert Storm database.

The Definition of F-117 Bomb Hits in Desert Storm

One of the primary reasons that reported hits are apparently in conflict with other information recorded on the 37th TFW database is that during Desert Storm, specific objective peacetime bomb hit criteria were replaced with subjective wartime criteria. According to former 37th TFW officials, bombs making impact more than 3 feet from a DMPI in peacetime training were considered "gross errors." (And as noted previously, bomb drops without video were classified as misses.) However, these officials told us that in wartime, they deemed these criteria no longer appropriate. In the words of one former wing intelligence officer, "A GBU-10 striking 4 feet from a radar will accomplish the objective of the mission." Thus, a bomb was judged to be a hit when 37th TFW officials concluded that it probably had an adverse effect on the enemy. For example, if the intended target was a specific bunker in a large ammunition storage facility and the bomb missed the intended bunker but hit a bunker nearby, the bomb was counted as a hit.

In its Desert Storm white paper, the Air Force reported that campaign planners' faith in the F-117 targeting system was so great that pilots were tasked to hit not merely a particular building or shelter "but a particular corner, a vent, or a door. In fact, if they hit the building, but not the particular spot, their sortie counted as a miss, not a hit."[26] We conclude that the 80-percent "direct" bomb hit rate claim is not fully justified. The level of bomb accuracy was clearly less than the characterization in the Air Force white paper. However, the subjective criteria and other data problems prohibit us from recalculating a fully documented rate.[27]

---

[26] Reaching Globally, Reaching Powerfully (1991), p. 24.

[27] We reviewed a selective sample of mission videos in which reported hits contained contradictory information to determine the feasibility of verifying hit data. We determined that hit data could not be comprehensively verified because of (1) missing video, (2) video records lost when tape was reused during the campaign, (3) video images that were poor, (4) mislabeling of video, and (5) video in which the impact image was inconclusive.

Appendix III
Aircraft and Munition Effectiveness in Desert Storm

Therefore, we estimate that the F-117 bomb hit rate is likely to have been somewhere in the interval between the upper bound asserted by the Air Force of 80 percent and a worst-case, lower bound of approximately 55 percent. The lower bound assumes that all the reported hits lacking corroborating support or in conflict with other available data are discounted.[28] Whatever the actual bomb hit rate for the F-117, it may well have been "unprecedented," "unparalleled," and higher than the rates achieved by any other aircraft in Desert Storm; however, the data on the F-117 as well as other aircraft are insufficient to make such characterizations.

Probability of Weapon Release

An aircraft's bombing accuracy or bomb hit rate is one of two essential variables that operational planners use in estimating the probability that a given target will be damaged to the desired level when a specific number of aircraft attack it.[29] The second variable required by planners is the probability of weapon release. Planners need to know not only the accuracy of a weapon system but also the likelihood that on a given sortie the aircraft will be able to release its weapons. The 37th TFW database allowed the calculation of the probability of weapon release for the F-117 in Desert Storm.

The probability of weapon release is a function of multiple probabilities of potential failures during a mission that would prevent an aircraft from arriving over a target and releasing its weapons. The potential aircraft failures include (1) mechanical failure; (2) mission kill by enemy aircraft, SAM, or AAA; (3) diversion in reaction to enemy air defenses; (4) inability to locate the intended target; (5) inability to acquire the target in time to effectively launch weapons; (6) inability to complete attack coordination, and (7) inability to release weapons after arriving at the target. The F-117 proved more prone to some of these failures than others. In Desert Storm, no F-117 failed to release because of enemy aircraft, SAMs, or AAA or because of reactions to enemy air defenses.[30] However, F-117s did

---

[28]Clearly, some of the data in conflict with reported hits are more convincing than others; we believe that it is likely that some of these cases can be justified as functional hits. However, some of the evidence is equally convincing that some of the reported hits should not have been credited (such as miss distances as great as 540 feet and hits credited when bomb impact was outside DLIR FOV). The data do not permit a bomb-by-bomb reassessment.

[29]The Joint Munitions Effectiveness Manual states that damage expectancy is determined by the probability of damage to a target (that is, bomb hit rate) times the probability of release. A complete assessment of the probability that a target will receive the desired level of damage would also need to consider the number of aircraft sorties tasked and the appropriate selection of munition type given the characteristics of the target.

[30]We discussed F-117 survivability in Desert Storm in appendix II.

Appendix III
Aircraft and Munition Effectiveness in
Desert Storm

experience mechanical problems and adverse weather. Table III.12 presents the number of each type of failure that resulted in aborts and prevented bombs from being dropped on tasked F-117 strikes.

Table III.12: Failures That Prevented Bombs From Being Dropped on F-117 Primary Strikes[a]

Final disposition	Number	Percent
Total primary strikes tasked	2,271	100.0
Weather aborts	412	18.1
Air aborts	140	6.2
Ground aborts	17	0.8
Total primary strikes where no bombs were dropped	569	25.1
Total primary strikes where bombs were dropped	1,702	74.9

[a]A primary strike is defined as one aircraft tasked to deliver one or more bombs on a specific DMPI during a single sortie.

Source: 37th TFW Desert Storm database.

As table III.12 shows, one-quarter of all F-117 primary strikes tasked were aborted, principally because of bad weather.[31] (As explained in app. II, poor weather made it difficult for F-117s to identify and acquire targets and could prevent lasers from illuminating targets for the bombs.) Thus, based on the Desert Storm experience, operational planners considering the use of the F-117 in a comparable scenario and environment would anticipate that the expected probability of a target's being damaged to the desired level would be based on the number of bombs tasked, reduced by the proven probability of bomb release (75 percent), and reduced further by the demonstrated hit rate (between 55 and 80 percent). Therefore, in Desert Storm, the probability of a target's receiving damage from a scheduled F-117 strike (that is, the probability of bomb release times the demonstrated hit rate) was between 41 and 60 percent.[32]

---

[31]In contrast, according to GWAPS, 3,154 Air Force sorties were canceled and 2,280 were aborted during Desert Storm and 69,406 sorties were flown, for a combined sortie cancellation and abort rate of approximately 8 percent. The GWAPS data include the range of deployed Air Force aircraft performing the full range of service missions. Thus, while data are not available to compare mission cancellation and abortion rates by strike aircraft, the available data do indicate that the F-117 was more vulnerable to poor weather in performing its mission than was the average Air Force aircraft. GWAPS, vol. V, pt. I (Secret) tables 76 and 174, pp. 267, 408.

[32]DOD provided the following comment in response to this finding in our draft report, "This statement corrects exaggerated information (80 percent hit rate) supplied in the DOD title V report. The difference in the report represents confirmed and corroborated hits. Although statistically different, the important point is that two out of every five bombs delivered were on target. This represents a quantum leap in bombing accuracy, especially when considering that the CEP for laser guided munitions are measured in feet, not hundreds of feet. Aircraft without a precision guided munition (PGM) capability could not repeatedly duplicate these results."

Appendix III
Aircraft and Munition Effectiveness in
Desert Storm

F-117 Effectiveness on the First Night of the Air Campaign

Lockheed, the primary contractor for the F-117, claimed after the war that

"During the first 24 hours [of the air campaign], 30 F-117s struck 37 high value targets, inflicting damage that collapsed Saddam Hussein's air defense system and all but eliminated Iraq's ability to wage coordinated war. The concept of modern air warfare had been changed forever."[33]

In April 1991, Lt. Gen. Horner, the Joint Force Component Commander in Desert Storm, testified before the Congress that

"The F-117 allowed us to do things that we could have only dreamed about in past conflicts. Stealth enabled us to gain surprise each and every day of the war. For example, on the first night of the air campaign the F-117s delivered the first bombs of the war against a wide array of targets, paralyzing the Iraqi air defense network."[34]

This claim is useful in assessing F-117 performance because the first night's missions exemplified the design mission of the aircraft: to strike selected high-value, well-defended targets with LGBs. In Desert Storm, these included the strategic air defense targets referred to—comprising primarily SOCs, IOCs, and key C^3 elements of the IADS.

To assess whether the F-117s were as effective as claimed on the first night, and specifically in contributing to the collapse of the IADs, we addressed the following questions: (1) What were the reported F-117 bomb hit rates on the first night of the campaign against all targets, and IADS-related targets in particular? (2) Can the damage done to IADS targets by the F-117s on the first night be separated out from damage done by other aircraft?

We found that the claim that the F-117s alone were crucial in collapsing the IADS on the first night of the campaign is not fully supported by strike, BDA, and other intelligence data. These data indicate that the F-117s achieved only partial strike success on the first night; many other coalition aircraft attacked IADS-targets at the onset of the campaign; and IADS capabilities were diminished but continued to operate and remain viable past the first night.

F-117 Hit Rate on Planned Aimpoints on the First Night

We examined the F-117 database to evaluate whether it supported the claim that the F-117s had hit all 37 targets to which they had been tasked during the first night of the air campaign. These data show that only

---

[33]Lockheed Corporation, "We Own the Night," Lockheed Horizons, Issue 30 (May 1992), p. 57.

[34]DOD 1992 appropriations hearings (Apr. 30, 1991).

Appendix III
Aircraft and Munition Effectiveness in
Desert Storm

57 percent of the targets were hit on the first night.[35] Further, approximately half of the reported bomb hits (16 of 31) did not have corroborating documentation or were in conflict with other available data. (See table III.13.)

Table III.13: 37th TFW Data on Bombs Dropped by F-117s During the First 24 Hours

Target	Category	DMPIs	Bombs tasked	AC tasked	Hits	Misses	No drops	Hits with data problems[a]
A	[DELETED]	1	2	1	0	0	2	0
B	[DELETED]	1	1	1	0	0	1	0
C	[DELETED]	2	2	2	1	1	0	1
D	[DELETED]	2	2	2	1	1	0	1
E	[DELETED]	2	2	2	1	0	1	0
F	[DELETED]	1	1	1	0	1	0	0
G	[DELETED]	1	1	1	1	0	0	1
H	[DELETED]	1	1	1	1	0	0	1
I	[DELETED]	1	1	1	1	0	0	0
J	[DELETED]	2	2	2	2	0	0	1
K	[DELETED]	1	1	1	0	1	0	0
L	[DELETED]	1	1	1	0	0	1	0
M	[DELETED]	2	3	2	3	0	0	0
N	[DELETED]	1	1	1	0	0	1	0
O	[DELETED]	1	1	1	0	0	1	0
P	[DELETED]	1	1	1	0	0	1	0
Q	[DELETED]	3	4	4	4	0	0	2
R	[DELETED]	1	1	1	1	0	0	1
S	[DELETED]	1	1	1	0	1	0	0
T	[DELETED]	2	2	2	0	2	0	0
U	[DELETED]	1	1	1	0	1	0	0
V	[DELETED]	2	2	2	0	2	0	0
W	[DELETED]	1	1	1	1	0	0	0
X	[DELETED]	1	1	1	1	0	0	1
Y	[DELETED]	4	4	2	2	1	1	0
Z	[DELETED]	1	1	1	1	0	0	0
AA	[DELETED]	1	1	1	1	0	0	0
BB	[DELETED]	2	2	2	1	0	1	0
CC	[DELETED]	1	1	1	1	0	0	1

(continued)

[35]Fifty-nine percent of the tasked targets were hit on the second night, for a two-night average of 58 percent. Although the claim was based only on the first night's 37 targets, we examined the data on the second night as well, to determine if the first night's performance was an anomaly.

Appendix III
Aircraft and Munition Effectiveness in
Desert Storm

Target	Category	DMPIs	Bombs tasked	AC tasked	Hits	Misses	No drops	Hits with data problems[a]
DD	[DELETED]	1	1	1	0	0	1	0
EE	[DELETED]	3	3	3	2	1	0	2
FF	[DELETED]	4	4	4	1	3	0	1
GG	[DELETED]	2	2	2	2	0	0	1
HH	[DELETED]	1	1	1	0	0	1	0
II	[DELETED]	1	1	1	0	0	1	0
JJ	[DELETED]	2	2	1	2	0	0	1
KK	[DELETED]	1	1	1	0	1	0	0
Total		57	60	[b]	31	16	13	16

[a]Reported hits that lack corroborating support or are in conflict with other available data.

[b]Column total would not equal sum of aircraft tasked because some aircraft were tasked to more than one DMPI.

Source: 37th TFW Desert Storm and Missions databases.

F-117 First-Night Hit Rate on IADS Targets

A key claim made for the F-117s is that their effectiveness in destroying IADS targets on the first night opened up holes that nonstealthy aircraft then used to successfully attack other targets. Fifteen of the 37 F-117 first-night targets were IADS-related. Because of weather aborts and misses, only 9 of these 15 F-117 targets (60 percent) were reported hit by the F-117s on the first night of the campaign. Table III.14 shows our analysis of the 37th TFW database and DIA BDA reports.

Appendix III
Aircraft and Munition Effectiveness in
Desert Storm

Table III.14: F-117 Hit Rate on Strategic Integrated Air Defense Targets on the First Night

| Target | Number | | | | | | | Battle damage assessment[a] | | | |
| | DMPIs | Bombs tasked | Aircraft tasked | Hits | Misses | No drops | Hits with data problems[b] | Success | | | Day[d] |
								Yes	No	I[c]	
A	1	2	1	0	0	2	0				
C	2	2	2	1	1	0	1		X		28
H	1	1	1	1	0	0	1	X			5
I	1	1	1	1	0	0	0		X		7
J	2	2	2	2	0	0	1		X		6
L	1	1	1	0	0	1	0				
M	2	3	2	3	0	0	0			X	2
Q	3	4	4	4	0	0	2		X		2
T	2	2	2	0	2	0	0		X		3
V	2	2	2	0	2	0	0		X		2
W	1	1	1	1	0	0	0	X			2
GG	2	2	2	2	0	0	1		X		3
HH	1	1	1	0	0	1	0				
II	1	1	1	0	0	1	0				
JJ	2	2	1	2	0	0	1		X		2
Total	24	27	17[e]	17	5	5	7	2	8	1	

[a]Assessment of first phase III report issued on target.

[b]Reported hits that lack corroborating support or are in conflict with other available data.

[c]Phase III assessment inconclusive.

[d]Day of Desert Storm on which first DIA BDA report on target was issued.

[e]Total does not equal sum of aircraft tasked; some aircraft were assigned more than one target.

Source: 37th TFW Desert Storm and Missions databases.

The table shows that 17 F-117s were tasked to deliver 27 LGBs on 15 IADS-related targets with a total of 24 DMPIs. According to the 37th TFW database, 5 of the scheduled 27 LGBs (19 percent) were not dropped, another 5 (19 percent) were misses; and 17 (63 percent) were hits. Of the 17 claimed hits, however, 7 (41 percent) either lacked supporting video or were in conflict with other available data. This means that there are unambiguous data supporting hits by 10 of the 22 LGBs (45 percent) that were dropped on IADS targets. The F-117s did not hit 6 of the 15 (40 percent) IADS targets to which they were tasked, 1 of which was the Air Defense Operations Center in Baghdad.

Appendix III
Aircraft and Munition Effectiveness in
Desert Storm

During Desert Storm, DIA produced phase III BDA assessments on 11 of the 15 IADS targets to which the F-117s were tasked on the first night. According to initial DIA BDA assessments of the IADS targets (most of which were made by the end of day 3 of the campaign), 2 of the 11 targets assessed were damaged sufficiently to preclude restrikes, 8 targets remained functional and were recommended for restrikes, and 1 could not be conclusively assessed.

In sum, the claim that the F-117s were responsible for collapsing the IADS on the first night appears open to question because (1) the F-117s did not hit 40 percent of their tasked targets on the first night and (2) of the 11 IADS-related targets attacked by F-117s and assessed by DIA, 8 were assessed as needing additional strikes. In addition, the Missions database shows that 167 other platforms (such as A-10s, F-4Gs, and F/A-18s) also struck 18 air defense-related targets (IOCs, SOCs, and radars) on the first night.

The lack of data on the exact degree to which most targets were damaged, and how that might have affected total integrated capabilities, precludes attributing greater effectiveness to the F-117s than to other systems. Thus, while, overall, the coalition was able to neutralize the IADS in the early days of the war, the data are insufficient to validate the claim that the F-117s alone were the critical element, above all on the first night of the air campaign.

Moreover, Air Force intelligence assessments of the extent to which the IADS was operating in the first few days of the war do not support the assertion that the system was "collapsed" during the first few hours of the first night. Daily intelligence summaries prepared during the war, called DAISUMs, characterized the IADS on the third day of the campaign as "crippled but information is still being passed" and "evidence of degradation of the Iraqi C^2 network is beginning to show." The DAISUMs also described overall Iraqi electronic warfare activity as low but radar and SAM activity in Baghdad and KTO as heavy. By the fifth day of the air war, the DAISUMs described the situation as, "In general, the Iraqi IADS is down but not out."

Aircraft Tasked to Downtown Baghdad

Related to the claim for F-117 effectiveness against IADS targets is a broader claim made by the Air Force concerning the overall value or survivability of stealth aircraft. The Air Force stated in its Desert Storm white paper that "the F-117 was the only airplane that the planners dared

**Appendix III
Aircraft and Munition Effectiveness in
Desert Storm**

risk over downtown Baghdad." The Air Force further stated that "so dangerous was downtown Baghdad that the air campaign planners excluded all other attackers, except F-117s and cruise missiles, from striking it."[36] Similarly, in joint testimony to the Congress on stealth and Desert Storm, Gens. Horner and Glosson stated "F-117s were the only aircraft that attacked downtown Baghdad targets—by most accounts more heavily defended than any Eastern Europe target at the height of the Cold War."[37] A virtually identical claim was made by Air Combat Command's Gen. Loh, also in congressional testimony.[38] Contrary to these statements, however, we found that strikes by other aircraft were not only planned but also executed against key targets in downtown Baghdad.

A CENTAF-prepared Master Attack Plan (MAP) identified all planned air campaign strikes for the first 72 hours of the air war. For the third day of Desert Storm, the MAP called for three large-package F-16 strikes against targets both in downtown Baghdad and against the nearby Baghdad Nuclear Research Facility. Forty F-16s in package G were assigned to strike 5 leadership targets in the heart of the city—the headquarters of Iraqi intelligence service, directorate of internal security, military intelligence, national air force, and Baath Party. Another 16 F-16s in package N were assigned to restrike military intelligence headquarters; 8 more were tasked to a sixth central city target, the Ministry of Information and Culture. Although planned, these attacks were canceled because of poor weather.

On day 3 of the campaign, the third and largest package (package Q) included 72 F-16s; 56 were tasked against the Baghdad Nuclear Research Facility, on the edge of the city and just 10 miles from the presidential palace. Eight F-16s were tasked against the Baghdad Petroleum Refinery, across the Euphrates River from central Baghdad and barely 2 miles from the presidential palace. Four each were tasked to restrike the air force and Baath Party headquarters. These attacks were carried out, and two F-16s in this package were lost.

Thus, the MAP for day 3 called for a total of 152 F-16s to strike targets within a radius of 10 miles of the presidential palace; 96 were specifically tasked to targets in the heart of the city. Moreover, those tasked to the

---

[36]USAF, Reaching Globally, Reaching Powerfully (1991), p. 19.

[37]DOD 1992 appropriations hearings (Apr. 30, 1991), p. 468.

[38]Gen. Loh, the "Value of Stealth," DOD 1992 appropriations hearings (Apr. 30, 1991), p. 2. Figure II.4 is an Air Force depiction of the use of F-117s and F-16s against the Baghdad Nuclear Research Facility to demonstrate the "value of stealth." Appendix XI addresses the claim that the comparative advantage of stealth aircraft delivering LGBs over conventional aircraft delivering unguided bombs was demonstrated in Desert Storm when both types of aircraft attacked the same Baghdad target.

**Appendix III
Aircraft and Munition Effectiveness in
Desert Storm**

nuclear research center were well within the threat ranges of SAM and AAA sites that defended Baghdad area targets, whether core or suburban. And as explained in appendix II, many types of aircraft struck targets in metropolitan Baghdad, which was heavily defended throughout, thus making the distinction about taskings over downtown Baghdad versus the metropolitan area somewhat moot.

While aircraft other than F-117s were not subsequently tasked against downtown targets after package Q on day 3 of the campaign, many types of bombers struck targets in the Baghdad metropolitan area repeatedly throughout the air campaign. And those attacks carried out at night resulted in either zero or minimal casualties for nonstealthy, conventional aircraft.

TLAM Effectiveness Claims

Extensive analysis of BDA imagery and other data on the effectiveness of Tomahawk land-attack missiles by the Center for Naval Analyses has found that TLAM performance in Desert Storm was well below the impression conveyed in DOD's title V report to the Congress, as well as in internal DOD estimates.

The title V report, while essentially silent about the missile's actual accuracy and effectiveness, notes that the "launching system success rate was 98 percent." (DOD, p. T-203.) CNA and DIA reported that the Joint Chiefs of Staff estimated in April 1991 (just a couple months after the conflict ended) that 85 percent of the TLAMs had hit their intended targets.[39] Three variants of TLAMs were used in Desert Storm: TLAM Cs, with conventional unitary warheads; and TLAM D-Is; and TLAM D-IIs, which dispense different types of conventional submunitions.[40]

---

[39] Joint CNA/DIA Research Memorandum 93-49, TLAM Performance During Operation Desert Storm: Assessment of Physical and Functional Damage to the TLAM Aimpoints, Vol. I: Overview and Methodology (Secret), March 1994, p. 21. CNA/DIA noted that JCS assumed that TLAMs were always responsible for all the damage at the aimpoint, even when it had been targeted by other U.S. weapons.

[40] This report and the CNA/DIA reports cited do not assess the performance of the TLAM D-IIs because of classification issues.

Appendix III
Aircraft and Munition Effectiveness in
Desert Storm

Number of TLAMs Launched and Type of Targets

During Desert Storm, a TLAM mission was loaded 307 times into a particular missile for launch from a Navy ship or submarine.[41] Of those 307, 19 experienced prelaunch problems. Ten of the 19 problems were only temporary, thus these missile were either launched at a later time or returned to inventory. Of the 288 actual launches, 6 suffered boost failures and did not transition to cruise. Of the 282 missiles that transitioned to cruise, 22 were TLAM D-IIs and 260 were TLAM Cs and D-Is.

Of the 38 targets attacked by TLAMs, 37 were attacked by the 260 TLAM Cs and D-Is. The 37 targets had a total of 173 individual aimpoints; they were aimed at 10 leadership targets: 6 C^3 targets, 3 air defense targets, 8 electric power targets, 4 oil-related targets, 4 chemical and missile targets, and 2 airfield targets. (The 38th target was targeted by TLAM D-IIs alone.) However, TLAMs were limited in the type of target to which they could be aimed, since they did not have anywhere near the "hard target" capability of a 2,000-pound bomb. CNA/DIA reported that although two TLAMs hit the Baghdad air defense operations center, they made only "small craters on the roof" of the 11-feet-thick reinforced concrete bunker.

Concentrated Launch Period

TLAM launches occurred overwhelmingly in the first 3 days of the war. Of the 260 TLAM Cs and D-Is that transitioned to cruise phase, more than 39 percent were fired in the first 24 hours; 62 percent were launched during the first 48 hours; just over 73 percent in the first 72 hours; and no TLAMs of any kind were launched after February 1, 1991, just 2 weeks after the war started. CNA/DIA offered no explanation for why there were no launches after February 1. However, CNA/DIA noted that on February 1, six TLAM Cs were fired in a "stream raid," all aimed at the Rasheed airfield; they arrived in the Baghdad area about 11 a.m., they were fired upon, and only two of the six arrived at the target. GWAPS reported that Gen. Schwarzkopf did not approve any additional TLAM strikes either because (1) television coverage of daylight strikes in downtown Baghdad proved unacceptable in Washington or (2) their use was deemed too expensive given its relatively small warhead and high cost.

---

[41]Some analysts may be more familiar with a lower figure of intended launches. However, as CNA/DIA stated, "a TLAM mission was loaded 307 times into a particular missile for launch (i.e., there were missile/mission pairs)." Of these, 10 missiles experienced "temporary problems" preventing launch when intended (some were launched later and some returned to inventory), and 9 had prelaunch failures. Subtracting these 19 missiles, there were 288 TLAM Desert Storm launches at the time intended. Since 307 missiles were originally matched to a mission, we used that number as the universe of TLAM launches. (For further discussion, see CNA/DIA, vol. I (Mar. 1994), pp. 70-72.)

Appendix III
Aircraft and Munition Effectiveness in
Desert Storm

Problems With BDA

Despite initial strong positive claims made for TLAM performance in Desert Storm, analysis of TLAM effectiveness was complicated by problematic BDA data. Multiple TLAMs were targeted to the same targets, and attacks by U.S. Air Force bombers with other weapons were also made against some TLAM targets before the targets could be assessed for BDA purposes. Thus, for many TLAMs, it was difficult to identify the damage a particular missile may have done, or to know whether it actually even reached the target, if the target was scheduled for attack by other weapons before BDA collection.

However, using BDA imagery and analysis, CNA/DIA's postwar analyses have shown that about as many TLAM Cs and D-Is failed to arrive at their intended targets—termed "no shows"—as are estimated to have hit their targets. Others arrived at the designated target area, but impacted so far away from the aimpoint as to only create a crater. Of the 260 TLAM Cs and D-Is that transitioned to cruise flight, 30 were TLAM Cs with "programmed warhead detonation"—airburst mode—that created damage effects that CNA/DIA stated could not be evaluated adequately by existing BDA imagery. Therefore, these 30 are excluded from CNA/DIA's assessment of the percentage of TLAMs that arrived at the target area and that hit their intended target. (Since there was no way to reliably ascertain any damage caused by the airburst mode TLAMs, it could not be determined how many arrived over the targets either.) Ranges in the estimates for arrival and hits reflect BDA uncertainties.

Table III.15 shows the number of TLAMs launched and the number of TLAM Cs and D-1s estimated by CNA/DIA to have arrived at their targets and to have caused some damage.

For those TLAMs for which CNA/DIA were able to interpret BDA data, an estimated [DELETED] percent hit their intended aimpoint. These [DELETED] missiles represented [DELETED] percent of all 307 attempted launchings. If the [DELETED]-percent hit rate for the 230 detectable TLAM Cs and D-Is was assumed to have been the case also for the 30 PWD TLAM Cs and the [DELETED] TLAM D-IIs that transitioned to cruise, then a total of [DELETED] TLAMs would have hit their intended targets, or [DELETED] percent of the 307 attempted launches.[42]

However, actual damage to targets may well have been even less than the [DELETED]-percent hit rate appears to imply, given that, as CNA/DIA noted, the methodology used to define a TLAM hit was "in some ways generous."

---

[42]There were [DELETED] PWD TLAM Cs and D-IIs that transitioned to cruise. The range is [DELETED] percent, which is [DELETED]. Adding [DELETED].

Appendix III
Aircraft and Munition Effectiveness in
Desert Storm

CNA/DIA stated that a hit was defined as "damage of any kind to the aimpoint or element containing the aimpoint." (CNA/DIA, p. 67.) This meant, CNA/DIA explained, that "if a TLAM impacts the dirt some distance from the target but causes even minor fragment or blast damage to its aimpoint element, it is counted as a hit." (CNA/DIA, p. 67.) CNA/DIA reported that there were [DELETED] such marginal hits; if they are excluded, the TLAM hit rate was [DELETED]-percent for nonairburst TLAMs.

Table III.15: TLAM Performance in Desert Storm

Phase of TLAM use	All	C and D-I only	All	C and D-I only
Missile/mission pairs	307	[DELETED]a	[DELETED]	[DELETED]
Successful launches	282	[DELETED]	[DELETED]	[DELETED]
Transition to cruise flight	b	[DELETED]	b	[DELETED]
Arrived in target areac	b	[DELETED]	b	[DELETED]
No shows at targetd	b	[DELETED]	b	[DELETED]
Hit or damaged target	b	[DELETED]	b	[DELETED]

aExcludes 10 TLAMs with "temporary problems" from base used to calculate percentages.

bData not available.

cExcludes 30 TLAMs with programmed warhead detonation or airburst mode that could not be assessed. Therefore, numbers and percentages at this line and below are based on a set of 230 non-airburst mode TLAMs. For further details, see CNA/DIA, TLAM Performance During Desert Storm (Secret), March 1994, pp. 2-3.

dAn additional [DELETED] TLAMs that arrived in their target areas impacted at distances at least five times greater than their predicted CEP (circular error probable)—that is, from [DELETED] from their aimpoints. These [DELETED] were not counted as "no shows" or as hits.

Source: CNA/DIA, vol. 1 (Secret), March 1994, pp. 71-72.

Beyond TLAM's [DELETED]-percent miss rate against intended targets, it demonstrated additional problems. The relatively flat, featureless, desert terrain in the theater made it difficult for the Defense Mapping Agency to produce usable TERCOM ingress routes, and TLAM demonstrated limitations in range, mission planning, lethality, and effectiveness against hard targets and targets capable of mobility. Specifically, CNA/DIA reported that mission failures resulted from three issues independent of the missile and were problems that existed before the missile was launched. First, mission guidance was not always clear and specific (12 TLAMs were expended against 12 aimpoints where objectives were vague). Second, supporting intelligence was not always accurate (five TLAM aimpoints were misidentified with respect to their function). And third, targets were not always within the capabilities of the TLAM warhead (five aimpoints were either mobile or too hardened for the TLAM warhead).

Appendix III
Aircraft and Munition Effectiveness in Desert Storm

Since the war, the Navy has developed a Block III variant of the TLAM. Its improvements include the use of Global Positioning System in TLAM's guidance system. With GPS, TLAM route planning is not constrained by terrain features, and mission planning time is reduced. Some experts have expressed the concern that GPS guidance may be vulnerable to jamming. Thus, until system testing and possible modifications demonstrate TLAM Block III resistance to electronic countermeasures, it is possible that the solution to the TERCOM limitations—GPS—may lead to a new potential vulnerability—jamming. Moreover, the Block III variant continues to use the optical Digital Scene Matching Area Correlator, which has various limitations. [DELETED]

In sum, TLAMs were initially believed to be extremely successful in hitting—and therefore damaging—their targets; however, subsequent intensive analysis shows that the hit rate for 230 TLAM Cs and D-Is was [DELETED] percent. Moreover, a stricter definition of a "hit" indicates a slightly lower rate of [DELETED] percent. TLAMs were aimed at just 38 targets, perhaps based on their limited capabilities against reinforced targets. While TLAMs offered a distinct alternative to having to deliver weapons from a manned aircraft, the data from Desert Storm suggest that there are important limitations to their effectiveness in terms of hit rate and capability of damaging a wide range of targets.

Weapon System Manufacturers' Claims

We assessed the accuracy of statements made by various U.S. manufacturers about the performance of their products that played a major role in the air campaign. Table III.16 presents manufacturers' statements and summarizes our finding on each product.[43]

---

[43]We culled statements from annual reports to stockholders, "10-K" annual reports to the federal government, and public advertisements appearing in a major weekly publication (Aviation Week and Space Technology).

Appendix III
Aircraft and Munition Effectiveness in
Desert Storm

Table III.16: Manufacturers' Statements About Product Performance Compared to GAO Findings

Manufacturer	Product	Statement	Finding
General Dynamics	F-16	"No matter what the mission, air-to-air, air-to-ground. No matter what the weather, day or night. The F-16 is the premier dogfighter."[a]	The F-16's delivery of precision air-to-ground munitions, such as Maverick, was impaired, and sometimes made impossible, by clouds, haze, humidity, smoke, and dust. Only less accurate unguided munitions could be employed in adverse weather using radar.
Grumman	A-6E	"A-6s . . . [were] detecting, identifying, tracking, and destroying targets in any weather, day or night."[b]	The A-6E FLIR's ability to detect and identify targets was limited by clouds, haze, humidity, smoke, and dust; the laser designator's ability to track targets was similarly limited. Only less accurate unguided munitions could be employed in adverse weather using radar.
Lockheed	F-117	Achieved "80 percent direct hits."[c]	The hit rate was between 55 and 80 percent; the probability of bomb release was only 75 percent; thus, the probability of a hit during a scheduled F-117 mission was between 41 and 60 percent.
		The "only aircraft to attack heavily defended downtown Baghdad."[c]	Other types of aircraft frequently attacked targets in the equally heavily defended metropolitan area; the Baghdad region was as heavily defended as downtown.
		"During the first night, 30 F-117s struck 37 high-value targets, inflicting damage that collapsed Saddam Hussein's air defense system and all but eliminated Iraq's ability to wage coordinated war."[d]	On the first night, 21 of the 37 high-value targets to which F-117s were tasked were reported hit; of these, the F-117s missed 40 percent of their strategic air defense targets. BDA on 11 of the F-117 SAD targets confirmed only 2 complete kills. Numerous aircraft, other than the F-117, were involved in suppressing the Iraqi IADS, which did not show a marked falloff in aircraft kills until day 5.
		"On Day 1 of the war, only 36 Stealth Fighters (less than 2.5% of the coalition's tactical assets) were in the Gulf theater, yet they attacked 31% of the 17 January targets."[d]	The 2.5-percent claim is based on a comparison of the F-117s to all deployed aircraft, including those incapable of dropping bombs. The F-117s represented 32 percent of U.S. aircraft capable of delivering LGBs with warheads designed to penetrate hardened targets. F-117s were tasked against 35 percent of the first-day strategic targets.
		"The F-117 reinstated the element of surprise."[c]	Other nonstealthy aircraft also achieved surprise. Stealth characteristics did not ensure surprise for all F-117 strikes; modifications in tactics in the use of support aircraft were required.
Martin Marietta	LANTIRN	Can "locate and attack targets at night and under other conditions of poor visibility using low-level, high speed tactics."[e]	LANTIRN can be employed below clouds and weather; however, its ability to find and designate targets through clouds, haze, smoke, dust, and humidity ranges from limited to no capacity at all.

(continued)

Appendix III
Aircraft and Munition Effectiveness in
Desert Storm

Manufacturer	Product	Statement	Finding
McDonnell Douglas	F-15E	An "all weather" attack aircraft.[f]	The ability of the F-15E using LANTIRN to detect and identify targets through clouds, haze, humidity, smoke, and dust was very limited; the laser designator's ability to track targets was similarly limited. Only less accurate unguided munitions could be employed in adverse weather using radar.
	TLAM C/D cruise missile	"Can be launched . . . in any weather."[g]	TLAM's weather limitation occurs not so much at the launch point but in the target area where the optical [DELETED].
		"Incredible accuracy"; "one of the most accurate weapons in the world today."[g]	From [DELETED] percent of the TLAMs reached their intended aimpoints, with only [DELETED] percent actually hitting the target. It is impossible to assess actual damage incurred only by TLAMs.
Northrop	ALQ-135 jammer for F-15E	"Proved itself by jamming enemy threat radars"; was able "to function in virtually any hostile environment."[a]	[DELETED]
Texas Instruments	Paveway guidance for LGBs	"Employable" in "poor weather/visibility" conditions.[h]	Clouds, smoke, dust, and haze impose serious limitations on laser guidance by disrupting laser beam.
		"TI Paveway III: one target, one bomb."[a]	Our analysis of a selected sample of targets found that no single aimpoint was struck by one LGB—the average was 4, the maximum was 10.
		"LGBs accounted for only 5% of the total ordnance. But Paveway accounted for nearly 50%" of targets destroyed.[a]	Data were not compiled that would permit a determination of what percentage of targets were destroyed by any munition type.

[a]From a company advertisement in Aviation Week and Space Technology, (1991).

[b]Grumman Annual Report, 1991, p. 12.

[c]Lockheed briefing for GAO.

[d]From Lockheed Horizons, "We Own the Night," Issue 30 (1992), p. 55, 57.

[e]Martin Marietta, 10-K Report to the Securities and Exchange Commission, 1992, p. 14.

[f]McDonnell-Douglas, "Performance of MCAIR Combat Aircraft in Operation Desert Storm," brochure.

[g]McDonnell-Douglas, "Tomahawk: A Total Weapon System," brochure.

[h]Texas Instruments, "Paveway III: Laser-Guided Weapons," brochure, 1992.

Table III.16 shows that each of the manufacturers made public statements about the performance of their products in Desert Storm that are not fully supported. We also found that although some manufacturers told us that they had only limited information available to them—to the point of relying on hearsay—this did not inhibit them from making unfounded assertions about system performance, attempting to create favorable impressions of their products. Finally, while the manufacturers' claims were often inaccurate, their assertions were not significantly different from, nor appreciably less accurate than, many of the statements of DOD officials and DOD reports about the same weapon systems.

Air Campaign Effectiveness Against Mobile Targets

Over the 38 days preceding the ground campaign, approximately 37,500 strikes were conducted against Iraqi forces in kill box areas, targeting tanks, armored personnel carriers (APC), and other tactical vehicles. Because there are few data on the precise number of munitions expended or sorties flown against tanks and other vehicles, and because it was impossible to systematically collect and compare BDA data to assess munition hit rates, it is also impossible to know what level of effectiveness was achieved in Desert Storm for the various munition types used.

Pilots reported that they had been able to destroy large numbers of vehicles on the ground—tanks, APCs, and trucks—as well as artillery pieces, before and during the ground campaign, especially with guided munitions such as LGBs and Maverick missiles. While much pilot frustration stemmed from the use of unguided bombs from medium to high altitudes, a number of limitations were also revealed in the use of guided munitions.

The Desert Storm databases do not provide data on attacks against specific vehicles; many such attacks are subsumed as strikes against kill boxes in the KTO. Interviews with pilots revealed that the effectiveness of munitions against small ground targets was constrained both by Desert Storm altitude delivery restrictions and the combined technical limitations of the aircraft, sensors, and munitions used, whether guided or unguided. At the same time, because Iraqi KTO forces tended to remain in place through the 38 days preceding the ground campaign—and often put tanks in recognizable formations—they were comparatively easy to identify.

As noted in appendix II, after day 2, aircraft delivery tactics were designed to maximize survivability—by dropping ordnance from medium to high altitudes—rather than to maximize weapon effectiveness. Most pre-Desert Storm training occurred at low altitudes where bombs are not subject to the high winds found in the gulf at high altitudes. It was the consensus of the Desert Storm veteran pilots we interviewed that unguided munitions were much less accurate from high altitude than from low.

Appendix III
Aircraft and Munition Effectiveness in
Desert Storm

Pilots reported that guided munition effectiveness also decreased somewhat from higher altitudes because (1) targets were more difficult to designate with lasers, (2) some computer software did not allow high-altitude bombing, and (3) the LGBs were also subject to the effects of wind. Depending on the missile sensors, guided munition delivery was also degraded, if not altogether prevented at times, by clouds, smoke, dust, haze, and even humidity.

The difficulty in identifying and targeting vehicles and other small ground targets, whether with guided or unguided munitions, was reflected in the findings of postwar studies by the Army's Foreign Science and Technology Center (FSTC) and the CIA that sought to distinguish the relative effectiveness of the air and ground campaigns in destroying Iraqi armor.

FSTC and CIA both found that the attrition of armored vehicles from guided munitions was probably less than was initially claimed for air power. FSTC personnel examined tanks that the Iraqis had left behind in the KTO.[44] Of 163 tanks analyzed, 78 (48 percent) were abandoned intact by the Iraqis or were destroyed by Iraqi demolition, presumably to deny them to the coalition, while 85 (52 percent) had sustained 145 hits. Of these hits, only 28 (17 percent) were assessed as having come from air-to-ground munitions.

Using aerial photography, the CIA identified the number of Iraqi tanks and APCs that did not move from areas where they were deployed during the entire air campaign to areas where ground fighting occurred and were therefore "destroyed or damaged during the air campaign . . . inoperable because of poor maintenance, or . . . abandoned."[45]

The CIA study examined the damage done to armored vehicles of 12 Iraqi divisions, 3 of them Republican Guard divisions. Of the 2,665 tanks deployed to those 12 divisions, the CIA estimated that 1,135 (43 percent) were destroyed by aircraft before the ground war and 1,530 (57 percent) were undamaged. Of 2,624 APCs, 827 (32 percent) were assessed as destroyed by aircraft; 1,797 escaped damage. The levels of attrition among divisions varied greatly, with the RG units experiencing the lightest

---

[44]The sample of tanks studied was not scientifically selected; it consisted simply of those that the study participants were able to locate and inspect.

[45]CIA, Operation Desert Storm: A Snapshot (Sept. 1993), last page. Even though some number of the vehicles were possibly abandoned or broken down because of lack of maintenance, the study's methodology credited all vehicles that did not move as vehicles killed by air attack; thus, the study may have overcounted the percentage of tanks, APCs, and artillery destroyed by air-to-ground munitions.

Appendix III
Aircraft and Munition Effectiveness in
Desert Storm

attrition, although there was substantial variation among them as well—from 13 to 30 percent of tanks destroyed before the ground campaign.[46]

In sum, although the CIA and FSTC studies each had methodological shortcomings, taken together, their findings suggest that while the air campaign may have been less effective than first estimated against these targets, it still destroyed (or rendered unusable) less than half the Iraqi armor in the KTO.

Air Campaign Effectiveness in Achieving Strategic Objectives

To what extent were each of the strategic objectives of the air campaign met? We addressed this subquestion in two parts. First, we reviewed the available outcome data for each category of strategic targets as possible indicators of the campaign's effectiveness in destroying different categories of targets. Second, we reviewed the available data and literature on the aggregate effectiveness of the campaign in meeting each of the strategic objectives.

Outcome Data by Strategic Target Category

The effectiveness of aircraft and munitions in the aggregate varied among the strategic target sets.[47] While the attainment of strategic objectives is determined by more than the achievement of individual target objectives, the compilation of individual target objectives achieved was one tool used by commanders during the war to direct the campaign. Table III.17 illustrates that just over half (53 percent) of the final DIA phase III reports concluded that the target had been destroyed or the objective had been met and no additional strikes were required. The percentage of targets assessed as fully destroyed in each category ranged from a low of 25 percent in the SCU category to a high of 76 percent in the NBC category.

---

[46]The Hammurabi, Madinah, and Tawakalna RG divisions experienced 13, 23, and 30 percent attrition of their tanks, respectively (for an average attrition of 21 percent). Nine regular army armored and mechanized divisions experienced an average tank attrition rate of 48 percent.

[47]The number of targets in each strategic target set where the target objectives had been successfully met was used as a measure of the effectiveness of aircraft and munitions in the aggregate. The determination of whether the target objective had been met was based on the final DIA phase III BDA report written on a target during the campaign.

Appendix III
Aircraft and Munition Effectiveness in
Desert Storm

Table III.17: Targets Categorized as Fully Successfully Destroyed and Not Fully Successfully Destroyed

Target category	Number FS	Percent FS	Number NFS	Percent NFS	Total
C³	73	57	55	43	128
ELE	13	57	10	43	23
GVC	13	52	12	48	25
KBX	a	a	a	a	a
LOC	35	67	17	33	52
MIB	18	31	40	69	58
NAV	4	29	10	71	14
NBC	16	76	5	24	21
OCA	24	65	13	35	37
OIL	9	38	15	62	24
SAM	18	69	8	31	26
SCU	6	25	18	75	24
Total	**229**	**53**	**203**	**47**	**432**

ªData were not available.

Although the rate of success varies across target categories, for several reasons these rates do not necessarily reflect the relative degree to which individual campaign objectives—as operationalized through the formation of target categories—were achieved. Desert Storm campaign goals were not necessarily achieved through the cumulative destruction of individual targets. For example, destroying x percent of all bridges does not automatically equate to reducing the capacity of the lines of communication by x percent, for several reasons: the bridges destroyed may not be the most crucial to the flow of supplies, intelligence may not have identified all of the bridges, and the enemy may effectively respond with countermeasures (such as pontoon bridges). In addition, not all targets are of equal importance. The value in destroying a key bridge over the Euphrates may well be higher than destroying a bridge in Baghdad with its numerous alternative bridges.

Another reason why the data in table III.17 must be interpreted with caution is that the partial damage to the majority of targets assessed as not fully successful could have contributed toward the attainment of the overall campaign objectives. Moreover, no criteria, and no data, exist to determine the absolute or relative effect of partially (or fully) damaged targets on the attainment of campaign objectives.

Appendix III
Aircraft and Munition Effectiveness in
Desert Storm

Further, table III.17 presents data only on targets for which BDA data exist. These targets constitute less than half of the targets in the Missions database, and they do not necessarily represent all of the targets in each category. In addition, relevant targets that should have been struck but were not on the list of strategic targets (such as unknown Iraqi NBC targets) are not represented among the targets in the table.

Air Campaign Effectiveness in Achieving Key Objectives

The Desert Storm air campaign had larger goals than simply damaging individual target. For example, it is one thing to destroy a dozen bridges; it is another to achieve the objective of effectively cutting supply lines. In this section, we examine the effectiveness of the air campaign with regard to several broad objectives that account for nearly all 12 of the strategic target categories shown in table III.17.[48] Because of their limitations, the data shown in table III.17 should be used only as supporting or partial evidence.

We augment those success rates with information from pilots, planners, and analysts summarized in table III.18, which compares the Desert Storm results as reported in DOD's title V report to our findings.

Table III.18: Desert Storm Achievement of Key Objectives

Target set	DOD title V result	Our finding
IADS and airfields	Air supremacy "attained." IADS "fragmented" within hours; medium- and high-altitude sanctuary created; however, AAA and IR SAMs remained a threat to the end. Iraqi air force "decimated."	Coalition rapidly achieved complete control of Iraqi and KTO airspace, almost uncontested by Iraqi aircraft. IADS fragmented over first few days, but autonomous SAM and AAA sites and IR SAMs remained serious threats. Integrated threat overstated; autonomous threat understated. 290 of 724 fixed-wing Iraqi aircraft destroyed, 121 escaped to Iran, and remainder not hit; 43 percent of air force intact and in Iraq at end of war.

(continued)

---

[48]The only strategic target category not clearly subsumed under one of several broader sets is that of naval-related targets, including port areas. These targets were not a major focus of our study. Both DOD's title V report and GWAPS reported that the air campaign was highly effective in eliminating Iraq's naval forces.

Appendix III
Aircraft and Munition Effectiveness in
Desert Storm

Target set	DOD title V result	Our finding
Leadership and command, control, and communications	Leadership forced to "move often," reducing C^3; telecommunications facilities destroyed but were often repaired.	52 percent of leadership and 57 percent of C^3 targets were successfully destroyed or damaged.
	Redundant and alternative communication facilities "were difficult to destroy."	Despite hits on C^3 nodes, Saddam was able to communicate with and direct Iraqi forces.
	Much of command structure was "degraded."	
Oil and electricity	80 percent of oil-refining capacity "damaged."	Data support title V report's assessment.
	National electric power grid "eventually collapsed."	
	Early disruption of primary sources negatively affected entire war industry capabilities.	
Scuds	Scud facility damage "less than previously thought."	No known destruction of mobile Scud launcher.
	Launches reduced after day 11, with some increase in last week and occasional large salvos.	Scud launches seemingly temporarily suppressed but end-of-war launches suggest large reserve may still exist.
	No destruction of mobile launchers confirmed; they were difficult to find.	Scud hunt level of effort overstated.
		No correlation between rate of launches and anti-Scud sorties.
Nuclear, biological, and chemical	Nuclear facility destruction "was incomplete"; damage to "known" nuclear facilities was "substantial"; however, nuclear program "did not suffer as serious a setback as desired."	76 percent of known NBC targets fully successfully destroyed.
	Chemical warfare program was "seriously damaged; 75 percent of production capability destroyed."	While known nuclear sites were severely or moderately damaged, overall program was virtually intact because only less than 15 percent of the facilities were known and, therefore, attacked.
	NBC destruction estimates "suffered from incomplete target set information."	
	Nuclear program virtually intact; only less than 15 percent of the facilities hit because of lack of knowledge about the program.	
Railroads and bridges (lines-of-communication)	Three-quarters of bridges to KTO destroyed; major food shortages for frontline forces; lines of communication in KTO effectively interdicted.	67 percent of LOC targets fully successfully destroyed.
		Iraqi ground forces experienced some shortages but, overall, remained adequately supplied up to ground war start.
Republican Guard and other ground forces in the KTO	Iraqi forces' overall combat effectiveness "reduced dramatically," "significantly degraded"; "not every Republican Guard division was hit equally hard."	Frontline troops and equipment apparently hit hard, but morale apparently very low before the air campaign.
	Those south of Basrah "received less damage."	Static tactics of Iraqi ground forces aided targeting.
	RG forces overall less damaged than frontline forces.	Some RG heavy armor divisions escaped with large inventory.

Appendix III
Aircraft and Munition Effectiveness in
Desert Storm

Air Supremacy

Using DOD's definition of air supremacy, we can state that the coalition rapidly achieved and maintained it—meaning that there was no effective opposition to coalition aircraft from the Iraqi air force within just a few days of the onset of the air campaign.[49] However, coalition aircraft were never safe from AAA or handheld IR SAMs while flying at either low or medium altitude at any time during the conflict, and actual damage to the Iraqi air force was less than implied by the claim of air supremacy.

The primary response of the Iraqi air force to coalition attacks and capabilities was either to flee to Iran or to try to remain hidden in hardened aircraft shelters or in civilian areas. As a result, after some initial resistance—including the likely shooting down of an F/A-18—the Iraqi air force retreated, offering little threat to either coalition aircraft or to coalition ground forces. At the same time, an estimated 290 (40 percent) of Iraq's 724 fixed-wing aircraft were destroyed in the air or on the ground by the coalition; another 121 escaped to Iran, leaving 313 (43 percent) intact and inside Iraq at the end of the war. GWAPS' conclusion that the "Iraqi Air Force was not completely destroyed by the war's end" may be an understatement, since more fixed-wing aircraft survived than were destroyed.[50] While the Iraqi air force never posed a serious threat to a qualitatively and quantitatively superior coalition force, more than enough of it survived to remain a regional threat.

Similarly, as evidenced by pilots' accounts and low-level losses that continued throughout the war, coalition aircraft were not able to defeat the AAA or portable IR SAM threats because of the very large number of these systems and the difficulty in finding such small, mobile, nonemitting systems. This meant that while coalition aircraft had a high-altitude sanctuary, medium- and especially low-altitude deliveries remained hazardous throughout the war.

Moreover, although radar-guided SAMs accounted for almost no damage or losses after the first week of the air war—because they were being launched <u>unguided</u>—the number of launches remained quite substantial <u>throughout</u> the campaign. About 151 SAMs were launched in the last 8 days of the air war, although only 2 resulted in loss or damage to coalition

---

[49]On January 27, 1991, Gen. Schwarzkopf declared that coalition air forces had achieved air supremacy. (DOD title V report to the Congress [Apr. 1992], pp. 124, 127, and 129. See glossary for definition.)

[50]GWAPS, vol. II, pt. II (Secret), p. 156. GWAPS also notes that there are some questions about the exact number of aircraft; this reflects data gaps and counting issues. Therefore, all numbers cited are estimates.

Appendix III
Aircraft and Munition Effectiveness in
Desert Storm

aircraft.[51] Eleven coalition aircraft were shot down in the last 3 days of the war, almost all at low altitudes (either in advance of the ground war or during it), from AAA or IR SAMs. Of a total 86 coalition aircraft lost or damaged during the war, 21 losses (25 percent) occurred in the last 7 days—long after air supremacy had been declared.

Leadership and Command, Control, and Communications

The effectiveness of the air war against the Iraqi "national command authority" is less clear than for air supremacy, not least because there is no readily quantifiable measure about what it would have meant to "disrupt" command, control, and communications. There are no agreed-upon yardsticks about how many communication nodes or lines need to have been destroyed, how much dispersion or degradation of authority fulfills the term "disrupt," or what it means to "isolate" Saddam from the Iraqi people or to force him to "cry uncle."

Moreover, while the kind of targets that were related to c^3 were fairly apparent, they were also diverse—including the "AT&T building," the presidential palace, numerous deeply buried command bunkers, military headquarters, telecommunication switching facilities, and so forth. Further, even if all these had been destroyed—and analysis of the DIA phase III messages shows that at least 57 percent of the c^3 category and 52 percent of the GVC were—the fact that c^3 could be and was maintained through radios meant that c^3 was very difficult to disrupt. In effect, the extent of communications disruption was "unknown."[52] It is clear, however, that the air campaign against the Iraqi leadership did not cause the regime to collapse and thereby preclude the need for a ground offensive.

Oil and Electricity

The attacks on electricity-related targets largely achieved their objective of sharply reducing generated electricity but apparently did not succeed in weakening popular support for the regime, as hoped by air war planners. Oil supplies were somewhat reduced by air attacks but not enough to affect the Iraqi forces. Table III.17 reports that 38 and 57 percent of the oil and electric facility targets, respectively, were assessed as fully successfully destroyed. These data are consistent with GWAPS and title V accounts of the damage to the oil and electricity infrastructure, which concluded that the campaign was more successful in achieving its goals in the electricity category than in the oil category.

---

[51]GWAPS, vol. II, pt. II (Secret), p. 140, fig. 10. Numbers are our estimates based on the bar charts shown in the figure.

[52]GWAPS, vol. II, pt. II (Secret), p. 348, notes that "the available evidence will not permit even a rough quantitative estimate as to how much Baghdad's national telecommunications and c^3 were disrupted by strategic air attack."

Appendix III
Aircraft and Munition Effectiveness in
Desert Storm

With regard to electricity, both accounts agree that attacks on electric power plants and transformer facilities in the first 2 days resulted in a fairly rapid reduction in generating capacity. By January 20, capacity had dropped from about 9,500 megawatts to about 2,500; after numerous restrikes against smaller plants, it was eventually reduced to about 1,000 megawatts, or about 15 percent of prewar capability. While the lights did go off in Baghdad as well as in much of the rest of central and southern Iraq, GWAPS found no evidence that this negatively affected the popularity of the Hussein regime.[53]

GWAPS notes that damage to electric generator halls was somewhat greater than had been planned. While the planners had wanted only the electrical transformers and switching systems hit, to avoid long-term damage, the pilots, perhaps unaware of these plans, hit the generators. Forcing the Iraqis to rely on secondary backup power sources was an undoubted hindrance to overall capabilities.

With regard to oil, the air campaign focused on reducing refining capability and destroying stored refined oil. Iraqi oil production was concentrated at three major refineries. According to GWAPS, the CIA estimated that more than 90 percent of the total Iraqi refining capability was rendered inoperative by air strikes. However, only about 20 percent of the refined product storage capacity was destroyed, perhaps because fewer than 400 sorties struck these facilities. Further, because Iraqi units had sufficient stocks to last for weeks, if not months, when the ground war started, the attacks on oil had no significant military impact on Iraqi ground forces.

Mobile Scud Launchers

The overall record against mobile Scuds strongly suggests that even under highly favorable circumstances—namely, in a condition of air supremacy with no jamming of airborne sensors and with Scud launches lighting up the night sky—the United States did not have the combination of real-time detection and prosecution required to hit portable launchers before they moved from their launch points. There is no confirming evidence that any mobile Scud launchers were destroyed, and data to support the deterrent effect of the Scud-hunting campaign are weak because the rate of firings does not appear to have been related to the number of anti-Scud sorties.

The launches of Scud missiles at Israel and Saudi Arabia forced a major unplanned diversion of air resources into trying to locate and target trucks and other vehicles being used as mobile launchers. Preventing these

---
[53]GWAPS, vol. II, pt. II (Secret), p. 308.

Appendix III
Aircraft and Munition Effectiveness in
Desert Storm

launches became an urgent mission, yet both GWAPS and DOD title V reported that there is not a single confirmed kill of a mobile launcher; a draft Rand analysis reached essentially the same conclusion.[54]

In 42 instances, F-15s on Scud-hunting missions were directed to an area from which a Scud had been launched but prosecuted only 8 to the point of delivering ordnance. However, both GWAPS and DOD credit the anti-Scud campaign with suppressing the number of launches after the initial 10 days of the war. There was a clear drop-off in Scud launches after day 10 of the war, but an increase again starting with day 36. The firing rate of Scuds averaged about 5 per day for the first 10 days—but with large daily variations—and declined to approximately 1 per day until the last week of the war, during which it averaged 3 per day.[55] The number of launches on a given day shows no consistent relationship to the number of planned counter-Scud sorties. This can be seen from the fact that while the number of anti-Scud sorties ranged from about 45 to 90 on days 2 through 12, the number of Scud launches varied from 0 to 14 per day during that period.

NBC Warfare Capabilities

The coalition's objective was to eliminate Iraq's capabilities to build, deploy, or launch nuclear, biological, or chemical weapons. The goal of eliminating Iraq's NBC capabilities was not even approximated by the air campaign; very substantial NBC capabilities were left untouched. An intelligence failure to identify NBC targets meant that the air campaign hit only a tiny fraction of the nuclear targets and left intact vast chemical and biological weapons stores.[56]

While 3 nuclear-related facilities were severely or moderately damaged by air power, these turned out to be only less than 15 percent of those identified by U.N. inspection teams after the war. The United Nations identified 16 "main facilities." Moreover, some facilities may have remained shielded from the United Nations. Therefore, effectiveness against this target category was probably even less than can be estimated from damage to known sites. The unclassified title V report stated (on p. 207) that the nuclear program "did not suffer as serious a setback as was desired."

---

[54]Rand, "Technology Lessons From Desert Storm Experience: A Preliminary Review and Assessment," draft report (Oct. 1991), p. 3 and chart 25.

[55]Institute for Defense Analyses, Desert Storm Campaign, P-2661 (Apr. 1992), p. I-16.

[56]It is fair to note that although the air campaign was not directly effective in destroying the vast majority of Iraq's NBC warfare capabilities by the end of the war, the campaign was instrumental in securing the coalition victory and motivating Saddam Hussein to accept U.N. resolutions and on-site inspection teams. Thus, the air campaign indirectly led to the achievement of this campaign objective following the cease-fire.

Appendix III
Aircraft and Munition Effectiveness in
Desert Storm

With regard to chemical warfare production facilities, DIA concluded that by February 20, 1991, a 75-percent degradation of production and filling facilities had been achieved. However, it was also the case that large stocks of chemical weapons were not destroyed: "it took numerous inspections and much effort after the war by U.N. inspectors to begin even to approach eliminating the bulk of Iraq's chemical weapons."[57] For example, in April 1991, Iraq admitted to the U.N. that it still had 10,000 nerve gas warheads, 1,500 chemical-weapon bombs and shells, and 1,000 tons of nerve and mustard gas. Later, it conceded that it still had 150,000 chemical munitions. Therefore, it is readily apparent that, as with the nuclear weapons targets, much was missed, either through lack of target information or through ineffective attacks.

For several years following the cease-fire, U.N. inspection teams were unable to find conclusive evidence that Iraq had produced offensive biological weapons. However, in mid-1995, in response to U.N. inspection commission evidence, the Iraqis admitted to producing large quantities of two deadly agents—the bacteria that cause botulism and anthrax—on the eve of the Gulf War. Several suspected production facilities were hit during the war, as were suspected research facilities at Taji and Salman Pak. In addition, a number of refrigerated bunkers believed to contain biological weapons were hit. DOD's classified title V report stated (on p. 224) that the biological warfare program "was damaged and its known key research and development facilities were destroyed. Further, most refrigerated storage bunkers were destroyed." Whether these constituted the entirety of Iraq's biological warfare program is not yet known.

Lines of Communication

Destroying railroads and bridges as well as supply convoys was seen as the key to meeting several related objectives—cutting supply lines to the KTO to degrade and demoralize Iraqi forces and blocking the retreat of those forces, leading to their destruction in the ground campaign. While large numbers of bridges, railroad lines, and other LOC targets were destroyed by air attacks, the sheer amount of in-place stocks, as well as the number of available transport vehicles, apparently served to keep most of the Iraqi ground forces adequately supplied, up to the start of the ground war. Thus, the goal of cutting lines of communication was only partially met.

Table III.17 indicated that approximately two-thirds of the LOC targets assessed were determined to be successfully destroyed. GWAPS and the

---

[57]GWAPS, vol. II, pt. II (Secret), p. 331.

**Appendix III
Aircraft and Munition Effectiveness in
Desert Storm**

title V report stated that so many bridges over the Euphrates and Tigris rivers were destroyed that supply flows were severely reduced to frontline troops. GWAPS stated (on p. 349) that "all important bridges [were] destroyed"; the title V report noted that three-fourths of the bridges from central Iraq to the KTO were destroyed or heavily damaged. It is estimated that attacks on LOC targets reduced the carrying capacity of traffic on the Baghdad-to-KTO highways from about 200,000 metric tons per day to about one-tenth that amount by the end of the war. In addition, damage to railroad bridges completely cut the only rail line from Iraq to Kuwait.

However, GWAPS noted (on p. 371) that the Iraqis' stocks of material in theater were so large that "by the time the ground war began, the Iraqi army had been weakened but not 'strangled' by air interdiction of its lines of communications." For example, at the start of the air campaign, Iraq had 40,000 to 55,000 military cargo trucks, 190,000 commercial vehicles, and 120,000 Kuwaiti vehicles. In addition, Iraq had 300,000 metric tons of ammunition in dozens of locations in the KTO; only an estimated 10 percent of this was destroyed before the ground war.[58] The GWAPS report stated that logistic movement difficulties within Kuwait may have resulted as much from Iraqi ineptitude as from air attacks; the effect of the latter is impossible to separate out. Moreover, despite the air attacks, GWAPS found that the Iraqi forces were adequately sustained overall throughout the air campaign, although some units reported food shortages.

Iraqi Ground Forces, Including the Republican Guard

Assessments differ about the extent to which the effectiveness of the Iraqi forces in the KTO was reduced before the ground war. Estimates of overall effectiveness must take into account not only the inventory of weapons but also morale and readiness. Moreover, not all equipment was equally valuable, and some, such as artillery, was potentially more lethal against an attacking force (including feared chemical munitions) but less important than tanks for degrading Iraqi offensive capabilities.

The Iraqi ground forces were diverse in a number of ways: the better-equipped, elite Republican Guards were kept relatively far back from the front while the lesser supplied frontline troops were heavily composed of ethnic groups out of favor and out of power within Iraq. Evidence from interviews with Iraqi prisoners of war suggests it was not just the air campaign that destroyed the effectiveness of their ground forces: they characterized themselves not as "battle hardened" after 8 years of war with Iran but, rather, as "war weary." U.S. Army intelligence summaries of the statements of prisoners stated the following:

---

[58]GWAPS, vol. II, pt. II (Unclassified), p. 194.

Appendix III
Aircraft and Munition Effectiveness in
Desert Storm

"War weariness, harsh conditions, and lack of conviction of the justice of the invasion of Kuwait caused widespread desertion in the Iraqi Army prior to the air campaign, but in some units the genuine foot race north [that is, desertion] really commenced when the bombs began to fall."[59]

In effect, the air campaign was a factor in that collapse of morale, but it was clearly not the only cause: the fact that the Iraqi forces were in a preexisting state of low morale cannot be ignored.

Another measure of the effect of air power against Iraqi ground forces is its destruction of Iraqi equipment. GWAPS stated that the operations plan set a requirement that Iraqi ground forces in the KTO were to be reduced to no more than 50-percent effectiveness by the start of the ground war. According to some sources, this meant a 50-percent reduction not in the number of weapons in each and every category but, rather, in overall capabilities. However, GWAPS stated (on p. 203) that phase III of the air campaign had been designed to "reduce Iraqi armor and artillery by that planned amount." The broad objectives were not only to reduce the capability of these units to inflict casualties but also—as the title V report states at least three times—to "destroy" the Republican Guard.

In effect, several competing objectives existed under the broader umbrella of meeting the goal of reducing the Iraqi ground forces by 50 percent. For while the commander in chief of the Central Command ordered that attrition against Iraqi frontline forces be maximized, this meant that fewer sorties were flown against the less-threatening "third echelon" Republican Guard divisions, and fewer against the Republican Guard heavy armor divisions, than against the infantry divisions closer to the front.[60] As a result, destruction of the three "heavy" Republican Guard divisions ("holding the bulk of all the armor") was considerably less than that against either the frontline forces or the Republican Guard infantry divisions.[61] All frontline forces had been reduced to less than 50-percent effectiveness just before the ground war, while most of the rear units were above 75-percent effectiveness. The consequence of the much greater weight of effort on the front lines was that very large numbers of Republican Guards and their armor were either not attacked or only

---

[59]Department of the Army, "The Gulf War: An Iraqi General Officer's Perspective," memorandum for the record, 513th Military Intelligence Brigade, Joint Debriefing Center (Mar. 11, 1991), p. 4.

[60]The title V report states that there were fewer sorties against the rearward Republican Guard units because they were better dug in and had better air defenses, requiring more air support and more sorties. The Republican Guard infantry divisions formed a "second echelon" reserve, well behind the front lines but in front of the heavy, armored divisions.

[61]GWAPS, vol. II, pt. II (Secret), p. 161.

Appendix III
Aircraft and Munition Effectiveness in Desert Storm

sporadically attacked during the air campaign. The end result was that many of these forces escaped back into central Iraq, leaving some of the most formidable Iraqi forces intact.

The CIA estimated that no more than about 30 percent of the tanks of the three key Republican Guard "heavy" divisions were destroyed by air power before the ground campaign. Total tank losses by the end of the ground war for those three heavy divisions were 50 percent, according to the CIA, compared to an estimated 76 percent for all Iraqi tanks in the KTO. Our analysis of the Missions database found that targets most closely associated with ground troops received by far the most strikes and the most bombs and bomb tonnage compared to other target categories. These targets received at least nine times more strikes, five times more bombs, and five times more bomb tonnage than the next highest strategic target category, MIB.

Whatever the exact cause of armor or personnel losses, the fact remains that large numbers of Republican Guard armor were able to avoid destruction or capture by U.S. ground war forces. They were then available to Saddam for maintaining his power and to threaten Kuwait in October 1994.

Summary

Many claims of Desert Storm effectiveness show a pattern of overstatement. In this appendix, we addressed the effectiveness of different types of aircraft and munitions used in Desert Storm and the overall effectiveness of the air campaign in achieving its objectives. The Desert Storm input and BDA data did not permit a comprehensive aircraft-by-aircraft or munition-by-munition comparison of effectiveness; however, we were able to combine input and outcome data to (1) reveal associations of greater and lesser success against targets between types of aircraft and munitions and (2) examine the effects of selected types of munitions and aircraft where they were used in similar ways. Thus, we were able to work within the data constraints to examine several aspects of aircraft, munition, and campaign effectiveness.

While the available Desert Storm input and outcome data did not allow direct effectiveness comparisons between all aircraft types, they did indicate that overall effectiveness varied somewhat by type of aircraft and more so by type of target category attacked. The data also revealed patterns of greater and lesser success against targets, both between types

Appendix III
Aircraft and Munition Effectiveness in
Desert Storm

of aircraft and munitions over the course of the campaign and with respect to individual target categories.

There was no consistent pattern indicating that the key to success in target outcomes was the use of either guided or unguided munitions. On average, targets where objectives were successfully achieved received more guided and fewer unguided munitions than targets where objectives were not determined to have been fully achieved. But in several target categories, the reverse was true. Nor were there major differences in the apparent effect of platform type on strike performance. When attacking the same targets with LGBs, the F-111Fs reported achieving only a slightly greater target hit rate than the F-117s. Similarly, there was little difference in the rates of success achieved by F/A-18s and F-16s when delivering the MK-84 unguided munition.

The results of our analyses did not support the claim for LGB effectiveness summarized by "one target, one bomb." Moreover, planners apparently ordered restrikes either because BDA revealed that one bomb did not achieve target objectives or they did not believe that "one target, one bomb" was being achieved.

Desert Storm data also do not clearly support a number of major DOD claims for the F-117. For example, according to some, the accuracy of the F-117 in combat may have been unprecedented; our estimates of the bomb hit rate for the F-117 show that it was between 55 and 80 percent. Of equal importance, the rate of weapon release for the F-117 during Desert Storm was only 75 percent—largely because of a weather abort rate far higher than for other strike aircraft. Thus, the effectiveness of scheduled F-117 strikes was between 41 and 60 percent. And the accuracy and effectiveness of the TLAM was less than generally perceived.

Our analysis of manufacturers' claims revealed the same pattern of overstatement. All the manufacturers whose weapon systems we reviewed made public statements about the performance of their products in Desert Storm that the data do not fully support. And while the manufacturers' claims were often inaccurate, their assertions were not significantly different from, nor appreciably less accurate than, many of the statements of DOD officials and DOD reports about the same systems' performance in Desert Storm.

Finally, we found that the available quantitative and qualitative data indicate that damage to several major sets of targets was less complete than DOD's title V report to the Congress made clear and, therefore, that the objectives related to these target sets were only partially met. The gap between what has been claimed for air power in Desert Storm and what actually occurred was sometimes substantial. In effect, even under the generally favorable tactical and environmental conditions prevalent during Desert Storm, the effectiveness of air power was more limited than initially expected (see app. V) or subsequently claimed.

In light of the favorable conditions under which the air campaign was pursued and the technological and numerical advantages enjoyed by the coalition, it would not have been surprising if the effectiveness of the individual aircraft and munitions had been quite high. However, the commander of the U.S. air forces clearly stated at the onset of the war that his top priority in the air campaign was survivability. Conducting the war from medium and high altitudes precluded some systems from being used in ways that would probably have maximized their effectiveness. At the same time, the basically flat terrain, the attainment of air supremacy, and the dearth of Iraqi countermeasures provided favorable delivery conditions. Aircraft, munitions, and campaign effectiveness, to the extent that they can be measured, should be extrapolated only with care to another enemy in another contingency.

Appendix IV
Cost and Performance of the Aircraft and Munitions in Desert Storm

This appendix compares the costs and performance of the aircraft and munitions used in the Desert Storm air campaign, as well as the results from them. Because the data collected in Desert Storm about the performance of weapon systems contain numerous inconsistencies in quality and quantity, they do not allow us to make a reliable cost-effectiveness comparison of all the systems under review.

For some aircraft, such as the F-117, there are relatively good data about the number of sorties conducted, while for others, such as the A-10, numerous questions remain about the most basic kind of performance data. For most systems, including the TLAM, there are relatively few instances in which the effects of a particular attack with a particular weapon on a given target can be separated out from other attacks on the same target. This is because BDA data often were not collected until after several attacks had occurred.

To approximate a measure of cost-effectiveness, we considered an aircraft's total program unit cost; sortie cost; and Desert Storm performance data such as survivability, sortie rate, and outcomes achieved by target category. Combining aircraft input and output performance data with cost estimates permits us to present as comprehensive a comparison as possible of the multiple weapon systems used in the air campaign.

Cost and Performance of Aircraft

Measures Used	The following measures assisted us in our comparative evaluation of the aircraft under review. Dollar costs are in constant fiscal year 1994 dollars.
Total Program Unit Cost	This measure includes research and development and procurement costs identified in DOD's periodic Selected Acquisition Reports to the Congress, to permit a comparison of aircraft per unit costs.
Desert Storm Cost Per Sortie	This is the cost to operate each type of aircraft under review on a typical sortie. These estimates of comparative costs were generated by the Air Force at our request, using Air Force and Navy data and an agreed-upon methodology.

Appendix IV
Cost and Performance of the Aircraft and
Munitions in Desert Storm

Average Desert Storm Sorties Per Day	This measure was derived by dividing total sorties for each aircraft under review by the 43 days of the air campaign and by the number of aircraft deployed. Since these averages were clearly dependent upon multiple factors—such as distance to target, which can vary greatly for identical Navy aircraft on different carriers or identical Air Force aircraft at different bases—there are various factors that can explain differences between aircraft on this measure.[1] However, it is a summary measure of overall aircraft <u>availability</u> and, as such, permits an understanding of the range of the comparative availability of each aircraft to perform its assigned mission at its own particular level of effectiveness, which can vary by type while not showing the explanation for differences. Availability is commonly regarded as advantageous, since it is assumed that it is better to be able to attack the enemy more rather than less in a given time period.
Desert Storm Casualty Rate	This measure permits a comparison of the survivability of aircraft, derived by dividing total sorties of each aircraft type by total lost and damaged aircraft of each type.
Number and Ratio of Guided and Unguided Munitions Delivered	This performance measure presents the type and number of munitions delivered, by aircraft type, on all target categories.
Total Tonnage and Average Tonnage Per Day Per Aircraft	This performance measure compares each aircraft's delivery of munitions, as measured by total Desert Storm tonnage and average tonnage per day per aircraft. The assumption is that, given a specific munition type, it is advantageous to deliver more rather than less tonnage per day against an enemy. This measure is, of course, complicated by variance in the type of munitions that different aircraft types deliver. Thus, it is also necessary to review the effect that the various aircraft types had on targets with their different munition combinations.
Environmental Flexibility	This measure compares aircraft on their capability to operate in two stressful environmental conditions: conducting combat flight operations at night and in adverse weather. First, we indicate whether an aircraft was used for both day and night strikes in Desert Storm (versus day or night only). Second, we indicate whether an aircraft had the capability to deliver munitions effectively under adverse weather conditions. We did not have sufficient data to know whether pilots chose to release bombs in poor weather regardless of accuracy degradation.

[1]Other factors can include, aircraft reliability and maintainability, mission planning requirements, aircrew fatigue and availability, and ability or inability to operate out of forward operating bases; all can vary by aircraft type.

Appendix IV
Cost and Performance of the Aircraft and
Munitions in Desert Storm

Predominant Target Taskings	The strategic target categories we measure accounted for three-quarters or more of an aircraft's Desert Storm strikes. By eliminating those categories for which only a comparatively small number of aircraft strikes were performed, we obtained an overall assessment of what target categories an aircraft was used most often against. This, we believe, is somewhat more useful and informative than simply tallying up the gross number of target categories an aircraft was used against, even if only a handful of strikes were flown in some categories. This latter methodology was used by the Air Force and DOD in descriptions of the F-117s' contribution to the air campaign.
Ratio of Targets Successfully and Not Fully Successfully Destroyed	Using the data discussed in appendix III, we compared the various aircraft on the overall ratio of targets they attacked that were, or were not, assessed as successfully destroyed. At best, these ratios reflect assessments of the level of success associated with the various aircraft, though not necessarily exclusively attributed to them.
Other Possible Measures	Numerous measures could be used in comparing Desert Storm air campaign systems, such as aircraft mission capable rates or aircraft range. We chose the measures that, in our view, offered the most useful ways in which to compare systems used in Desert Storm, again taking into account data availability and limitations. Thus, for example, rather than comparing mission capable rates, we compared sortie rates actually flown in the air campaign: we believe it more informative to measure that a combat sortie was actually flown than that an aircraft was determined "mission capable" yet may not have actually flown a combat mission. Similarly, aircraft range was not compared because the availability of tanker aircraft in Desert Storm tended to mask differences between aircraft on this dimension. (However, if fewer tankers are available in future conflicts, range differences among aircraft could have a significant effect on availability.) Finally, it is important to emphasize that no single measure should automatically be given greater weight than others in assessments of aircraft or munitions. The comparison we proffer here intentionally presents multiple dimensions on which to assess air campaign systems, not least because of the data reliability problems already discussed. Further, aircraft have different missions, and effectiveness on one type of mission may have been achieved through design requirements that greatly limit performance on other missions. Therefore, no one single cost or performance measure will consistently capture all that should be known or understood in comparing one aircraft type to another.

Appendix IV
Cost and Performance of the Aircraft and
Munitions in Desert Storm

Overall Results

Table IV.1 presents cost and performance data for the aircraft under review.

The following appear to be the major points that can be drawn with regard to the issue of Desert Storm aircraft cost and performance. Comparatively, none of the air-to-ground aircraft examined demonstrated overall consistently superior performance across the measurable performance indicators. Similarly, no aircraft performed consistently poorly on all or most of these dimensions.

Neither single-role bombers, nor multirole fighter-bombers demonstrated obvious superiority compared to others in the air-to-ground role. Defensive air-to-air missions were predominantly performed by single-role air-to-air aircraft, with single-role F-15Cs credited with over 85 percent of Desert Storm air-to-air kills. While multirole aircraft did perform some support and some air-to-air missions, their participation by no means eliminated the need for single-role air-to-air and support aircraft. The evidence from Desert Storm points to the usefulness of single-role aircraft in their respective missions and the usefulness of multirole aircraft most predominantly in the air-to-ground mission.

The data in table IV.1 reveal no clear link between the cost of either aircraft or weapon system and their performance in Desert Storm. Neither relatively high-cost nor low-cost air-to-ground aircraft demonstrated consistently superior performance across a range of measures such as sortie rate, survivability, amount of munitions delivered, and participation in successful target outcomes.

Appendix IV
Cost and Performance of the Aircraft and
Munitions in Desert Storm

Table IV.1: Cost and Performance of Major U.S. and U.K. Desert Storm Air-to-Ground Aircraft and TLAM

Platform	Cost — Total program unit cost[a]	Cost — Sortie[b]	Combat sortie — Average per day per aircraft	Combat sortie — Rate of lost and damaged aircraft per sortie	Munitions delivered — Number guided	Munitions delivered — Number unguided	Ratio
F-117	$111.2[e]	$15.7	0.7	0	2,000	4	500:1
F-111F	$68.3	$24.9	0.9	0.0011	2,935	586	5:1
F-15E	$39.1 without LANTIRN $46.5 with 2 LANTIRN pods	$11.5	1.0	0.0009	1,669	14,089	1:8
A-6E	$39.3	$27.8	1.1	0.0031	623	17,588	1:28
F-16	$18.9 without LANTIRN $22.6 with 1 LANTIRN pod	$5.9	1.2	0.0006	159	38,438	1:242
F/A-18	$35.9	$17.2	1.2	0.0022	368	11,179	1:30
GR-1	$32 - $57.3[f]	g	0.9	0.0076	497	1,346	1:3
A-10	$11.8	g	1.4[h]	0.0023	4,801	g	g
B-52	$163.8[j]	g	0.6	0.0029	36[k]	71,885	1:1,196
TLAM	$2.85	$2,855.0	g	[DELETED][l]	297	0	i

Platform	Munitions delivered — Total tonnage	Munitions delivered — Tonnage per aircraft per day	Strike conditions	Predominant target categories[c]	FS:NFS ratio[d]
F-117	1,990	1.10	Night only; no weather capability	C³, LOC, MIB, NBC, OCA	1.4:1
F-111F	2,004	0.71	Night only; limited by weather	KBX, LOC, OCA	3.2:1
F-15E	5,593	2.71	Mostly night; very few day missions; limited by weather	KBX, OCA, SCU	1.0:1
A-6E	5,715	1.16	Mostly night; some day; limited by weather	KBX, NAV	1.1:1
F-16	20,866	1.93	Mostly day; some night; limited by weather	KBX, OCA	1.5:1
F/A-18	5,513	0.74	Day and night; limited by weather	C³, KBX, OCA	0.8:1
GR-1	1,090	0.38	Day and night; limited by weather	KBX, OCA, OIL	1.2:1
A-10	g	g	Mostly day; some night; no weather capability	KBX	g
B-52	25,422	8.69	Mostly night; some day; no weather limitation	KBX, MIB	0.7:1
TLAM	144	3.30[m]	Day and night; limited by weather	C³, ELE, GVC, NBC, SCU	1.1:1

(Table notes on next page)

**Appendix IV
Cost and Performance of the Aircraft and
Munitions in Desert Storm**

^aIn millions of fiscal 1994 dollars.

^bIn thousands of fiscal 1994 dollars. Generic aircraft sortie costs, not specific Desert Storm sortie costs. Total program unit cost and sortie cost for the TLAM are the same because a combat sortie for the TLAM requires the physical destruction of the missile.

^cTarget categories in which approximately three-quarters of all strikes by aircraft type were directed.

^dBased on the analysis in appendix III and summarized in table III.1.

^eLockheed data expressed in "then-year" dollars. DOD data exist but are classified at the "special access required" level. Because the specific "then-year" dollars were not identified by year and amount, we were unable to convert them to fiscal 1994 dollars. Even though this figure understates the cost of the F-117, it is the best figure we could obtain.

^fEstimated costs obtained from public sources.

^gData were not available.

^hA-10 sorties may have been undercounted; thus, 1.4 may be too low.

ⁱData were not applicable.

^jIncludes $6.8 billion in acquisition costs for 102 aircraft and $9 billion in modifications since the B-52H was deployed in the early 1960s. A portion of the $9 billion spent on modifications were for upgrades of its strategic-nuclear capability or upgrades subsequently superseded by other modifications. The data we received from the Air Force did not specifically identify those modification costs relevant to the B-52s as used in Desert Storm. Also, the total program unit costs attributed to other aircraft could be understated somewhat in comparison to the B-52. Cost data for all aircraft other than the B-52 were obtained from Selected Acquisition Reports. However, these reports, which include modification costs, are no longer issued after airframe production ceases. Thus, modification costs for out-of-production aircraft are not captured on these reports and are not reflected in table IV.1. Therefore, the costs cited here tend to overstate the B-52's cost relative to the other aircraft.

^kThe B-52 launched 35 CALCMs (conventional variants of the air-launched cruise missile).

^lTLAM losses are based on a study by CNA/DIA that found that of the 230 TLAM C and D-I models launched, an estimated [DELETED] did not arrive at their target areas.

^mTonnage per day for TLAMs is its total tonnage (144 tons) divided by the number of days in the entire air campaign (43).

Virtually every type of aircraft and the TLAM demonstrated both significant strengths and limitations. For example, no F-117s were lost or damaged; it was the platform of choice among planners for nighttime strikes against stationary, point targets, yet it was employable in only highly limited conditions. The much older, nonstealthy F-111F achieved a somewhat higher target hit rate than the F-117 against targets attacked by both with the same type of munition (although the F-111F expended more munitions per target). The low-cost A-10s and F-16s made large contributions in terms of missions flown and bomb tonnage delivered and performed as well on other measures, such as survivability rates. However, neither was

**Appendix IV
Cost and Performance of the Aircraft and
Munitions in Desert Storm**

equipped to deliver LGBs, and the F-16's potential effectiveness with unguided munitions was diminished by operating from medium and high altitudes. B-52s delivered much more tonnage individually and as a force than any other aircraft, but accuracy from high altitude was low.[2]

Similarly, the F-16s delivered about 21,000 tons of bombs, but this worked out to only 1.93 tons daily per aircraft, compared to 2.71 tons for the F-15Es; F-15Es, however, accounted for only about one-quarter as much total tonnage as the F-16s. Thus, on one performance measure, the F-15Es look better than the F-16s, but much less impressive on another. In addition, the F-15Es had sortie costs about double those of the F-16s but also delivered a much greater ratio of guided-to-unguided munitions (1 to 8 versus 1 to 242). This was a result, in part, of the command decision to assign the available LANTIRN targeting pods, and thus the ability to deliver LGBs, to F-15Es rather than to F-16s; it was also a result, in part, of the decision to assign all but a few Maverick missiles to A-10s rather than to the F-16 units that were trained to employ them.

A comparably mixed picture can be seen for all the other aircraft under review. Overall, therefore, the data in table IV.1 present an inconclusive picture when it comes to rank-ordering the costs and performance of the aircraft as they were used in Desert Storm.

Comparative Strengths and Limitations of Aircraft Types

To facilitate comparative assessment of the aircraft, we examined the extent to which the data above, in combination with data discussed in appendixes II and III, can address four questions that involve aircraft acquisition issues of concern to the Congress:

1. Did the F-117 stealth bomber differ in air-to-ground combat performance and effectiveness from nonstealth aircraft, and what was the contribution of stealth technology to the outcome of the air campaign?

2. What were the contributions of single-purpose aircraft versus the multirole or dual-role aircraft recommended by DOD's "Bottom-Up Review"?

3. Was there a relationship between aircraft cost and performance?

4. How did the TLAM cruise missile perform compared to various aircraft?

---

[2]See Operation Desert Storm: Limits on the Role and Performance of B-52 Bombers in Conventional Conflicts (GAO/NSIAD-93-138, May 12, 1993).

Appendix IV
Cost and Performance of the Aircraft and
Munitions in Desert Storm

Stealth Versus Nonstealth Aircraft

Stealth was one of many options used to achieve portions of what was accomplished in the air campaign. It could not serve to achieve all objectives given its operating limitations. For example, it was not designed to, and in Desert Storm it did not, engage targets (1) that were mobile and required searching, (2) that were large "area targets" requiring coverage by dozens of bombs, or (3) that planners wanted to attack during the day. Most notably, the F-117's bomb hit rate was between 55 and 80 percent, and equally important, its weapon release rate was only 75 percent.

In addition, in some respects, other aircraft may have equaled the F-117 on the very dimensions for which special claims had been made for it. The limited data available showed that the F-111F missions were about as successful in hitting common targets. Pilots of aircraft other than the F-117 reported that they, too, achieved surprise on many, and in some cases most, attacks, according to an Air Force criterion for the success of stealth—namely that defensive fire from SAMs and AAA did not commence until after the first bombs detonated. While the F-117 attacked targets in every strategic category—more than any other aircraft—in some categories, very few strikes were conducted, and every type of aircraft under review attacked targets in no less than three-fourths of the categories. And unlike several other aircraft, the F-117 never faced the daytime air defenses that turned out to be the war's most lethal.

As the second most expensive aircraft in our study—costing almost twice as much as the next most costly aircraft—the F-117 did not perform as well as several other aircraft on the sorties- and tons-per-day measures. For example, the F-15Es averaged 1 mission per day (about 50 percent higher than the 0.7 average for F-117s) and averaged 2.71 tons of released munitions per day (246 percent more than the F-117 average). The F-16s averaged 1.2 sorties daily (70 percent more) and delivered 75 percent more tonnage daily than the F-117s.

To maintain stealth, F-117s can carry bombs only internally; this limits them to two LGBs. As a result, each F-117 was clearly very limited in the number of aimpoints it could hit before having to return home. Also, the F-117s were based more than 1,000 miles from Baghdad, which meant a round-trip mission as long as 6 hours with multiple refuelings. One Air Force explanation for this basing decision was the need to keep the F-117s out of range of Scud missiles. Another explanation was that the air base at Khamis Mushayt was one of only a select few in-theater bases with sufficient hangars to house the F-117 fleet and protect its sensitive radar absorptive coating from the elements. Another possible reason for the

**Appendix IV
Cost and Performance of the Aircraft and
Munitions in Desert Storm**

F-117s being based so far away was the fact that a complex and time-consuming mission planning process was necessary to exploit its stealth characteristics. The time this mission planning system took and the fact that the F-117 was able to conduct combat operations only at night could have meant that the time required to fly between Khamis Mushayt and the Saudi border was not the key limiting factor on the F-117's Desert Storm sortie rate. Moreover, unlike other aircraft, such as the A-10 and the F-16, the F-117 did not fly from a more distant main operating base to a forward one from which multiple sorties were generated.

Other Desert Storm aircraft were also limited by their distance from targets. For logistics reasons, most B-52s flew from far more distant bases than the F-117s, resulting in a slightly lower 0.6 average on daily sorties. In contrast, the B-52s had nearly eight times the daily average munition delivery (8.69 tons versus 1.10 tons) because of their greater carrying capability. Navy planes on carriers in the Red Sea were similarly limited in terms of sortie rates because of the distance from targets and carrier rotations.[3] The A-6Es averaged 1.1 daily sorties and 1.16 tons per day in munitions. The F/A-18s averaged nearly the same number of daily sorties (1.2), but delivered only an average of 0.74 tons of munitions per day, approximately two-thirds that of the F-117s. F-111Fs were based 525 nautical miles from the Iraqi border, some F-16s were 528 nautical miles from the border, and some F-15Es were about 250 nautical miles away. Thus, distance to targets was clearly a factor in various aircrafts' sortie rates, but it was not the only factor; additional reasons included complex mission planning requirements, logistics needs, inability to operate out of forward operating bases, and requirements to operate only from aircraft carriers that could not be deployed close by.

Nevertheless, distance to target alone cannot explain performance, since the F-111Fs averaged 0.9 sorties per day (28 percent higher than the F-117s) but released only 0.7 tons of munitions per day per aircraft—36 percent below the F-117's average. Similarly, the British, Saudi, and Italian air-to-ground variants of the Tornado flew slightly more sorties per day (0.9), yet they delivered less than half the daily tonnage (0.4).

At the same time, the F-117s were not able to perform tasks routinely carried out by other aircraft because of the operating trade-offs that were necessary to enable them to be stealthy and to deliver LGBs. Such routine

---

[3]Sortie rates and munition payloads cited here are for all Navy aircraft, from both Red Sea and Persian Gulf carriers and for Marine Corps F/A-18s and A-6Es based on land.

Appendix IV
Cost and Performance of the Aircraft and Munitions in Desert Storm

tasks include strikes in poor weather or under any conditions in daylight or dusk, attacks against mobile targets that required searching, and missions that required deviation after takeoff from planned flight paths.

However, to the extent that air defense systems depend on radar, it is surely an advantage to be less detectable by radar than other aircraft, and the available evidence suggests that in Desert Storm, the F-117 was not easily detectable by radar. However, nonstealthy aircraft were also able to escape engagement by radar-based defense systems by other means such as by being masked by jamming support aircraft or by virtue of the physical destruction of radars by SEAD aircraft such as the F-4G. Moreover, given the widespread jamming that occurred in Desert Storm, the availability of fighter protection, as well as the relatively rapid degradation of the Iraqi IADS, it is clear that the F-117s sometimes also benefited from these support factors and did not always operate independent of them.

Single-Role Versus Multirole Aircraft

In its October 1993 "Bottom-Up Review," DOD expressed a strong preference for multirole as opposed to "special-purpose" aircraft because "multi-role aircraft, capable of air superiority, strike, and possible support missions have a high payoff."[4] The use of both types of aircraft in Desert Storm permits a comparison on some dimensions of their performance and contribution.

The Navy F/A-18 was the only multirole aircraft that was actually employed in both air-to-ground strikes and air-to-air engagements. A large number of F/A-18 missions, especially in the early stages of the air war, were escort, and one F/A-18 was credited with two air-to-air kills. Although the F-16 and the F-15E were equipped with guns and missiles for self-defenses, neither of these Air Force multirole aircraft performed any escort or air-to-air missions. Air-to-air engagements for Air Force aircraft were the domain of the single-role, air-to-air, F-15C, which was neither equipped nor tasked to air-to-ground missions.[5] While the exercise of air-to-air capability by Air Force multirole aircraft was apparently strongly discouraged, air supremacy meant that there was limited need for air-to-air

---

[4] DOD, Report on the Bottom-Up Review, Les Aspin, Secretary of Defense, (Oct. 1993), p. 36. Secretary of Defense William J. Perry endorsed the Bottom-Up Review and has not altered the review's advocacy of multirole aircraft over special purpose aircraft.

[5] U.S. F-15Cs were credited with 31 coalition air-to-air kills, 87 percent of the Desert Storm total. F-14s were also assigned to the air-to-air mission; however, none had any air-to-air kills of fixed-wing aircraft (though one enemy helicopter was shot down by an F-14).

**Appendix IV
Cost and Performance of the Aircraft and
Munitions in Desert Storm**

capability, and what did exist was adequately covered by F-15Cs and F-14s.[6]

With regard to support roles, F/A-18s and F-16s employed HARM missiles and other munitions to suppress enemy air defenses. However, this supplemented rather than eliminated the role played by specialized F-4Gs, EF-111s, and EA-6Bs—all of which were used extensively in SEAD or jamming.

The data available permit a limited comparison of multirole aircraft and more specialized, single-role bombers (F-117, F-111F, A-10, A-6E, GR-1, and B-52) in the air-to-ground mission. In terms of unit cost, the single-role aircraft are both the most and the least expensive (the B-52 and the F-117 versus the A-10).[7] In terms of the average daily sorties, only the single-role A-10 exceeded the multirole F-16's and F/A-18's rate of 1.2 per day. Excluding the B-52, multirole aircraft had the highest as well as the lowest average daily munition tonnage; the F-15E was the highest, at 2.71 tons, and the F/A-18 was the lowest, at 0.74 tons.

On other performance measures, the two aircraft types appear to be generally indistinguishable. All were very survivable, most had comparable overall night and weather capability, as well as similar night and weather limitations, and most delivered a mix of guided and unguided munitions.

In terms of the ratios reflecting rate of participation against successfully and not fully successfully destroyed targets, the single-role F-111F had the highest ratio and the single-role B-52 had the lowest ratio. However, the multirole F/A-18 had a ratio that was nearly identical to that of the B-52, and the multirole aircraft with the highest ratio—the F-16 at 1.5:1—had a ratio that was 47 percent of the F-111F's 3.2:1.

In sum, in air-to-air combat, multirole aircraft had only minimal opportunity, accounting for only 2 of 38 air-to-air kills. Some multirole aircraft were used in air-to-air support SEAD missions, but their use did not halt the need for aircraft specialized for those type of missions. Both single and multirole aircraft appeared at both ends of the cost scale. As a generic type, multirole aircraft did not demonstrate any major payoff in the air-to-air role since the more specialized F-15Cs accounted for almost all

---

[6]Pilots told us that Gen. Horner said the first F-16 pilot to unload his bombs in order to attack an Iraqi aircraft would be "sent home."

[7]In terms of sortie cost, the single-role A-6E and the F-111F were high and the multirole F-16, F/A-18, and F-15E were lowest and lower; however, it is not clear whether it was the A-6's and F-111F's much older age than the multirole aircraft that explains their higher cost or their single role.

**Appendix IV
Cost and Performance of the Aircraft and
Munitions in Desert Storm**

air-to-air kills. In the air-to-ground role, multirole performed at the same overall level as specialized aircraft. Generally, the multirole aircraft did not perform as multirole aircraft in Desert Storm.

However, using Desert Storm data, it is not possible to reach firm conclusions about the multirole aircraft's potential payoff, relative to single-role aircraft. With greatly varying total program unit costs, as well as a wide range of daily average bomb tonnage dropped and especially the apparent lack of need for multirole aircraft on missions other than air-to-ground attack, the case for or against multirole and single-role aircraft is not readily apparent solely from Desert Storm experiences.

Relationship Between Aircraft Cost and Performance

It is often asserted that, on average, the more that something costs—such as a passenger car—the better it is, compared to similar things that cost less. A more expensive automobile is assumed to possess certain performance qualities that make it superior to a low-cost car: it might accelerate more quickly, handle more precisely, or ride more comfortably. Moreover, these advantages are assumed not to have limitations that would prevent the car from being used as frequently as one chose or under a wide variety of conditions. Similarly, a common impression of military hardware is that an airplane that costs much more than others would have greater capabilities that distinguish it from other aircraft, making it overall a "better" aircraft. While this perception may appear to be simplistic, it has been sufficiently widespread, even among military experts, to warrant examination in light of the Desert Storm data. Moreover, DOD commonly justifies very costly aircraft and other weapons to the Congress, and to the public, on the grounds that they are more capable than other aircraft and they offer unique capabilities that warrant the greater cost.

In this section, we consider aircraft total program unit costs and whether there was any discernible correlation between those costs and the Desert Storm performance measures cited above. As noted above, at $111 million and $164 million, respectively, the F-117 and B-52H cost far more than the next most expensive aircraft under review (the $68 million F-111F). The A-10, at $12 million, was the least expensive U.S. air-to-ground aircraft in Desert Storm; the F-16—with one LANTIRN pod—was the next least expensive at $23 million.

<u>Survivability and Operating Conditions.</u> In terms of aircraft survivability, high- and low-cost aircraft were almost identical at night and at medium-to-high altitudes (as shown in app. III, statistically speaking, there was no meaningful difference in the survivability rates of any of the Desert

Appendix IV
Cost and Performance of the Aircraft and
Munitions in Desert Storm

Storm air-to-ground aircraft). Most high- and low-cost aircraft were able to operate both day and night, although high-cost F-117s, F-111Fs, and F-15Es were used almost exclusively in the more survivable nighttime environment. In effect, in general, high cost did not correlate with improved survivability, although it may correlate with it in the case of the F-117, which, as intended, operated only at night and at medium altitudes—an environment where substantially fewer aircraft casualties occurred in Desert Storm.

In terms of other environmental conditions, there was no pattern of high-cost aircraft offering consistently better performance in adverse weather. Indeed, the more costly aircraft with LGB capability were more likely to be vulnerable to weather degradation than were aircraft that used unguided ordnance. For, while both types of aircraft delivered guided and unguided ordnance, most of the more costly aircraft delivered more guided, relative to unguided, bombs.[8] One reason for this was that low-cost aircraft were not equipped to deliver LGBs, which can partially account for aircraft cost differentials.[9] Whether the capability to deliver LGBs versus unguided munitions made the platform more or less effective would depend on an assessment of the relative merit of those munition types, discussed later in this appendix.

Number Deployed. All other things being equal, one would expect that the more costly an aircraft, the fewer would be available to be deployed in combat, since fewer would likely have been produced.[10] This proved to be the case in Desert Storm, with 251 F-16s and 148 A-10s deployed compared to 42 F-117s, 48 F-15Es, and 66 F-111Fs. Although obvious, it may be worth recalling that, in terms of total program unit costs, a single F-117 costs

---

[8]Two prominent exceptions to this are the high-cost B-52, which delivered very few guided munitions, and the low-cost A-10, which delivered about 4,800 guided Maverick missiles.

[9]For example, providing the low-cost A-10 with LGB-capability would, at a minimum, raise the A-10 unit price by about $7.4 million by adding two LANTIRN pods, to $19.2 million, an increase of 63 percent. This increase would, however, result in the A-10's continuing to be the lowest cost aircraft under review. It should also be noted that since the war, the relatively low-cost F-16 has been equipped with both types of LANTIRN pods, thus enabling it to deploy LGBs.

[10]The statistical correlation between aircraft unit cost and numbers deployed was $r = -0.54$. Unit cost data for the Tornado was calculated as the average of the highest and lowest fiscal 1994 unit cost figures that were available. The number of Tornado GR-1s deployed to Desert Storm was taken from the British AOB for February 1991 cited in the British Ministry of Defense Gulf War Lessons Learned report. The number of all other aircraft deployed to Desert Storm was taken from DOD's title V report.

Because the number of aircraft deployed to battle is likely to be related to the number available for deployment, we also examined, where the data permitted, the correlation between the number of aircraft produced and unit cost. The correlation was $r = -0.54$, indicating that more costly aircraft are produced in smaller numbers, thus leaving fewer available for deployment, relative to less costly aircraft. GR-1 data are not included because production numbers for these aircraft were unavailable.

Appendix IV
Cost and Performance of the Aircraft and
Munitions in Desert Storm

about as much as about 9 A-10s; a single F-111F equals 3 F-16s with LANTIRN pods.

Thus, in assessing an overall force, the appropriate comparisons should not be between one high-cost aircraft and one low-cost aircraft because to acquire equal forces of the two would obviously require vastly different amounts of money. A more appropriate way to measure aircraft forces might be the number of aircraft that an equal amount of acquisition funding can purchase. For example, the fleet of 42 F-117s deployed to Desert Storm cost $4.7 billion to develop and build, while the three times larger fleet of 148 A-10s cost $1.7 billion; that is, 106 additional aircraft for $3 billion less. Similarly, for the same amount of money, very different sized fleets, and capability, can be procured. For example, $1 billion in funding would procure 9 F-117s or 85 A-10s. The Desert Storm performance data reveal that the 9 F-117s would have carried out fewer than 7 sorties per day; in contrast, the 85 A-10s would have flown 119. While the design missions of the two aircraft differ substantially, their use in Desert Storm demonstrated that they are not necessarily mutually exclusive. Nearly 51 percent of the strategic targets attacked by the stealthy F-117s were also attacked by less costly, conventional aircraft—such as the F-16, F-15E, and F/A-18.[11]

Based on its performance in Desert Storm, advocates of the F-117 can argue that it alone combined the advantages of stealth and LGBs, penetrated the most concentrated enemy defenses at will, permitted confidence in achieving desired bombing results, and had perfect survivability. Advocates of the A-10 can argue that it, unlike the F-117, operated both day or night; attacked both fixed and mobile targets employing both guided and unguided bombs; and like the F-117, it suffered no casualties when operating at night and at medium altitude. In short, the argument can be made that to buy more capability, in the quantitative sense, the most efficient decision could be to buy less costly aircraft. Moreover, to buy more capability in the qualitative sense, it may be a question of what specific capability, or mix of capabilities, one wants to buy: in the F-117 versus A-10 comparison, each aircraft has both strengths and limitations; each aircraft can do things the other cannot. Therefore, despite a sharp contrast in program unit costs, based on their use, performance, and effectiveness demonstrated in Desert Storm, we find it inappropriate to call one more generally "capable" than the other.

---

[11]The incompleteness of A-10 strike data prevents our identifying the extent, if any, to which, A-10 and F-117 target taskings overlapped. However, each type of aircraft performed 40 or more strikes in the following strategic target categories: C^3, KBX, OCA, SAM, and SCU.

Appendix IV
Cost and Performance of the Aircraft and
Munitions in Desert Storm

The data did not demonstrate a consistent relationship between the program unit cost of aircraft and their relative effectiveness against strategic targets, as measured by the ratio of fully successful to not fully successful target outcomes for the set of strategic targets attacked by each type of aircraft. For example, while the high-cost F-111F had the highest ratio of all aircraft reviewed, the relatively low-cost F-16 had a higher ratio than either the F-117 or the F-15E, both of which were on the high end of the cost scale. The F/A-18, in the middle of the cost scale, had a low ratio of participation against successfully destroyed targets relative to unsuccessfully destroyed targets, but the medium-cost A-6E had a ratio that was higher than or equivalent to the F-15E and F-117, both much higher cost aircraft. However, the F-117 and the F-111F, two high-cost, LGB-capable aircraft, ranked first and third in participation against successful targets.[12]

Summary. We found no clear link between the cost of either aircraft or weapon system and their performance in Desert Storm. Aircraft total program unit cost does not appear to have been strongly positively or negatively correlated with survivability rates, sortie rates or costs, average daily tonnage per aircraft, or success ratio of unguided-to-guided munition deliveries. No high-cost aircraft demonstrated superior performance in all, or even most, measures, and no low-cost aircraft was generally inferior. On some measures low-cost aircraft performed better than the high-cost ones (such as sortie rate, sortie cost); on some measures, the performance of low- and high-cost aircraft was indistinguishable (such as survivability and participation against targets with successful outcomes).

TLAM Cruise Missile Compared to Aircraft

The Navy's TLAM cruise missile is substantially different from the aircraft reviewed. Its unit cost of approximately $2.9 million is clearly well below that of any aircraft, but because it is not reusable, it had the highest cost per sortie. Moreover, there were major categories of strategic targets (mobile, very hard, or buried targets) that it was inherently incapable of attacking or destroying. Also, like many guided munitions, the TLAM's optical guidance and navigation system (employed in the last portion of flight) can be impeded by [DELETED].[13] This means that the costs of

---

[12]Participation by each type of air-to-ground aircraft against targets assessed as fully successful targets was as follows: F-117 = 122, F-16 = 67, F-111F = 41, A-6E = 37, F/A-18 = 36, F-15E = 28, B-52 = 25, and GR-1 = 21. No data were available for the A-10. The TLAM participated against 18 targets assessed as fully successful. Participation against FS targets by type of aircraft is a function of two factors—the breadth of targets tasked to each type of aircraft (see app. III) and their FS:NFS ratio as presented previously.

[13]Even if the P(k) for a single TLAM against a given target is [DELETED], no less than [DELETED] missiles would be required to guard against reliability failure if the target is deemed to have urgent or high value.

Appendix IV
Cost and Performance of the Aircraft and
Munitions in Desert Storm

hitting any given target are substantial, given that TLAMs are single-use weapons.

These TLAM characteristics must be balanced against the fact that its employment does not risk an aircraft or its pilot. There is, of course, essentially immeasurable benefit to avoiding the loss or capture of pilots. However, TLAMs are limited in their applicability compared to some aircraft because many target types (for example, very hard targets) are not vulnerable to TLAMs or are not feasible as TLAM targets (for example, mobile ones). Further, given the TLAM's high-unit cost and demonstrated P(k), consideration must be given to whether a given target is sufficiently valuable to be worth using a TLAM. High costs mean that relatively few targets in an air campaign would be worth targeting with TLAMs, especially if aircraft survivability is high.

Cost and Effectiveness of Munitions

A review of the cost and use of the air-to-ground munitions in Desert Storm supplements the foregoing assessment of aircraft to examine what aircraft-munition combinations may have been the most effective in the air campaign. The GWAPS study presented data on air combat-related ordnance expended in Desert Storm by U.S. forces. Neither a separate breakout nor ordnance dropped by other coalition air forces was available.[14] Five major types of ordnance were released by U.S. air-to-ground aircraft in Desert Shield and Desert Storm. Table IV.2 shows these and their cost.

---

[14]The ordnance included cruise missiles, of which 35 were CALCMs launched from B-52s, and 297 TLAMs from Navy ships and submarines. We include both types of missiles because they were integral to the air campaign in terms of their targets and their role in the planning of the air campaign.

Appendix IV
Cost and Performance of the Aircraft and
Munitions in Desert Storm

Table IV.2: Desert Shield and Desert Storm Air-Related Ordnance Expenditures by U.S. Forces

	Number	Cost[a]
Bombs and noncruise missiles		
Unguided bombs	210,004	$432.0
Guided bombs	9,342	298.2
Antiradiation missiles	2,039	510.9
Air-to-surface guided missiles	5,448	549.1
Total	**226,833**	**$1,790.2**
Cruise missiles		
TLAMs	297	$861.3
CALCMs	35	52.5
Total	**332**	**$913.8**
Total bombs and missiles	**227,165**	**$2,704.0**

[a]In millions of fiscal 1990 dollars.

Source: GWAPS, vol. v, pt. I (Secret), pp. 581-82, and DOD Selected Acquisition Report on TLAM.

It is evident from table IV.2 that while the vast majority of the expended ordnance was unguided—92.4 percent—the inverse was true for cost. About 84 percent of cost was accounted for by the 7.6 percent of ordnance that was guided. If the 332 cruise missiles are excluded—with their extremely high unit costs—unguided ordnance still represented about 92.6 percent of the total number expended, but the percentage of cost for ordnance that was guided decreases to 75.9 percent.

The points summarized in table IV.3 concerning the relative strengths and weaknesses of guided and unguided munitions are supported in the discussion below.

Appendix IV
Cost and Performance of the Aircraft and
Munitions in Desert Storm

Table IV.3: Relative Strengths and Limitations of Guided and Unguided Munitions in Desert Storm

Measure	Relative strengths	Relative limitations
Guided		
Cost	No demonstrated strengths. LGBs, Mavericks, and other guided munitions were much more expensive than unguided munitions.	High unit cost; cost ratio of LGBs to unguided unitary bombs ranged up to 48:1; for Mavericks, 164:1.
Survivability	Varying amounts of standoff capability avoided defenses collocated with the target. LGB and other guided munition use permitted medium- and high-altitude releases while retaining accuracy, thus reducing aircraft vulnerability to AAA and IR SAMs.	Standoff capability did not negate defenses not at the target. [DELETED]
Operating characteristics	Night-capable, clear weather (except for most EO guidance systems); some correctable accuracy degradation from high winds.	Adverse weather, clouds, smoke, dust, haze, and humidity either eliminated or seriously restricted employment. Sometimes required precise intelligence and more demanding mission planning.
Effectiveness	Sometimes highly accurate even from high altitudes, even against point targets; lower likelihood of collateral damage.	"One target, one bomb" is an inappropriate and illusive characterization of LGB effectiveness; no consistent relationship between use of guided munitions and targets that were successfully destroyed.
Unguided		
Cost	Low unit cost; made up 92 percent of the munitions used but only 16 percent of munitions cost.	No cost disadvantages identified.
Survivability	Permitted higher pilot situation awareness and more ready ability to maneuver to evade threats.	Little or no standoff capability from defenses at target except for use at high altitude, which severely degraded accuracy.
Operating characteristics	Exploited radar bombing systems impervious to weather but only for missions requiring limited accuracy.	Nonradar unguided bombing systems had virtually as many limitations from weather, smoke, dust, and so on as guided munition sensors; accuracy seriously degraded by winds, especially when used at medium-to-high altitude.
Effectiveness	Of all munitions used, 92 percent were unguided; unguided munition use was an essential part of the air campaign, especially against area targets and ground forces.	Not accurate from medium-to-high altitude against point targets. Higher likelihood of collateral damage; no consistent relationship between use of unguided munitions and targets that were successfully destroyed.

Weighted Average Munition Costs

We analyzed and compared the munitions used in Desert Storm, calculating the weighted average unit cost for each munition, which is based on the different numbers of each type used and their unit cost. Table IV.4 compares these costs for unguided unitary bombs, unguided cluster bombs, LGBs, the IR/EO guided GBU-15, and the Maverick and Walleye air-to-surface munition.

The data in table IV.4 show that there are very large differences in the unit costs between the categories of guided and unguided munitions, as well as

**Appendix IV
Cost and Performance of the Aircraft and
Munitions in Desert Storm**

substantial cost variations within each category. The unguided unitary bombs used in the air campaign cost, on average, $649 each, while LGBs cost, on average, more than $31,000 each—a cost ratio of about 1:48. The cost ratio of the average unguided unitary bomb to the other major type of guided munition, the Maverick, was 1:164. Even the cost for more expensive unguided cluster munitions was just one-fifth the average LGB and one-eighteenth the cost of a Maverick.[15]

In terms of munition expenditures, 17 times more unitary unguided bombs were dropped than LGBs and 30 times more unguided unitary bombs than Mavericks. Six times more cluster munitions were used than LGBs, 11 times more clusters than Mavericks.

---

[15]Some unguided munitions were more expensive than some guided: CBU-89s cost four times more than GBU-12s, [DELETED].

Appendix IV
Cost and Performance of the Aircraft and
Munitions in Desert Storm

Table IV.4: Unit Cost and Expenditure of Selected Guided and Unguided Munitions in Desert Storm[a]

Munition	Unit cost	Number expended	Total cost	Average unit cost[b]
Unguided unitary				
MK-82LD	$498	69,701	$34,711,098	
MK-82HD	1,100	7,952	8,747,200	
MK-83	1,000	19,018	19,018,000	
MK-84GP	1,871	9,578	17,920,438	
MK-84HD	2,874	2,611	7,504,014	
M-117	253	43,435	10,989,055	
Subtotal		152,295	$98,889,805	$649
Unguided cluster				
CBU-52/58/71	2,159	7,831	$38,497,129	
CBU-87	13,941	10,035	139,897,935	
CBU-89	39,963	1,105	44,159,115	
CBU-72	3,800	254	965,200	
CBU-78	39,963	209	8,352,267	
MK-20	3,449	27,987	96,527,163	
Subtotal		57,421	$328,398,809	$5,719
Laser guided				
GBU-10	$22,000	2,637	$58,014,000	
GBU-12	9,000	4,493	40,437,000	
GBU-16	150,000	219	32,850,000	
GBU-24	65,000	284	18,460,000	
GBU-24/109	5,000	897	76,245,000	
GBU-27	75,539	739	55,823,321	
GBU-28	100,000	2	200,000	
Subtotal		9,271	$282,029,321	$30,421
IR GBU-15	$227,600	71	$16,159,600	$227,600
IR and EO Maverick				
AGM-65B	$64,100	1,673	$107,239,300	
AGM-65C	110,000	5	550,000	
AGM-65D	111,000	3,405	377,955,000	
AGM-65E	101,000	36	3,636,000	
AGM-65G	269,000	177	47,613,000	
Subtotal		5,255	$536,993,300	$102,187
Walleye II				
AGM-62B	$70,000	133	$9,310,000	$70,000
Total		224,446	$1,271,680,835	

[a]In fiscal 1990 dollars.

[b]The weighted average unit cost for each general munition type takes into account the different numbers of each munition type actually used.

Source: GWAPS, vol. V, pt. I (Secret), pp. 581-82.

Similar to our findings regarding the relationship between aircraft cost and numbers deployed, the data in table IV.4 show that the more costly a munition, the fewer were expended, for both guided and unguided

**Appendix IV
Cost and Performance of the Aircraft and
Munitions in Desert Storm**

categories of munitions.[16] More than 150,000 unguided unitary bombs were expended, costing just under $100 million, while in contrast, the 9,271 LGBs used cost over $282 million. Only 5,255 Maverick missiles were used, but these cost over $536 million, or 30 percent of all noncruise missile costs, while representing about 2.3 percent of ordnance expended. Even if cruise missile costs are included, Mavericks were 21.5 percent of total ordnance costs, or nearly 10 times their share of total ordnance numbers.

Munition Costs to Attack Targets

The data available permit us to calculate the munition costs to attack the targets assessed in appendix III as fully successfully destroyed and not fully successfully destroyed. These data are shown in table IV.5, grouped into target categories, for targets that we were able to evaluate from DIA phase III damage assessments. Data for the A-10 are not included, for the reliability reasons noted previously.

---

[16]The Pearson correlation coefficient between the number of munitions expended and cost was negative and moderate in size, $r = -0.42$. The correlation between the number of unguided munitions expended and unguided munition cost was $r = -0.44$, while the correlation between the number of guided bombs expended and munition cost was slightly stronger $r = -0.52$, although still in the moderate range.

Appendix IV
Cost and Performance of the Aircraft and
Munitions in Desert Storm

Table IV.5: Number and Cost of Munitions Expended by Target Category and Success Rating

Target	Rating	Number of BEs[a]	Munitions expended	Munitions per BE	NFS:FS	Total BE targets	Total cost per BE[b]	NFS:FS
C³	FS	62	974	15.7	2.41	105	$190	1.58
	NFS	43	1,626	37.8			300	
ELE	FS	10	1,298	129.8	1.92	14	391	0.30
	NFS	4	996	249.0			119	
GVC	FS	10	139	13.9	0.90	21	186	1.91
	NFS	11	133	12.1			356	
LOC	FS	28	605	21.6	2.47	40	300	1.01
	NFS	12	641	53.4			302	
MIB	FS	17	4,814	283.2	1.11	50	1,590	0.69
	NFS	33	10,378	314.5			1,091	
OCA	FS	22	7,682	349.0	0.73	34	4,661	0.95
	NFS	12	3,059	254.9			4,445	
OIL	FS	4	1,017	254.3	0.44	16	447	1.07
	NFS	12	1,353	112.8			478	
NAV	FS	3	132	44.0	2.10	13	323	4.13
	NFS	10	939	93.9			1,334	
NBC	FS	15	1,458	97.2	2.79	20	1,600	2.72
	NFS	5	1,354	270.8			4,346	
SAM	FS	10	189	18.9	0.63	14	51	4.84
	NFS	4	48	12.0			248	
SCU	FS	5	972	194.4	0.90	20	929	1.52
	NFS	15	2,633	175.5			1,416	

[a]BEs attacked exclusively by cruise missiles are not included.

[b]Costs are in thousands of fiscal 1991 dollars. As official data on the cost of British munitions were not available to us, we assumed that the cost of the U.K. 1000 LGB was equivalent to the GBU-10, the most common U.S. LGB.

Few, if any, consistent patterns can be discerned from the data shown in table IV.5. Among targets rated FS, the average number of munitions used per BE ranged from about 12 to 350; among NFS targets, the average per BE ranged from 12 to 315. The ratio of munitions used on targets rated NFS versus FS within each category also showed great variation—from 0.44 for OIL (on average, less than half as many munitions were used on OIL targets rated NFS as on those rated FS) to 2.8 for NBC targets (NBC NFS targets received nearly three times as many munitions per BE as those rated FS). Moreover, in 5 of the 11 target categories, more munitions were expended

Appendix IV
Cost and Performance of the Aircraft and
Munitions in Desert Storm

on FS targets than on NFS targets; however, in 6 categories, the NFS targets received more munitions than FS ones. In other words, success across categories did not clearly correlate with the amount of munitions delivered.

Weapon costs and target success showed some degree of pattern, but it was counterintuitive: in most categories, nonsuccess was more costly than success in terms of the munitions employed. In three categories (ELE, MIB, and OCA), the successfully attacked target costs were higher than those not fully successful. In the other eight categories, target costs were higher for the NFS targets.

To control for outliers, or unrepresentative data from small samples, we looked at the two categories that received the most munitions, MIB (15,192 weapons on both FS and NFS) and OCA (10,741 total weapons). Even between these two categories there were notable variations. The ratio of weapons used on NFS versus FS targets was 1.11 for MIB and 0.73 for OCA—that is, in one target category, FS targets received more munitions on average than NFS targets, and in the other category, they received less. The same was true of cost—in one category FS targets had higher munitions costs, on average, than NFS targets and in the other target category, the relationship was reversed. In addition, the cost of weapons used for each FS target was about three times greater for OCA than for MIB ($4.7 million for OCA targets versus $1.6 million for MIB targets). Also, because there were less than twice as many munitions used against FS OCA targets as FS MIB targets, it is apparent that more expensive munitions per unit were used against OCA targets than MIB targets. However, the ratio of success against MIB targets was more favorable than against OCA targets.

Any generalizations must be tempered by the fact that the data are incomplete in at least three regards: (1) A-10 weapons expenditures are absent, and these aircraft conducted approximately 8,000 combat sorties during Desert Storm, although the great majority were in the KBX category not listed in table IV.4; (2) the 357 BE-numbered targets for which FS and NFS evaluations could be made are a subset of all targets with BEs and a considerably smaller subset of all targets against which munitions were delivered during the air campaign; and (3) data on TLAMs and CALCMs are not included.

Given these limitations, the data shown must be treated as indicators of Desert Storm performance, not definitive measures. Two conclusions seem apparent: (1) there was great variability in the number and cost of

**Appendix IV
Cost and Performance of the Aircraft and
Munitions in Desert Storm**

munitions used to attack targets, whether successfully or unsuccessfully, and (2) neither greater numbers of munitions used nor greater munition costs consistently coincided with success across target categories. In 6 of 11 categories, greater numbers of munitions used coincided with NFS, and in 8 out of 11 comparisons, greater cost of munitions more closely coincided with NFS assessments.

The use of guided and unguided munitions against the rated targets can also be compared. Costs of the weapons delivered, per BE, in each target category are illustrated in table IV.6. (Note, data on TLAMs and A-10s are not included; therefore, both the weight of effort and costs are somewhat understated.)

Two points can be made from the data shown in table IV.6. First, in 8 of the 11 target categories, the cost per BE of precision-guided munitions used on FS targets exceeded the cost of unguided munitions. The same is true of the NFS targets in 7 of 11 categories. However, in all cases but one (GVC, NFS), more unguided munitions were used than guided munitions against any target, whether it was successfully destroyed or not. Thus, even though more unguided munitions were almost always used than guided, the cost to use guided munitions was usually greater.

Perhaps more importantly, the data in table IV.6 permit an analysis of whether an increase in the number of either guided or unguided munitions coincided with successfully destroyed targets. In only 4 of 11 categories, more PGMs were used on average against the FS than NFS targets; in 7 of 11, more PGMs were used against NFS targets. In 5 of 11 categories, more unguided munitions were used against the successfully destroyed targets. In other words, the data do not show that a key difference between successfully and not fully successfully destroyed targets was that the former were simply bombed more than the latter. This was the case for both types of munitions, PGMs and unguided.

Appendix IV
Cost and Performance of the Aircraft and
Munitions in Desert Storm

Table IV.6: Munition Costs Associated With Successfully and Not Fully Successfully Destroyed Targets

Target	Successfully destroyed				
	Number of BEs[a]	PGMs per BE	PGM cost per BE[b]	Unguided munitions per BE	Unguided cost per BE[b]
C³	62	3.5	$160.4	12.2	$29.6
ELE	10	2.0	307.3	127.8	83.4
GVC	10	5.9	167.3	8.0	19.0
LOC	28	6.2	261.7	15.0	38.3
MIB	17	16.3	982.7	266.9	607.5
NAV	3	4.3	287.0	39.6	35.9
NBC	15	19.3	1,194.5	77.9	405.4
OCA	22	51.9	3,498.4	297.0	1,162.6
OIL	4	0	0	254.2	446.6
SAM	10	0.8	22.4	18.1	28.9
SCU	5	11.6	243.9	182.8	685.3
Total	**186**	**12.1**	**$730.7**	**91.5**	**$277.0**

Target	Not fully successfully destroyed				
	Number of BEs[a]	PGMs per BE	PGM cost per BE[b]	Unguided munitions per BE	Unguided cost per BE[b]
C³	43	3.8	$254.4	34.0	$45.8
ELE	4	0.5	11.0	248.5	107.9
GVC	11	7.7	345.2	4.4	10.4
LOC	12	10.7	281.4	42.7	20.3
MIB	33	7.5	775.1	306.9	316.3
NAV	10	9.1	1,210.6	84.8	123.7
NBC	5	51.0	4,051.7	219.8	294.6
OCA	12	39.7	3,355.6	215.3	1,089.6
OIL	12	0.3	25.1	112.5	452.9
SAM	4	4.8	104.5	7.3	143.9
SCU	15	6.0	372.0	169.5	1,043.7
Total	**161**	**9.7**	**$761.9**	**134.1**	**$314.6**

[a]BEs attacked exclusively by cruise missiles are not included.

[b]Costs are in thousands of fiscal 1991 dollars. As official data on the cost of British munitions were not available to us, we assumed that the cost of the U.K. 1000 LGB was equivalent to the GBU-10, the most common U.S. LGB.

Appendix IV
Cost and Performance of the Aircraft and
Munitions in Desert Storm

Pilot's Views on Guided Versus Unguided Munitions

With regard to the effectiveness of individual munitions, the Desert Storm data do not permit a comprehensive comparison, since the effects of one type of weapon were almost never identified before other weapons hit the target. However, pilots did report both pluses and minuses with both guided and unguided munitions.

With guided munitions, pilots reported three negative consequences as delivery altitude increased. First, because the slant range to targets was increased by higher altitude, [DELETED].

Second, the higher altitude deliveries made LGBs more subject to winds, and pilots had to correct the [DELETED].

A third problem reported by F-117 and F-15E pilots was the need to revise some of the computer software for LGBs to accommodate the higher altitude tactics. [DELETED]

While each of these problems affected accuracy, they were correctable or caused problems only on the margin. The accuracy problems encountered by unguided munitions were more difficult, if not impossible, to overcome. Pilots of virtually every type of aircraft remarked that they had little confidence in hitting point targets with consistent accuracy from high altitudes with unguided bombs.

Several reasons were cited. First, pilots stated that much of their training before Desert Shield had been for low-altitude tactics. As a result, some pilots had to learn high-altitude bombing techniques either just before or during the war. Second, the Persian Gulf region experienced winds that were both strong (as much as 150 mph in jet streams) and unpredictable. The high-altitude tactics exacerbated the effects of these winds wherever they occurred, [DELETED].

As a result, pilots reported considerable difficulty attacking small, point targets, such as tanks, from high altitude with unguided bombs. Some expressed a high level of frustration in being assigned to do so and said that it was simply inappropriate, even "ridiculous," to expect that unguided bombs were capable of hitting a target like a tank from high altitude with any consistency. It was also clear that such inaccuracy made unguided munitions inappropriate for use in inhabited areas, where civilian assets could easily be hit in error.

Appendix IV
Cost and Performance of the Aircraft and
Munitions in Desert Storm

The large number of circumstances using unguided munitions was described by pilots as both appropriate and effective. These included military units in the field or other large, area targets, such as buildings or complexes of buildings, when not near civilian areas.

Attacks on Bridges

Beyond the experiences and observations of pilots, the data permit some analyses that shed some additional insights about the relative effectiveness and cost of different munition types.

CNA was able to analyze U.S. Navy attacks against certain bridges that employed LGBs, unguided bombs, and Walleye electro-optical guided bombs.[17] The CNA data and analysis are only one of a few instances where it is possible to link target damage with the use of specific types and numbers of munitions. The analysis separated out the effects of attacks with the different munitions, and it found 29 strikes on bridges where the BDA was unambiguous—that is, when no other attack was scheduled between the time of the attack and the collection of the BDA.

The study found that in eight strikes against bridges using Walleye, [DELETED]. The same rate of success was found when unguided munitions were used—[DELETED].[18] CNA data also reveal that, on average, more unguided munitions were delivered per bridge strike than guided munitions. On Walleye missions, an average of 1.3 bombs were used per strike. When LGBs were employed, an average of 3.2 were delivered per strike. And when unguided bombs were selected, an average of 15 were used per bridge.

Table IV.7 presents the cost of each type of munition employed and calculates the average cost of munitions per dropped span.

---

[17]CNA, Desert Storm Reconstruction Report; Volume II: Strike Warfare (Secret), Alexandria, Va.: 1992.

[18]Using these data, CNA concluded (on p. 6-41) that "Irrespective of weapon employed, for those bridge strikes with directly associated BDA, 17 percent of the strikes dropped a [bridge] span. When considering individual weapon types, the percentages of strikes resulting in dropped spans are similar, although the percentage for LGB/GBU strikes is somewhat higher. When the indeterminate BDA cases are considered, the individual results become indistinguishable."

Appendix IV
Cost and Performance of the Aircraft and
Munitions in Desert Storm

Table IV.7: Number and Cost of Munitions Used in Naval Air Attacks on 13 Bridges in Desert Storm

Munition type	Number	Cost[a]	Spans dropped	Average munitions per span dropped	Total cost per span dropped
Walleye	8	$560,000	[DELETED]	[DELETED]	[DELETED]
LGB	34	1,260,000	3	11.3	420,000
Unguided	85	120,052	1	85.0	120,052

[a]The range in costs of guided munitions used against these bridges was from $22,000 for the GBU-10 to $150,000 for the MK-83 LGB. The range in costs for unguided munitions was from $498 for the MK-82 to $1,871 for the MK-84.

Based on table IV.7, we find that (1) far fewer—as few as one-tenth—the number of guided munitions than unguided were required, on average, to destroy a bridge; (2) there is an inverse relationship regarding cost—that is, the cost to drop a span with guided munitions was three-to-four times more than the cost of unguided munitions; and (3) as with our previous analysis, the Desert Storm evidence did not substantiate the "one-target, one-bomb" claim—rather, on average, 11 laser-guided bombs were used for each span dropped. (See app. III.)

These conclusions must be treated cautiously. The sample is from only 13 bridges and consists only of Navy aircraft and munitions. Within these limitations, the data support our previous findings concerning the relationship between the cost and effectiveness of guided and unguided munitions and the numbers actually used to achieve target objectives.

Other Bridge Attack Analysis

Using the Missions database and the phase III BDA messages, we performed a second analysis of attacks against bridges. The phase III messages included 24 bridges attacked by both Air Force and Navy aircraft. Nineteen of these were successfully destroyed; five were not. The BDA did not, in these cases, allow any distinctions of what munition type effected the damage. Using the munition cost data in table IV.4, we calculated the munition cost to successfully destroy a bridge with both Air Force and Navy aircraft and guided and unguided munitions. The results are shown in table IV.8.

Appendix IV
Cost and Performance of the Aircraft and
Munitions in Desert Storm

Table IV.8: Munitions Costs to Attack 24 Bridges in Desert Storm

Assessment of bridges attacked	Average				
	Guided munitions	Cost of guided munitions[a]	Unguided munitions	Cost of unguided munitions[b]	Cost of bridges attacked[c]
FS	10.8	$237,600	18.2	$34,052	$271,652
NFS	7.2	158,400	14.2	26,568	184,968

[a]This assumes that the guided munition used was the GBU-10, with a unit cost of $22,000.

[b]This assumes that the unguided munition used was the MK-84 GP, which pilots stated to be the unguided munition of choice against bridges. The unit cost of this munition was $1,871.

[c]The average costs to attack bridges presented in tables IV.7 and IV.8 are not directly comparable for two reasons. First, the chronological BDA and strike data compiled by CNA allowed the calculation of costs up to and including the first successful strike against a bridge. Unambiguous chronological BDA and strike data were not available through the missions and phase III databases; thus, costs include strikes before, during, and after the initial successful attack. Second, the criteria for success are different. In the CNA study, the criterion was "span dropped." In our interpretation of DIA's phase III messages, the criterion was that the mission objective was met, which often equated with the absence of a restrike recommendation. In addition, ambiguous BDA was included in the NFS category.

While these data do not distinguish the effects of different types of munitions, they do support many of the points made earlier. First, as with the CNA data, it is clear that while fewer guided munitions were used, their cost was substantially higher. Second, in both analyses, about 11 LGBs were used per destroyed bridge. Thus, the data from the CNA analysis—with unambiguous BDA—suggest that our analysis of the number of LGBs dropped per successful target—in this case a bridge—is not inappropriate. It also reinforces the point that it is misleading to characterize LGBs as "one-target, one-bomb" weapons. Third, and finally, there are so few cases where BDA permits a reliable analysis of the exact number of a specific type of munition used per successful mission; thus, the data available from Desert Storm do not permit supportable general conclusions about the comparative effectiveness of guided versus unguided munitions.

Survivability

One characteristic pilots cited as a strong advantage of guided munitions over unguided was the ability to release a munition at a substantial standoff distance from a target, thereby limiting exposure to any defenses at the target.[19] There were, however, limitations to the advantages of

[19]Different guided munitions could be delivered at standoff distances greater or lesser than others: specifically, the IR version of the GBU-15 had a standoff capability of up to [DELETED]. Maverick missiles stood off at slant ranges of [DELETED]. Unpowered LGBs were described by some pilots as having a limited standoff capability.

**Appendix IV
Cost and Performance of the Aircraft and
Munitions in Desert Storm**

standoff capability. [DELETED] A-10 pilots noted that Iraqi defenses were not always directly collocated with the target, with the result that launching a weapon from maximum delivery range could still expose aircraft to defenses not at the target. Standoff capability distanced aircraft from defenses collocated with the target, but that was not necessarily all the defenses.

Another factor cited by pilots about guided munitions was the relatively high workload required to employ them. [DELETED][20]

[DELETED]

Pilots delivering unguided munitions experienced different problems: vulnerability to AAA was high when releasing at the low altitude that maximized the accuracy of unguided munitions. Thus, CENTAF's order to cease low-level deliveries after the third day of the campaign meant a trade-off of reduced accuracy with unguided bombs for improved survivability.

In sum, delivery tactics for guided and unguided munitions both compromised aircraft survivability but in different ways. The advantage of guided munitions to standoff from a target's defenses varies by PGM type, and some pilots reported that standoff from target defenses did not always ensure standoff from all relevant defenses. Moreover, guided munitions can make aircraft more vulnerable [DELETED], while maximum accuracy for unguided bombs requires more dangerous low-altitude delivery.

Operating Characteristics

As discussed in appendix II, night, clouds, haze, humidity, smoke, dust, and wind had significant, but different, effects on guided and unguided munitions. Delivery of guided munitions was either limited or prevented altogether by weather or other conditions that impaired visibility. In contrast, when weather and other environmental conditions affected infrared or optical search sensors for unguided munitions, they could still be delivered with radar. Doing so meant that the ability to identify valid targets among relatively indiscriminate radar returns was usually poor and accuracy from high altitude was also poor, but the employment of unguided munitions was still possible.

---

[20]The "heads down" and subsequent situational unawareness problem was much less of a problem in two-seat aircraft (the F-15E, A-6E, and the D model of the F/A-18). In these, the pilot could concentrate on external threats while the weapon systems officer performed the "heads down" tasks necessary to deliver the guided munition. However, this advantage of two-seat air-to-ground aircraft did not appreciably reduce the "wings level" time of the aircraft.

**Appendix IV
Cost and Performance of the Aircraft and
Munitions in Desert Storm**

Another operating characteristic was the support that the different munition types normally required. Pilots reported varying levels of intelligence and mission planning they needed for guided and unguided munitions. For example, [DELETED]. (In F-111F LGB missions, such as "tank plinking," detailed information and planning were not necessary.) Although they strongly preferred receiving detailed target and mission planning data, pilots using unguided munitions reported that they often had less support. For example, B-52 pilots stated that they sometimes received new targets just before takeoff, or even when they were en route to a previously planned target, but the new targeting information was sometimes little more than geographic coordinates.

In addition, "precision" for guided munitions requires not only precise accuracy from the munition but also precise intelligence support. Pinpoint accuracy is impossible if the right aimpoint is unknown.

In sum, to achieve accuracy, guided munitions were normally more limited by weather and by their support and intelligence needs than unguided munitions. In contrast, unguided munitions were usable in poor weather, but they were also less accurate.

Summary

In this appendix, we found that each type of aircraft and munition under review demonstrated both significant strengths and weaknesses. There was no consistent pattern indicating that either high-cost or low-cost aircraft or munitions performed better or were more effective in Desert Storm.[21]

The limited data do not show that multirole aircraft were either more or less effective in the air-to-ground capacity than more specialized, single-role aircraft. However, air-to-air missions were predominantly performed by single-role air-to-air aircraft, and while multirole aircraft did perform some air-defense escort and some support missions, their use did not eliminate the need for single-role, air-to-air, and other support aircraft. The evidence from Desert Storm would seem to suggest the usefulness of single-role aircraft in their respective missions and the usefulness of multirole aircraft most predominantly in the air-to-ground mission.

---

[21]Despite the absence of an overall, consistent pattern, there were clearly cases where both types were ineffective: weather either seriously degraded or rendered unusable guided munitions; high-altitude deliveries made unguided munitions highly inaccurate, according to pilots who termed the use of unguided munitions against point targets, "ridiculous." Conversely, there were conditions where the data indicated that both munitions were effective.

Appendix IV
Cost and Performance of the Aircraft and Munitions in Desert Storm

The high-cost F-117 stealth bomber has significant operating limitations that affect when, where, and how it can be used; its target hit rate appears to have been matched by the F-111F against similar targets. Although the F-117 was often, but certainly not always, tasked against different targets, on certain performance dimensions—such as sortie rate, operations in weather, and tonnage delivered—it did not match the performance of several moderate-and even low-cost aircraft.

Guided munitions are many times more costly than unguided munitions, and their employment was constrained by poor weather, clouds, heavy smoke, dust, fog, haze, and even humidity. However, guided munitions were less affected by winds and, unlike unguided munitions, they were more consistently accurate from medium-to-high altitude. Although quite inexpensive and less restricted by low visibility, unguided munitions cannot reliably be employed against point targets from the medium and high altitudes predominantly used in Desert Storm.

Both guided and unguided munitions have important implications for aircraft survivability. To be accurate, unguided munitions need low-altitude delivery, which in Desert Storm was found to be associated with too many casualties. While guided munitions can be accurate from high altitude, their standoff capability does not necessarily protect them from defenses not at the target. [DELETED]

While guided munitions are clearly more accurate from medium and high altitudes, their high unit cost means that they may not be the least expensive way to attack certain targets, sometimes by a considerable margin, compared to unguided bombs. There was no apparent pattern indicating that guided munitions were, overall, more effective than unguided munitions in successfully destroying targets or that the difference between targets that were successfully destroyed and that were not fully successfully destroyed was simply that the latter were not attacked as often as the former by either guided or unguided munitions.

The TLAM cruise missile demonstrated a high-cost sortie rate, low survivability, and severe employment limitations. Its accuracy was substantially less than claimed; however, unlike any aircraft, its use does not risk an aircraft or, more importantly, its pilot.

Appendix V
Operation Desert Storm Objectives

In an address to the Congress on August 5, 1990, 3 days after Iraq's invasion of Kuwait, President George Bush stated that the U.S. national policy objectives in the Persian Gulf were to

- effect the immediate, complete, and unconditional withdrawal of all Iraqi forces from Kuwait;
- restore Kuwait's legitimate government;
- ensure the security and stability of Saudi Arabia and other Persian Gulf nations; and
- ensure the safety of American citizens abroad.[1]

Initially, U.S. forces were deployed as a frontline deterrent to an Iraqi attack on Saudi Arabia. However, almost immediately, planning began for an offensive air campaign aimed at forcing an Iraqi withdrawal from Kuwait and accomplishing the other national policy objectives. Between early August 1990 and January 16, 1991, the phase of the campaign named Operation Desert Shield, U.S. and coalition planners drew up a series of increasingly refined and progressively more ambitious offensive campaign plans.[2] The plans changed as the number and size of U.S. and coalition forces committed to the campaign increased, but we did not review each variation in these plans. Rather, we present the plan as it stood on the eve of the war, to understand better what the goals of the campaign were as it was about to start. In addition, we examine how the offensive campaign's goals were to be operationalized in terms of phases and targets.

Desert Storm Campaign Objectives

On the eve of the offensive campaign, the commander in chief of the Central Command issued his operational order (OPORD) to U.S. and coalition forces to carry out Operation Desert Storm. The OPORD was almost identical to the operations plan that had been distributed to U.S. forces earlier in the month.

According to the OPORD (p. 5), the

---

[1]Cited in DOD's title V report, p. 30, and GWAPS, vol. I, pt. I: Planning (Secret), p. 87.

[2]During the course of Desert Shield, more than 25 countries joined the coalition to oppose Iraq's invasion of Kuwait and enforce U.N. sanctions against Iraq. Nine coalition members (in addition to the United States) participated in the Desert Storm air campaign; the remaining countries contributed either to the ground and maritime campaigns or in a supporting capacity (for example, medical teams, supply ships, and financial aid). Approximately 16.5 percent of the combat sorties during the air campaign were flown by non-U.S. forces. About 5 percent were flown by the United Kingdom; the others were flown by the aircraft of other coalition members.

Appendix V
Operation Desert Storm Objectives

"offensive campaign is a four-phased air, naval and ground offensive operation to destroy Iraqi capability to produce and employ weapons of mass destruction, destroy Iraqi offensive military capability, cause the withdrawal of Iraqi forces from Kuwait, and restore the legitimate government of Kuwait."

To achieve these general objectives, the OPORD further stated that offensive operations would focus on the following theater objectives:

- "attack Iraqi political/military leadership and command and control (c^2);
- "gain and maintain air superiority;
- "sever Iraqi supply lines;
- "destroy chemical, biological, and nuclear capability; and
- "destroy Republican Guard forces."[3]

According to OPORD, the offensive campaign would be executed in four phases, of which the first three essentially involved the air campaign and the last, the ground offensive. Although each phase had its own specific objectives, the OPORD stated (on p. 6) that execution would not necessarily be sequential and that "phases may overlap as objectives are achieved or priorities change." In effect, the plan recognized the need for flexibility in the face of changing circumstances.

According to the OPORD, phase I—the strategic air campaign— would start the offensive and was estimated to require 6 to 9 days to meet its objectives. The OPORD stated (on p. 9) that the

"strategic air campaign will be initiated to attack Iraq's strategic air defenses; aircraft/airfields; strategic chemical, biological and nuclear capability; leadership targets; command and control systems; Republican Guard forces; telecommunications facilities; and key elements of the national infrastructure, such as critical LOCs, electric grids, petroleum storage, and military production facilities."

The amount of damage to be inflicted on each of these target categories was not stated, but the OPORD noted (on p. 9) that "repaired or reconstituted targets will be re-attacked throughout the offensive campaign as necessary."

Phase II—the attainment of air superiority in the Kuwait theater of operations—was estimated to begin sometime between day 7 and day 10 and to require 2 to 4 days, ending no later than D+13 (days after D-Day). The OPORD stated (on p. 9) that

---

[3]The operations plan states that the Iraqi leadership was to be "neutralized"; this wording does not appear in the OPORD.

Appendix V
Operation Desert Storm Objectives

"air superiority in the Kuwait theater of operations will be established by attacking aircraft/airfields, air defense weapons and command and control systems in order to roll back enemy air defenses. . . . The ultimate goal of this phase is to achieve air supremacy through the KTO."

Phase III—battlefield preparation—was estimated to start sometime between D+9 and D+14 and to require 6 to 8 days. The OPORD noted (on p. 10) that phase III would involve

"attacking Iraqi ground combat forces (particularly RGFC units) and supporting missile/rocket/artillery units; interdicting supply lines; and destroying command, control and communications systems in southern Iraq and Kuwait with B-52s, tactical air, and naval surface fires . . . . The desired effect is to sever Iraqi supply lines, destroy Iraqi chemical, biological, and nuclear capability, and reduce Iraqi combat effectiveness in the KTO by at least 50 percent, particularly the RGFC. . . . [Moreover,] the purpose . . . is to open the window of opportunity for initiating ground offensive operations by confusing and terrorizing Iraqi forces in the KTO and shifting combat force ratios in favor of friendly forces."[4]

Phase IV—the ground offensive—had no estimated concrete start day in the OPORD, since it was dependent on achieving at least some of the goals of the first three phases, most especially that of degrading overall Iraqi ground force effectiveness by 50 percent. Nor did the OPORD cite the anticipated duration of phase IV. However, in a December 20, 1990, briefing, the CENTAF Director of Air Campaign Plans estimated that the ground offensive would require 18 days, with the total campaign taking 32 days.

Centers of Gravity

The OPORD further stated that Iraq had three centers of gravity (COG) to be targeted for destruction throughout the offensive campaign. These were Iraq's (1) national command authority, (2) NBC capability, and (3) the Republican Guard forces. The operations plan of December 16, 1990, cited the identical COGs, but also included a matrix "showing the phase in which each theater objective becomes the focal point of operations." (See pp. 9-10.) This matrix is reproduced in table V.1.

---

[4]After the war, a considerable controversy arose over whether the 50-percent criterion referred to overall Iraqi ground force capabilities in the KTO or to the actual number of vehicles to be destroyed. Based on the actual order presented here, it appears to have been the broader criterion, relating to the effectiveness of the units.

Appendix V
Operation Desert Storm Objectives

Table V.1: Desert Storm Theater Objectives and Phases

Theater objective	Phase I: strategic air campaign	Phase II: Kuwait theater of operations air supremacy	Phase III: battlefield preparation	Phase IV: ground offensive
Disrupt leadership and command and control	X			
Achieve air supremacy	X	X		
Cut supply lines	X	X	X	X
Destroy NBC capability	X		X	
Destroy Republican Guard	X		X	X
Liberate Kuwait City				X

Source: CENTCOM operations plan, December 16, 1990, p. 10.

Potential Effectiveness of Air Power

Air power was intended to be used in all four phases but clearly would dominate the first three phases, which preceded the ground offensive. According to one of the key planners of the air campaign, it was hoped that the ground offensive would be rendered unnecessary by the effectiveness of the coalition air force attacks against Iraqi targets.[5] A senior Desert Storm planner we interviewed told us that the strategic air campaign (phase I) would concentrate on leadership-related targets deep inside Iraq, with the goal of forcing Iraqi leader Saddam Hussein to "cry uncle." If destruction of key leadership facilities—ranging from the presidential palace to critical communications nodes to military headquarters—did not result in an Iraqi collapse, then the elite Republican Guard units in the KTO would be hit next.[6] It was hoped that Saddam Hussein would flinch if severe destruction were inflicted on the Republican Guard, a key prop of Iraqi power. Finally, according to one key Black Hole planner (see glossary), if those attacks did not result in an Iraqi retreat, then the air campaign would continue with massive attrition of the Iraqi frontline forces, followed by a ground offensive.

As noted above, the OPORD did not specify the precise level of damage to be inflicted during phase I on a broad variety of strategic targets. This probably reflected the planners' focus on "an effects-based plan." That is, rather than concentrating on achieving a specific level of damage to individual targets or target sets, the goal was to achieve a greater impact,

---

[5] See DOD title V report, p. 135.

[6] The KTO area included RG units deployed as part of the attack on Kuwait in the area of Iraq immediately north of Kuwait.

Appendix V
Operation Desert Storm Objectives

such as shutting down the national electric power grid or paralyzing the ability of the Iraqi leadership to transmit orders or receive information from field units. Therefore, it was more important to destroy critical nodes, such as the generating halls of electric power plants or the telephone switching centers in Baghdad, than to flatten dozens of less important targets. Further, as a number of observers have noted, in certain categories, the goal was not to destroy them for years to come but, rather, to severely disrupt Iraqi capabilities temporarily. (This was particularly true with regard to oil production and electrical generation but not true for NBC targets.)

In sum, and not for the first time in armed conflict in this century, it was hoped that the shock and effectiveness of air power would precipitate a collapse of the opponent before a ground campaign. Failing that, it was expected that sufficient damage could be inflicted on enemy ground forces to greatly reduce casualties to the coalition ground forces.

These goals help explain, in part, the early concentration on key strategic targets in the opening hours and days of the air campaign. To operationalize these goals, the U.S. air planners divided fixed targets in Iraq and the KTO into the 12 categories cited in appendix I. (See table I.1.)

The air planners assigned targets within each of these categories to different aircraft, deciding which specific targets to hit and when. It is essential to realize that each of these categories is quite broad; many of the targets that fell under a single category varied considerably, along numerous dimensions. Perhaps most important, the number of aimpoints at a given target type, such as an airfield, could range from a few to dozens, depending on the number of buildings, aircraft, radar, and other potential targets at the location. Similarly, nuclear-related and military industrial facilities contained varying numbers of buildings, each considered an aimpoint.

In addition, each target category contained targets that had varying degrees of hardness, creating different levels of vulnerability. For example, "leadership" targets ranged from "soft" targets such as the presidential palace and government ministry buildings to bunkers buried tens of feet beneath the earth and virtually invulnerable to conventional weapons. Bridges, a part of the "railroad and bridges" category, varied in terms of the number of arches, the type of material used to construct them, width, and other factors that could significantly affect the number and type of weapons required to destroy them. In effect, any interpretation of the

Appendix V
Operation Desert Storm Objectives

number and kind of weapons and platforms required to inflict desired damage on a broad target category must start with the understanding that a tremendous range of targeting-related variables existed within a given category. (For a more complete list of the kinds of targets contained within each broad category, see app. I.)

In an analysis of the intended effects of the air campaign, GWAPS grouped the 12 target sets into 7 categories and, in greater detail than the OPORD, stated the air campaign's goals based on an analysis of Desert Storm documents and interviews with many participants. Table V.2 summarizes this analysis.

Table V.2: Operational Strategic Summary of the Air Campaign

Target sets	Desired or planned effects
Integrated air defense and airfields	Early air superiority
	Suppress medium- and high-air defenses throughout Iraq
	Contain and destroy Iraqi air force
Naval targets	Attain sea control—permit allied naval operations in northern Persian Gulf
Leadership, telecommunications, and C^3	Pressure and disrupt governmental functioning
	Isolate Saddam Hussein from Iraqi people and forces in the KTO
Electricity and oil	Shut down national grid—minimize long-term damage
	Cut flow of fuels and lubricants to Iraqi forces—no lasting damage to oil production
NBC and Scuds	Destroy biological and chemical weapons
	Prevent use against coalition
	Destroy production capability
	Destroy nuclear program—long term
	Prevent and suppress use of Scuds—destroy production and infrastructure
Railroads and bridges	Cut supply lines to the KTO—prevent retreat of Iraqi forces
RG and other ground forces in the KTO	Destroy the Republican Guard
	Reduce combat effectiveness of remaining units by 50 percent by G-day (start of the ground war)

Source: Analysis of GWAPS, vol. II, pt. II (Secret), p. 353, table 25.

Appendix V
Operation Desert Storm Objectives

Discussion

Table V.2 shows that some target sets were intended to be destroyed completely by air power, while others were to be damaged to a degree that would prevent their use during the conflict and for a short-term period afterward. Two of the three key COGs cited above—NBC and the RG—were slated for complete destruction, as were the Scuds that could deliver nuclear, biological, or chemical warheads. Although there was no explicit goal to topple the Hussein regime, some observers believe that effectively crippling the RG units might have encouraged regular army officers to attempt a coup d'état. In effect, the goals of the air campaign were almost surely more ambitious than simply to "disrupt" the Iraqi leadership.

In addition, the goal of cutting supply lines to the KTO could only be accomplished by effectively cutting all bridges and railroads while also preventing supply trucks from using existing roads or alternative routes, such as driving on the flat desert.

To achieve the results hoped for, the Desert Storm air planners put together a list of strategic targets to be attacked during the first 2 to 3 days of phase I, the strategic air campaign. This list grew during the months of planning, from 84 targets in late August 1990 to 476 by the eve of the war. The increase in the number of targets reflected several factors, not the least of which was that as coalition aircraft numbers deployed to the region rose dramatically, so too did the capability to hit many more targets during a very short period of time. In addition, the months of preparation had permitted the development of intelligence about critical targets and their locations and refinements in the plan to maximize the potential shock to Iraq.

The increase in the targets, by set, is shown in table V.3. (Note that the bottom two categories—"breach" and SAMs—are actually components of other categories. "Breaching" would normally be a tactical battlefield preparation mission; SAMs are part of strategic air defense.)

Because this growth in both target sets and number of targets has been thoroughly analyzed in previous studies, we review here only several major points. According to a number of analyses, the increase in the RG category (from 12 to 37 targets) reflected the CENTCOM CINC's concern that these units be destroyed as essential to maintaining regional stability after the end of the war. In his view, these units not only propped up the Iraqi regime but also gave it an offensive ground capability that had to be eliminated.[7]

---

[7]GWAPS, vol. I, pt. I (Secret), p. 173.

Appendix V
Operation Desert Storm Objectives

Table V.3: Target Growth, by Category, From the Initial Instant Thunder Plan to January 15, 1991[a]

Target category	Instant Thunder	9/13/90	10/11/90	12/1/90	12/18/90	1/15/91
SAD	10	21	40	28	27	58
NBC	8	20	20	25	20	23
SCU	[b]	[b]	[c]	[c]	16	43
GVC	5	15	15	32	31	33
C³	19	26	27	26	30	59
ELE	10	14	18	16	16	17
OIL	6	8	10	7	12	12
LOC	3	12	12	28	28	33
OCA	7	13	27	28	28	31
NAV	1	4	6	4	4	19
MIB	15	41	43	44	38	62
RG	[b]	[d]	[d]	[d]	12	37
Breach	0	0	[b]	[b]	0	6
SAM	0	0	[b]	[b]	0	43
Total	**84**	**174**	**218**	**238**	**262**	**476**

[a]Instant Thunder was the initial air campaign plan prepared by Air Force planners only days after the Iraqi invasion of Kuwait.

[b]Not available.

[c]Scuds included in NBC category.

[d]Republican Guard included in MIB category.

Source: GWAPS, vol. I, pt. I (Secret), p. 195.

Similarly, the air planners feared that a "premature" Iraqi surrender, after only a short strategic air campaign, would preclude the destruction of much of Iraq's offensive military capabilities, particularly NBC. Therefore,

"as the plan execution date grew closer and additional aircraft arrived in country . . . planners sought to spread sorties across as many of the target categories as possible, rather than concentrate on the neutralization of all or more targets in one category before the next became the focus of attacks."[8]

While seeking to eliminate as much Iraqi offensive capability as possible, as quickly as possible, air planners also had to allocate a large portion of the early strikes to the phase II goal of achieving air superiority, according to most analyses of the conflict. This reflected the CENTAF commander's

[8]GWAPS, vol. 1, pt. I (Secret), p. 174.

Appendix V
Operation Desert Storm Objectives

priority of minimizing aircraft losses. It was believed that this could be achieved only by rendering ineffective the Iraqi integrated air defense system, a highly centralized, computerized defense incorporating hundreds of radar-guided SAMs and about 500 fighter aircraft. A second goal was to prevent the Iraqis from attacking coalition units with aircraft delivered chemical or biological weapons, much less with conventional ones. The fear of nonconventional weapon attacks also generated requirements to destroy as many Scud missiles and launchers as possible. This target category was broken out from the chemical set by December 18, 1990, and then increased from 16 to 43 targets by the eve of the war.[9]

Finally, air superiority was essential to prevent the Iraqis from detecting or disrupting the movement of a huge coalition ground force in Saudi Arabia to execute a surprise attack on Iraqi forces from the west rather than through their front lines.

Two to Three Days Planned

As noted above, only the first 2 to 3 days of the strategic air campaign were planned in great detail, with the remainder to be based on the damage done to the high-priority targets that would be hit in the first 48 to 72 hours. A master attack plan was prepared for the first 72 hours, but actual air tasking orders were prepared for only the first 48 hours, because the CENTAF commander believed that plans would have to be changed given the results of the first 2 days. Using BDA intelligence, planners anticipated that some targets would have to be restruck, while new ones could be hit once BDA showed that those of the highest value were destroyed or sufficiently damaged. Sixty percent of the 476 targets designated by January 16, 1991, were to be hit during the first 72 hours, including "34 percent [of the targets attacked] . . . in the strategic air defense and airfield categories."[10]

Thus, by the eve of the war, an extremely detailed yet flexible air campaign plan was ready to be formulated, using forces that had been deployed to carry out the campaign.

---

[9]It was also believed that Iraq would launch Scud attacks on Israel in an attempt to bring that country into the war, thereby breaking apart the allied coalition, with its many Arab state participants. As events unfolded, this fear was justified, and a massive effort was devoted to suppressing Scud launches.

[10]GWAPS, vol. I, pt. I (Secret), p. 197.

Appendix V
Operation Desert Storm Objectives

Aircraft Deployed to the Conflict

There was very substantial variation in the proportion of U.S. air-to-ground aircraft deployed to the gulf, compared to the total number available of each kind of aircraft. Table V.4 shows the maximum number of each kind of U.S. air-to-ground platform sent to the gulf, the total worldwide U.S. inventory for each aircraft, and the percentage that the Desert Storm deployment represented of total inventory for that particular aircraft.

Table V.4: Number and Percent of Inventory of U.S. Air-to-Ground Aircraft Deployed to Desert Storm

Aircraft	Number deployed	Total U.S. inventory (1990)	Number deployed as percent of U.S. inventory
F-111F	66	83	80
F-117	42	56	75
B-52	68	118	58
F/A-18D	12	29	41
F-15E	48	125	38
A-6E	115	350	33
F/A-18A/C	162	526	31
A-10	148	565	26
F-16	251	1,759	14

Source: DOD's title V report, vol. III, appendix T.

It seems reasonable that a number of factors would have played roles in determining the numbers deployed for any given type of aircraft, including (1) the total inventory, which varied tremendously (from as few as 29 to 1,759); (2) the perceived need or role for the aircraft; and (3) the estimated likely effectiveness of the aircraft. It is not clear from planning or other documents which of these factors (or other ones) determined the different percentages of the worldwide inventory for each type of aircraft that was eventually allocated to the gulf. However, in general, the smaller the U.S. inventory of a particular type of aircraft, the larger the proportion of that inventory that was dedicated to Desert Storm.

Summary

In this appendix, we identified the KTO objectives: (1) attack Iraqi leadership and command and control, (2) achieve air superiority, (3) sever Iraqi supply lines, (4) destroy Iraq's NBC capability, and (5) prepare the battlefield by attacking RG and other ground forces.

The U.S. objectives were to be achieved by conducting a four-phase campaign, the first three phases of which constituted exclusively an air

Appendix V
Operation Desert Storm Objectives

campaign. Phase I—the strategic air campaign—would start the offensive and address the centers of gravity and most of the 12 strategic target categories. Phase II—the attainment of air superiority over Iraq and in the Kuwait theater of operations—was initiated simultaneously with phase I. Phase III—battlefield preparation—involved attacking Iraqi ground combat forces (particularly RG units) to reduce Iraqi combat effectiveness in the KTO by at least 50 percent. Finally, came phase IV—the ground offensive—during which coalition ground forces would be supported by the coalition air forces.

The air campaign plan continued to evolve from the initial Instant Thunder plan proposed in August 1990 until the eve of the campaign. During this time, the number of target categories remained nearly constant, but the number of targets grew from 84 to 476. A substantial portion of the U.S. air-to-ground inventory was dedicated to Desert Storm to service the many targets. The planners expected that the air campaign objectives could be decisively achieved in days or, at most, weeks. On the eve of the campaign, detailed strikes had been planned for only the first 48 to 72 hours. Subsequent strikes on strategic targets were expected to be planned based on the results achieved in the initial strikes.

Appendix VI
Basic Structure of the Iraqi Integrated Air Defense System

The country was divided into four sectors, each controlled by a sector operations center and each reporting directly to the national air defense operations center (ADOC) in Baghdad. The integrated air defense system was highly centralized, [DELETED]. Each SOC transmitted data back to intercept operations centers, which in turn controlled SAM batteries and fighter aircraft at air bases.

There were [DELETED] IOCs across the four sectors in Iraq feeding data to individual SOCs. Each IOC was optimized to direct either SAM or fighter aircraft against incoming enemy aircraft. Each IOC was connected to observer and early warning area reporting posts (RP) [DELETED].

Figure VI.1 shows the four IADS sectors in Iraq, the Kuwait sector, the RPs, IOCs, SOCs, ADOC, and the communication lines among these components.

There were about 500 radars located at approximately 100 sites, [DELETED].[1] [DELETED][2]

Figure VI.1: The Iraqi Air Defense Network

[FIGURE DELETED]

Source: [DELETED]

Evidence on IADS Capabilities

IADS Could Only Track a Limited Number of Threats

Despite the numerous components of the IADS, its actual operating capabilities were quite limited. The system was designed to counter comparatively limited threats from Israel and Iran, with each SOC capable of tracking [DELETED]. While sufficient against an attack from either

---

[1] GWAPS, vol. II, pt. I (Secret), p. 83.

[2] SPEAR (Secret), December 1990, p. 3-11.

Appendix VI
Basic Structure of the Iraqi Integrated Air Defense System

regional opponent, the system was inadequate to cope with a force of hundreds of aircraft and unmanned aerial decoys. [DELETED][3]

IADS Design Made the System Easy to Disrupt

[DELETED]

IADS Design Was Known in Detail to U.S. Intelligence

Another advantage that the coalition had in attacking the IADS is that all internal designs of the KARI computer system that controlled it [DELETED].[4] [DELETED]

Iraqi SAMs Were Old or Limited in Capability

Some key Iraqi antiair weapons were either quite old, well understood by U.S. intelligence, or limited in range and capability. SAMs with the greatest range, SA-2s and SA-3s, had been deployed 30 years earlier, putting them at the end of their operational lifespan. Moreover, both the USAF and other coalition air forces had long established countermeasures to these systems.

[DELETED]

The four types of SAMs just discussed—SA-2s, SA-3s, SA-6s, and SA-8s—along with Roland, were those that entirely comprised the SAM defenses of the five most heavily defended areas of Iraq: Baghdad, Basrah, Tallil/Jalibah, H-2 and H-3 airfields, and Mosul/Kirkuk. [DELETED]

AAA Guns Were Not Radar-Guided

While linked to the IADS, AAA guns were mostly unguided and used in barrage-style firing against attacking aircraft. Still, even unguided barrage-style AAA remained a considerable threat to attacking aircraft required to fly above 12,000 feet for most of the war.

The Iraqi Air Force Failed to Play a Role

With a substantial portion of the Iraqi air force destroyed, inactive, or fleeing to Iran early in the campaign, the threat was severely reduced since part of the effectiveness of the IADS depended on vectoring its fighters to attacking aircraft.

---

[3]SPEAR (Secret), December 1990, p. 3-25. Similarly, DIA reported that the IADS "could track only a limited number of threats and was [DELETED]." DIA, BDA Highlights (March 22, 1991), p. 26.

[4]USAF, History of the Strategic Air Campaign: Operation Desert Storm (Secret), p. 258.

Appendix VII
Pre-Desert Storm Missions and Actual Use

F-117	The F-117 was originally only intended for selected missions against heavily defended, high-value targets. The F-117's unique "low-observable" design narrows the range of its mission capability compared to other nonstealthy aircraft.

Before the war, planners primarily tasked the F-117s to high-value, heavily defended, air defense, C³, leadership, and NBC targets in and around Baghdad. The targets actually attacked by the F-117s became somewhat more diverse as the war progressed. According to an F-117 after-action report, the doctrinal target list for the F-117 "went out the window." |
| F-111F | Pre-air campaign mission plans for the F-111F focused on low-altitude air interdiction against strategic targets, such as airfields, radar sites, and chemical weapons bunkers. However, like all other aircraft, almost all Desert Storm missions were conducted at medium-to-high altitude. Another deviation from pre-Desert Storm mission planning for the F-111F were LGB strikes against tanks commonly referred to after the war as "tank plinking."

The F-111F was the only Desert Storm aircraft to deliver the GBU-15 and the 5,000-pound laser-guided, penetrating GBU-28. |
| F-15E | Pre-Desert Storm plans focused largely on an air interdiction role for the F-15E. However, the F-15E minimally participated in the overall air interdiction effort. Rather, F-15E missions were predominantly Scud hunting, reconnaissance, and antiarmor missions in kill boxes.

The F-15E is one of three U.S. Air Force LGB-capable platforms, yet the majority of the bomb tonnage delivered by the F-15E was unguided. Because of the limited number of LANTIRN targeting pods, only one-quarter of the F-15Es deployed to the Persian Gulf had the capability of autonomously delivering LGBs. |
| A-6E | Pre-Desert Storm plans involved air interdiction for A-6s with some emphasis on attacking airfields and Iraqi air defenses located at airfields. A-6s conducted air interdiction missions against a range of Desert Storm strategic targets, delivering the bulk of the bombs dropped on naval targets. |

Appendix VII
Pre-Desert Storm Missions and Actual Use

F-16	Initial air campaign plans tasked F-16s mostly during the daylight hours in large strike packages against targets such as airfields, chemical weapons storage areas, Scud missile production facilities, Republican Guard locations, leadership targets, and military storage facilities. Several strikes against strategic targets in the Baghdad area occurred during the first 2 weeks of the war. F-16s conducted a proportionately large number of strikes against C^3, NBC, OCA, and OIL targets. F-16 pilots told us that their missions further evolved at the end of the war to patrolling highways and rivers and striking and harassing targets of opportunity such as trucks, repaired bridges, and barges.
F/A-18	F/A-18s were initially assigned to carry out suppression of enemy air defenses, fleet defense combat air patrol, escort of other strike aircraft, and attacks against a range of ground targets. As Iraqi threats against Navy aircraft carriers were degraded, the number of F/A-18 CAP sorties was reduced while those allocated to interdiction increased. However, the F/A-18's lack of an autonomous laser for delivery of LGBs was cited in DOD's title V report as a shortcoming.[1]
A-10	When planners began to construct the air campaign plan, they did not anticipate tasking the A-10 against strategic targets. However, the role of the A-10 in the campaign evolved as the events of the war unfolded. The lower air defense threat in Scud launching areas enabled planners to task the A-10 against these targets and to capitalize on the A-10's large payload capacity and loitering ability. Intense AAA and IR SAM threats encountered near RG targets motivated the Air Force to largely assign the A-10s to lower threat areas. According to the pilots we interviewed, combat air support performed by the A-10 was difficult and nontraditional. For example, much of it was performed at night for both the Marines and the Army, when a key problem was how to identify targets. Although the A-10 is generally considered a day-only aircraft, two squadrons flew night missions [DELETED].
B-52	Over two-thirds of the B-52 missions were directed against Iraqi ground forces, with the remainder against targets such as military industrial

---

[1]See Naval Aviation: The Navy Is Taking Actions to Improve the Combat Capabilities of Its Tactical Aircraft (GAO/NSIAD-93-204, July 7, 1993), for more information on F/A-18 limitations in Desert Storm.

Appendix VII
Pre-Desert Storm Missions and Actual Use

facilities, electrical power plants, and airfields. B-52s flew just over 3 percent of the total air combat missions, but because of the aircraft's uniquely large payload, these accounted for 30 percent of the total bomb tonnage released.[2]

The Strategic Air Command officially reported the B-52 CEP to be [DELETED]. This level of inaccuracy resulted from the high winds that affected unguided bomb ballistics and from an error introduced by a contractor in misidentifying the ground coordinates of targets.

British Tornado, GR-1

The British Tornado had a visible and consistent role in the strategic air campaign, being one of the few non-U.S. coalition aircraft assigned missions in the final, command-approved, version of the Master Attack Plan. A primary planned mission for the Tornado was attacking runways with the JP233 munition at very low altitude. However, the combination of four British Tornado losses in the first week of the air campaign and the command decision to go to medium-altitude operations brought an end to these planned missions.

In the remaining 5 weeks of the air campaign, the primary Tornado mission was air interdiction at medium altitude against a variety of target types. Many of the new targets were point targets, like hardened aircraft shelters and bridges believed to necessitate LGBs. Because the Tornado had no laser self-designation capability, buddy lasing tactics with the British Buccaneer aircraft were attempted. A British Ministry of Defense report suggests that the buddy lasing experience demonstrated the need for laser self-designation capability in the Tornado.[3]

---

[2]See Operation Desert Storm: Limits on the Role and Performance of B-52 Bombers in Conventional Conflicts (GAO/NSIAD-93-138, May 12, 1993).

[3]British Ministry of Defense, The Gulf Conflict: Lessons Learned, p. 8-6.

Appendix VIII
Weight of Effort and Type of Effort Analysis

The weight of effort and type of effort indices permitted us to examine the relative contributions of the air-to-ground platforms and revealed the overall magnitude of the weight and type of effort that was expended against the strategic target sets established pursuant to the military objectives of the Persian Gulf War. In this appendix, we report results not included in appendix I.

WOE Platform Comparisons

Collectively, military industrial base, offensive counterair and kill box target sets received most of the weight of effort from the air-to-ground platforms reviewed here, and KBX targets received by far the most strikes, the most bombs, and the most bomb tonnage. BE-numbered targets in the KBX target set received at least 9 times more strikes, 5 times more bombs, and 5 times more bomb tonnage than the next highest ranking strategic target set in this regard. The comparisons indicate that the F-111F and the F-117 accounted for the majority of the guided bomb tonnage delivered against strategic targets, while the B-52 and the F-16 accounted for the majority of the unguided bomb tonnage delivered.

The B-52 and the F-16 accounted for the majority of unguided ordnance delivered against KBX targets. Respectively, they delivered approximately 32 million and 31 million pounds of bombs on KBX targets. The F-15Es participated most exclusively against Scud targets. Of the PGM tonnage delivered on C^3, NBC, and MIB targets, the F-117 accounted for most of it. Weight of effort on NAV targets was almost exclusively the domain of Navy platforms, where the A-6E accounted for much of the weight of effort. The Navy platforms did contribute a considerable WOE against KBX targets. The only non-U.S. coalition platform reviewed here—the British Tornado, GR-1—did not contribute a majority of WOE on any of the strategic target sets.

Figure VIII.1 shows the number of strikes by each platform against all 12 target categories. Relative to other platforms, the F-16 was a predominant force against KBX targets, accounting for at least 51 percent of the total strikes. The number of strikes conducted by the F-16s, F/A-18s, F-111Fs, A-6Es, F-15Es, and the B-52s on KBX targets was the largest number of strikes that each conducted compared to other strategic target categories. Figure VIII.1 also shows that the majority of the Desert Storm platforms expended more of their strike efforts on KBX targets than on any other strategic target category.

Appendix VIII
Weight of Effort and Type of Effort Analysis

Figure VIII.1: Target Category Strikes, by Platform

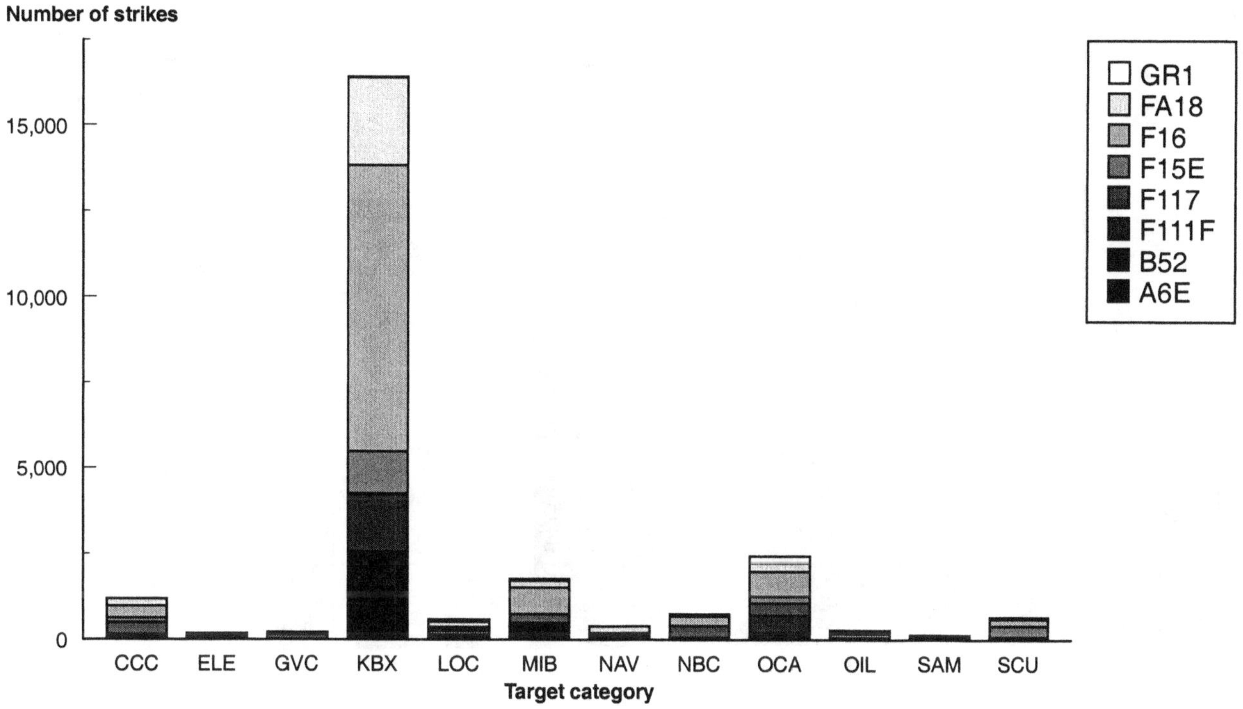

Number of strikes

[Bar chart with legend: GR1, FA18, F16, F15E, F117, F111F, B52, A6E. Y-axis shows 0 to 15,000+. X-axis categories: CCC, ELE, GVC, KBX, LOC, MIB, NAV, NBC, OCA, OIL, SAM, SCU. Target category.]

Figure VIII.2 depicts strike data for the selected platforms against the target categories, excluding KBX targets.

Appendix VIII
Weight of Effort and Type of Effort Analysis

Figure VIII.2: Target Category Strikes, by Platform, Excluding KBX Targets

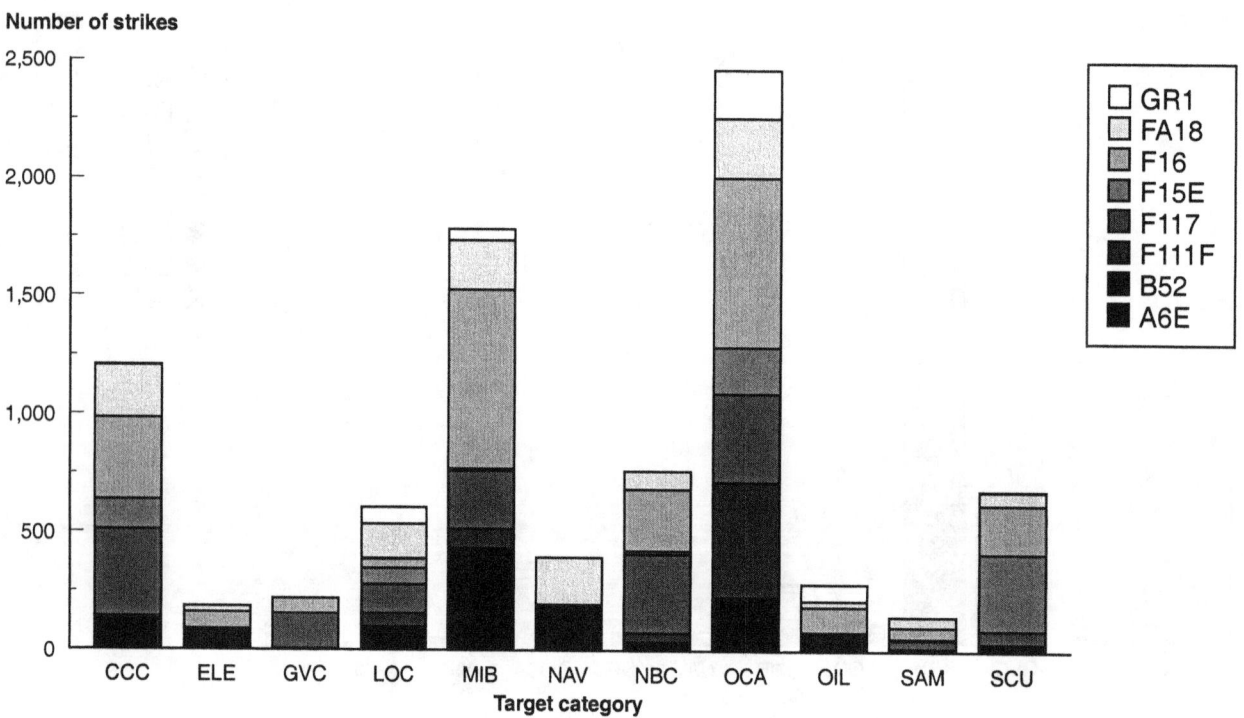

When KBX strikes are removed, figure VIII.2 more clearly shows other patterns, particularly that more strikes were expended on the MIB and OCA target categories relative to other target categories. In addition to being one of the strategic target sets, MIB targets often served as "dump" targets or secondary targets, while the OCA target set was associated with the Desert Storm objective of achieving air supremacy and would be expected to be given a considerable weight of effort.

Similar to F-16 strike data against KBX targets, the F-16 stands out in terms of the number of strikes conducted against OCA, MIB, ELE, and OIL target sets. One factor that can account for this is that more F-16s were deployed to the Persian Gulf theater than any other aircraft.

Appendix VIII
Weight of Effort and Type of Effort Analysis

Compared to other target sets, the F-111F delivered more strikes on the OCA target category. This coincides both with the stated mission capability of the F-111F, as well as the Desert Storm plans for the F-111F, which focused predominantly on an air interdiction role.

The F-15E conducted the largest number of strikes against Scud targets. In contrast to other platforms, the F-15E was not a significant part of strike efforts on any other target category. The F-117 conducted the most strikes on the C^3 target category, the GVC target category, and the NBC target category. Figure VIII.3 shows the number of bombs delivered by air-to-ground platforms against the strategic target sets.

Figure VIII.3: Bombs Delivered, by Platform

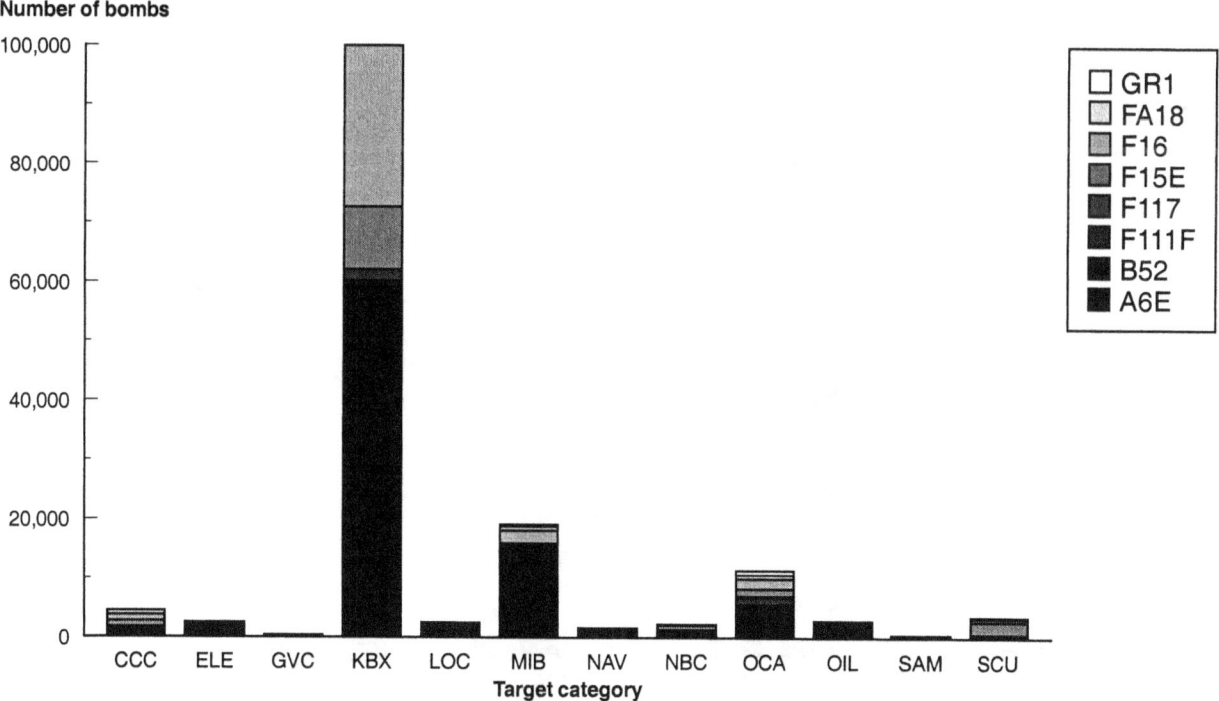

Appendix VIII
Weight of Effort and Type of Effort Analysis

Figure VIII.3 shows that the number of bombs delivered on KBX targets was at least four times as great as the number of bombs delivered on the MIB target set, the next highest.

Figures VIII.3 and VIII.4 show that the B-52 delivered more bombs against 7 of 12 target categories (ELE, KBX, LOC, MIB, NBC, OCA, and OIL). The F-16 was second only to the B-52 in bombs delivered against MIB and OCA strategic targets. Together with the data from the KBX target category, the F-16 is second to the B-52 in number of bombs delivered against the KBX, the MIB, and the OCA strategic target sets. The A-6E dominated strategic targets in the NAV target set, and the F-15E delivered substantially more bombs on Scud targets compared to the other platforms.

Figure VIII.4: Bombs Delivered, by Platform, Excluding KBX Targets

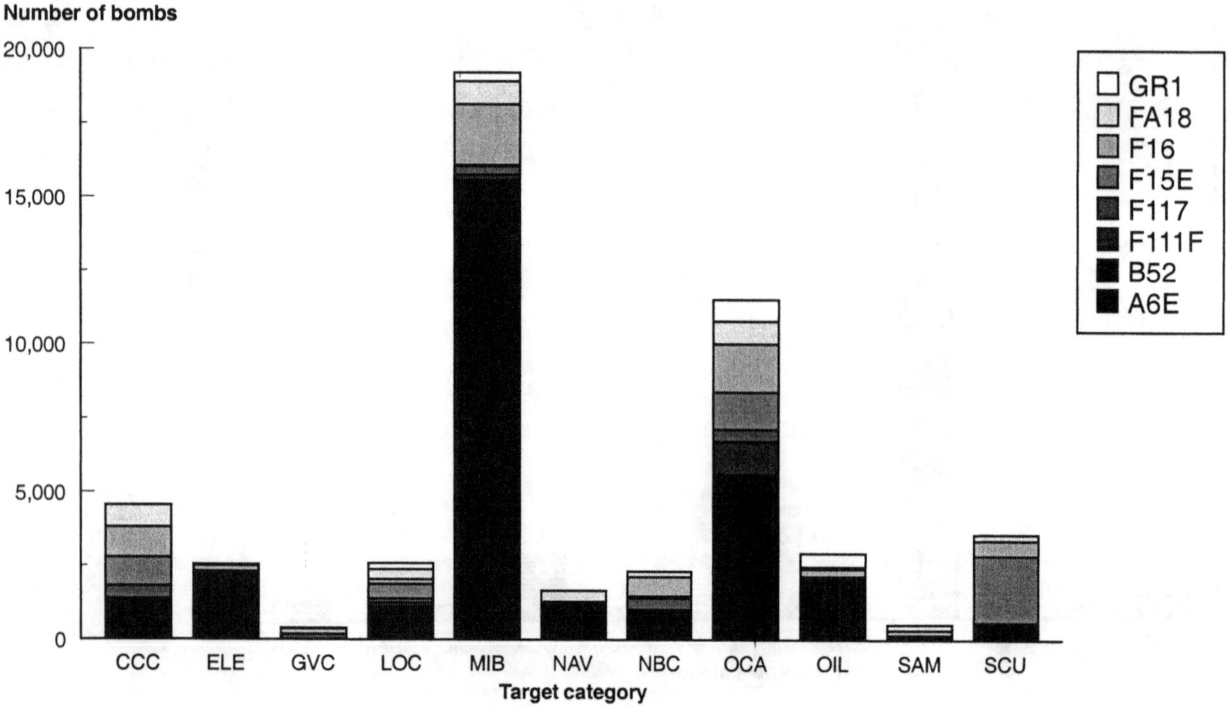

Appendix VIII
Weight of Effort and Type of Effort Analysis

Similar to the number of bombs delivered against target categories, figure VIII.5 shows that the most bomb tonnage was delivered on the KBX, MIB, and OCA target sets.

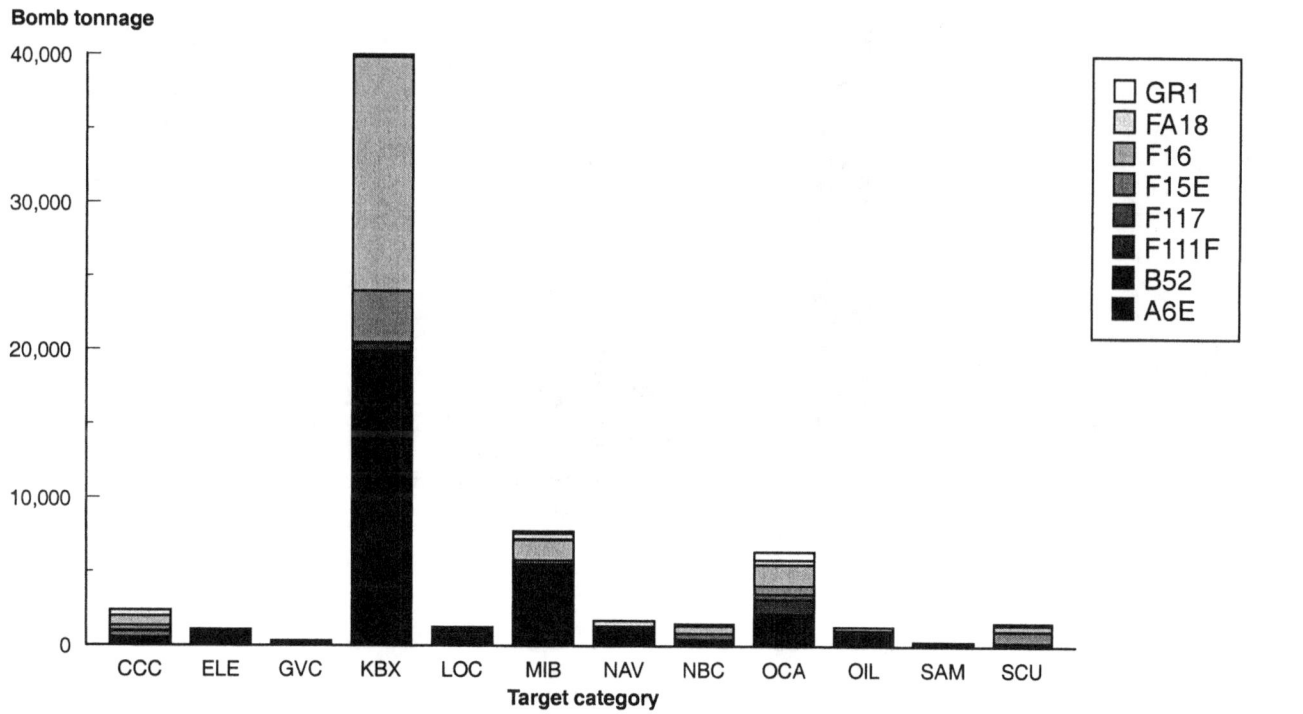

Figure VIII.5: Bomb Tonnage Delivered, by Platform

B-52s delivered more bomb tonnage, relative to the other platforms against strategic targets in the ELE, KBX, MIB, OCA, and OIL target categories. The F-16 delivered in excess of 31 million pounds of bombs on KBX targets. This is second only to the B-52, which delivered approximately 32 million pounds of bombs. (See fig. VIII.6.)

Appendix VIII
Weight of Effort and Type of Effort Analysis

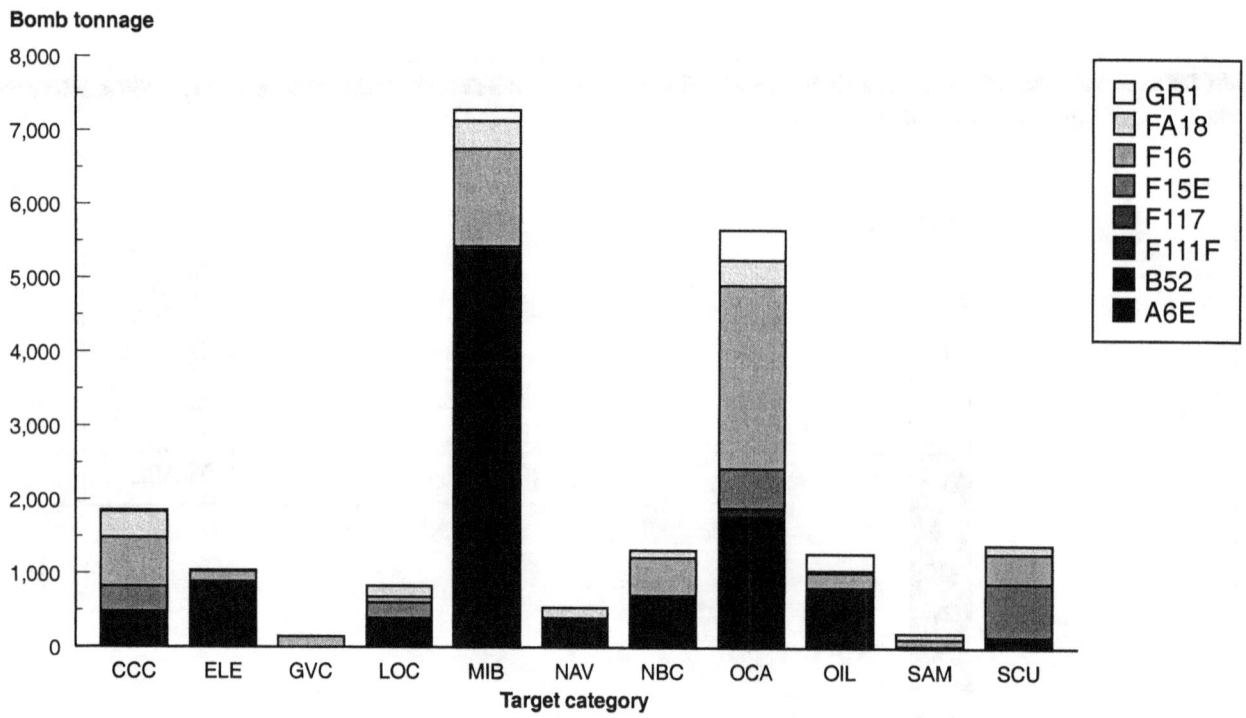

Figure VIII.6: Bomb Tonnage Delivered, by Platform, Excluding KBX Targets

Figure VIII.6 shows that the F-16 delivered more bomb tonnage on C^3 and NBC targets than on the other platforms. The F-15E delivered more bomb tonnage on Scud targets than on any other strategic target set. With regard to F-15E efforts against Scud targets, all of the WOE indices (number of BEs, number of strikes, number of bombs, bomb tonnage) converge to indicate that the F-15E was the predominant force on Scud targets and was not a principal part of the weight of effort on other strategic target categories.

Figure VIII.6 does not indicate that among the various platforms tasked to C^3, LOC, NAV, NBC, OCA, and SAM targets, a single platform is distinctive in terms of the bomb tonnage delivered. The data show distinctive variability in sources of bomb tonnage delivered against ELE, MIB, OIL, and to some degree, SCU targets. B-52 bomb tonnage accounts for this distinction

Appendix VIII
Weight of Effort and Type of Effort Analysis

against all these target sets except for Scud targets, which were accounted for by the efforts of the F-15E.

TOE Platform Comparisons

The type of effort measures indicate the quantity of guided and unguided bomb tonnage delivered by the selected air-to-ground platforms. Figure VIII.7 shows PGM tonnage delivered by platforms.

The most PGM tonnage was delivered against OCA targets. A factor that can account for this is that many OCA targets were hardened aircraft shelters and were attacked with LGBs. F-111Fs delivered in excess of 1.7 million pounds of bombs on OCA targets. F-111Fs also delivered the most PGM tonnage on KBX targets, which largely reflects F-111F tank-plinking efforts using LGBs. Compared to the other platforms, the F-117 accounted for the bulk of the PGM tonnage delivered on C^3, NBC, and MIB targets.

Figure VIII.7 shows that the F-15E delivered a majority of guided bomb tonnage on Scud targets and that this was the only strategic target category in which the F-15E contributed the majority of the PGM tonnage. This pattern is expected because the F-15E received most of its tasking to Scud targets and because the wing had limited PGM capability.

Appendix VIII
Weight of Effort and Type of Effort Analysis

Figure VIII.7: PGM Tonnage Delivered, by Platform

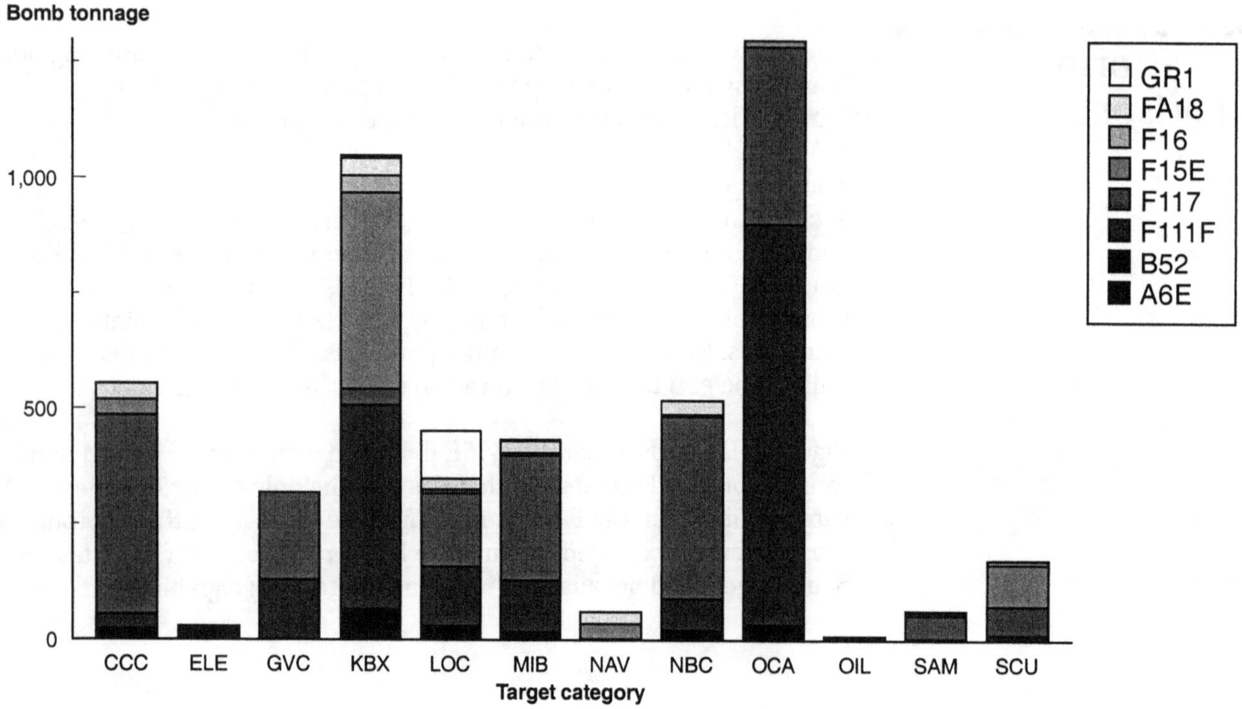

Figure VIII.8 shows that not only were very sizable amounts of unguided bomb tonnage delivered against BE-numbered KBX targets, but the unguided bomb tonnage delivered against KBX targets, relative to the other strategic target categories, was immense.

Appendix VIII
Weight of Effort and Type of Effort Analysis

Figure VIII.8: Unguided Tonnage Delivered, by Platform

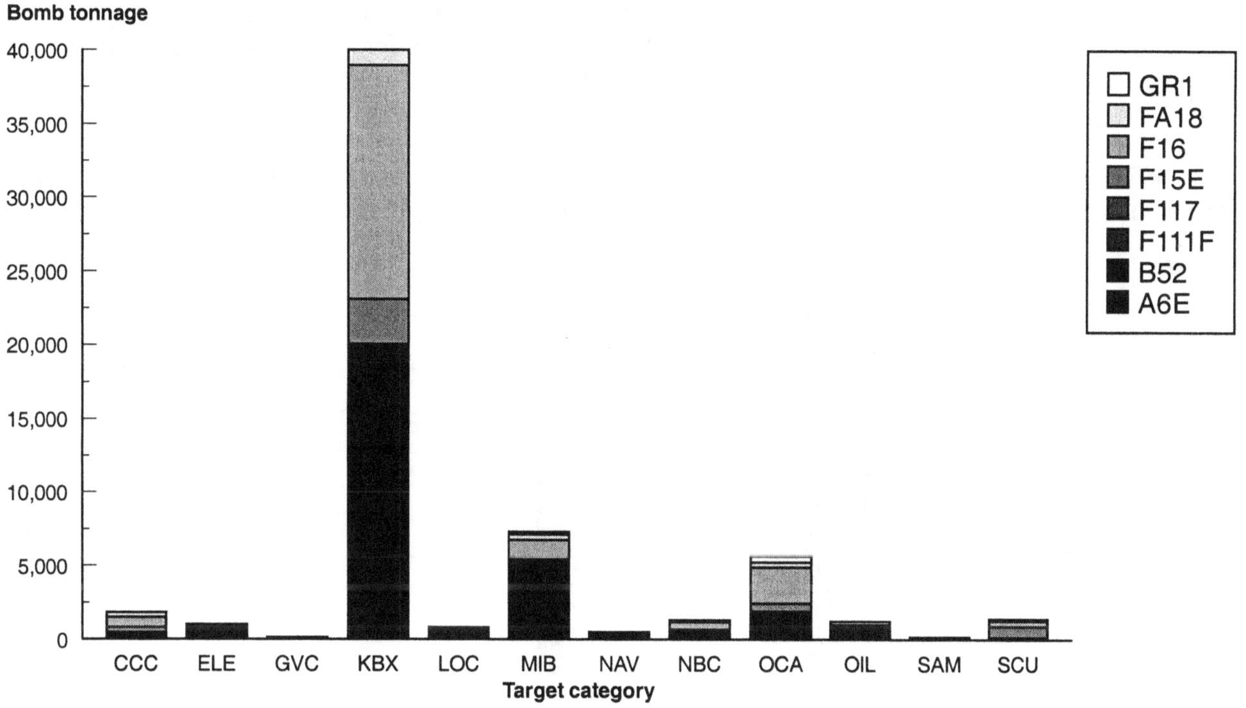

Approximately 78 million pounds of unguided bombs were delivered against ground targets located in kill boxes. Comparatively, F-16 and B-52 are the two platforms that accounted for the preponderance of unguided bomb tonnage delivered here. B-52s accounted for approximately 32 million pounds; F-16s approximately 31 million pounds, at least two-thirds of the total unguided bomb tonnage delivered on BE-numbered KBX targets. Figure VIII.8 also shows that the B-52 accounted for the majority of unguided bomb tonnage delivered against MIB targets.

Figure VIII.9 indicates that more unguided bomb tonnage was delivered against targets in the MIB and OCA strategic target categories than in the other strategic target categories.

Appendix VIII
Weight of Effort and Type of Effort Analysis

The F-16 delivered more of the unguided bomb tonnage against strategic targets in the C³, GVC, NBC, and OCA categories, and it was second to the F-15E in unguided bomb tonnage delivered against targets in the SCU category. Summing across all target categories and comparing to other platforms, B-52s and F-16s accounted for the preponderance of bombs delivered against strategic targets.

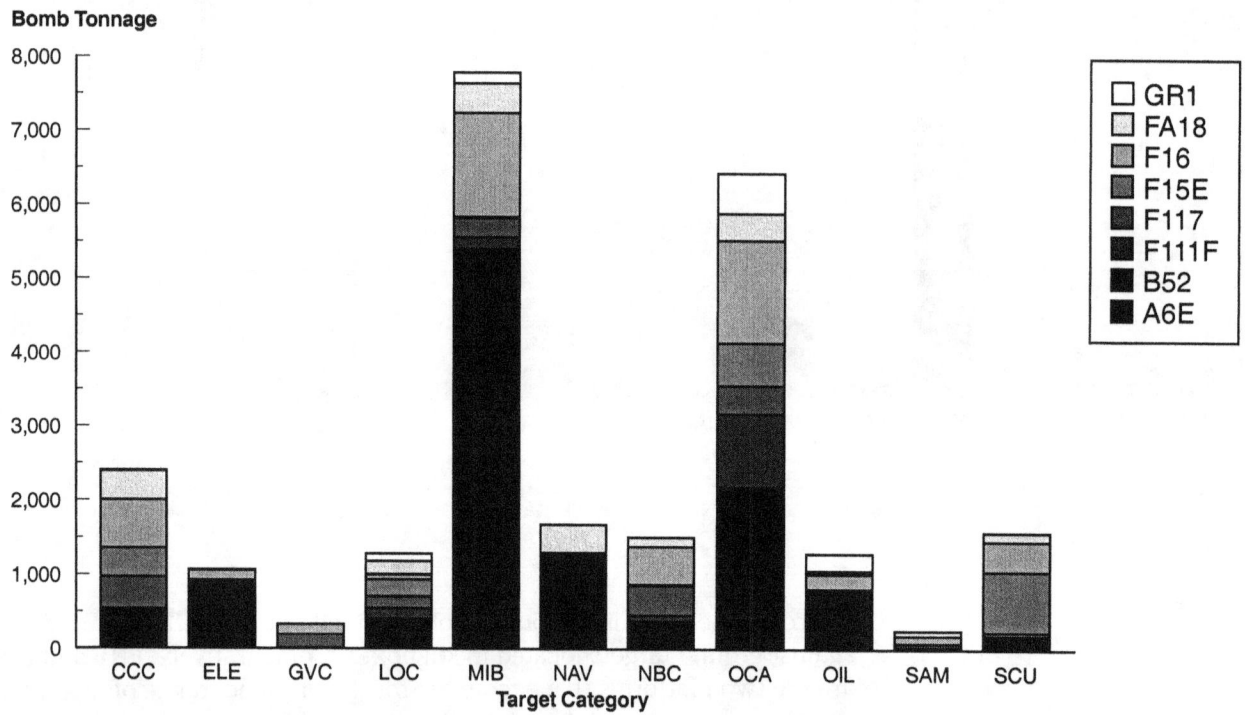

Figure VIII.9: Unguided Tonnage Delivered, by Platform, Excluding KBX Targets

Appendix IX
Target Sensor Technologies

Radar	Radar systems vary from older, low-resolution ground-mapping radars on the F-111F and B-52 to much newer, high-resolution target detection synthetic aperture radar on the F-15E. The basic forms of radar are pulse and continuous-wave types. Both detect targets by transmitting radio waves and then searching for return radio waves reflected from those targets in order to determine information about the location and speed of targets.
Electro-optical	Electro-optical systems exist as a sensor on munitions, such as the EO version of the Maverick missile, and as separate systems, such as night vision goggles. EO-guided weapons carry a miniature TV sensor or camera in the nose that senses targets that provide suitable visible (dark or light) contrasts. Night-viewing systems operate by magnifying the tiny amount of light available from the sky, even in the darkest night.
Infrared	Imaging infrared systems are sometimes integral to the aircraft (Pave Tack, TRAM, and FLIR/DLIR on the F-111F, A-6E, and F-117, respectively) and are sometimes a part of a pod or munition attached to the exterior of the aircraft (such as LANTIRN for the F-15E and F-16 and the IR version of Maverick on the A-10). IR systems lock onto targets by focusing on heat sources. Imaging IR systems are virtually infrared TV cameras, which create a heat image of a target and then rely on signal processing to lock onto a designated part of the heat image, rather than simply the hottest part of the image, as nonimaging IR systems do.
Other Sensor Systems	Other sensor systems using the technologies discussed above were employed in Desert Storm, and other technologies were used to supplement, or supplant, the systems described above. These systems were not integral to the aircraft, themselves, nor to the munitions carried by them; they were mostly either on separate platforms used before or concurrently with the strike aircraft, or they consisted of additional equipment employed by pilots. In the former category were target images provided by intelligence or reconnaissance sensors and sometimes made available to aircrew at the mission planning stage. Pilots of virtually all aircraft reported that receipt of such images and target planning materials were extremely important for mission planning, target study, and mission success, although needed materials were often unavailable or of poor quality. Pilots of aircraft delivering guided munitions stated this was especially true for them because they were often tasked to attack a

Appendix IX
Target Sensor Technologies

specific building, or a section of a building, and they needed the aids and cues available in target images to ensure accurate selection of the desired aimpoint.

While hardly a technology, a key "sensor system" was human vision. Although limited to clear weather, pilots from several aircraft reported confidence that they could hit a target, even with unguided bombs, as long as they could see it. At night, some pilots attempted to target visually by using illumination flares. Varying success with this method was reported by some A-10 and F/A-18 pilots, while A-6E pilots said they found it nearly impossible to find targets using flares.

Another system used by pilots, especially those in aircraft without infrared systems (A-10 and F/A-18), was handheld binoculars during the day and night vision goggles at night. With binoculars, pilots reported varying levels of success in finding and identifying targets from medium and high altitude during the day. Binoculars required unimpeded clear weather conditions and imposed a high workload on pilots in single seat aircraft. Pilots also reported that night vision goggles were ineffective for identifying valid targets on the ground at 10,000 feet or higher.

Appendix X
Combat Support Platforms

Reconnaissance Platforms

[DELETED] reconnaissance platforms, including TR-1As, U-2s, RF-4Cs, RC-135s, and S-3A/Bs were deployed to the Persian Gulf theater. Reconnaissance platforms provided support to combat aircraft by serving as airborne intelligence collection platforms, and they could also provide communications and electronic and photographic intelligence on enemy targets or situations.

In Desert Storm, intelligence from reconnaissance platforms was used for target study, to plan strike missions, and for BDA purposes. U-2/TR-1 intelligence was used in strike missions against Scud missile launchers, ships, Iraqi tanks, armored vehicles, and artillery.

Before the air campaign began, airborne intelligence collectors, such as RC-135s and U-2/TR-1s, flew near the Iraqi-Saudi border and gathered data on the nature of the Iraqi air defense system.

Surveillance Platforms

There were approximately [DELETED] airborne surveillance and control platforms, comprised of E-8 JSTARS, E-3 AWACS, E-2C Hawkeye, and U.S. Marine Corps OV-10s. Respectively, these surveillance platforms provided early-warning surveillance for Navy aircraft carriers (E-2C), command and control for Desert Storm air defense forces (AWACS), identification of friend or foe (IFF) capability, and airborne surveillance of ground targets (JSTARS). Because of the large number of aircraft simultaneously operating during the air campaign, AWACS was critical for IFF, [DELETED]. Marine Corps OV-10s conducted radio relay and visual reconnaissance missions on ground troop targets and maintained 24-hour coverage over the battlefield once the ground war started.

Notable from the Gulf War was JSTARS, which flew its first operational mission in Desert Storm. JSTARS collected intelligence on the movement of Iraqi ground forces in the KTO and other parts of the theater where ground troops were situated. [DELETED]

Electronic Combat Platforms

Platforms that conducted electronic combat missions or electronic warfare in a combat-support role included EF-111s, EC-135s, EC-130s, and EA-6B aircraft. These aircraft conducted missions that either involved jamming of enemy radars or attempted the destruction of radar sites with the use of HARM missiles or tactical air-launched decoys, within the range of enemy radars, for deception purposes. Because electronic combat support missions helped disinfect target areas of threats to strike aircraft,

Appendix X
Combat Support Platforms

they facilitated the ability of primary strike aircraft to conduct attacks on targets.

ABCCC

EC-130Es served as airborne battlefield command, control, and communication (ABCCC) combat support platforms. ABCCC was designed to provide real-time command and control over air forces. With ABCCC, commanders on the ground could relay real-time information on war developments and, if necessary, ABCCC could then relay information to aircraft, providing a near real-time response mechanism to unfolding events. ABCCC provided support to F-15Es operating in kill boxes by providing target deconfliction information before bomb deliveries. ABCCC also provided real-time ATO and BDA information to some units, which pilots pointed out as helpful to mission planning and strike activity given the large time lags in the formal ATO and BDA dissemination process.

Appendix XI
The Experience of F-16s and F-117s at the Baghdad Nuclear Research Facility

The Air Force has repeatedly claimed that an F-117 mission against the Baghdad Nuclear Research Facility at Osirak was a major success, following a failed mission by F-16s. It cites this case as a prime example of the accuracy and effectiveness of stealth aircraft with precision munitions over conventional aircraft with unguided munitions.

On the third day of the campaign, a large conventional daylight strike by 56 F-16s with unguided bombs attacked the nuclear complex, which was one of the three most heavily defended areas in Iraq. The results were assessed as very poor. Gen. Glosson told the Congress that, in contrast, "four nights later, we launched a third package [of F-117s] . . . three out of four reactors were destroyed."[1]

To verify the claim, we sought to answer the following questions:

- What was the frequency and number of F-16 and F-117 strikes on this target?
- Were aircraft other than the F-16 and the F-117 tasked against the target?
- When did DIA report that the target was functionally destroyed?

According to DIA, the nuclear research facility was not fully destroyed following the F-117 strikes on day 6 of the campaign. DIA produced seven phase III battle damage assessments on the target beginning on the second day of the campaign. The final phase III report, which was issued on February 26, day 42 of the campaign, concluded that the ability to conduct nuclear research or processing at the site was severely degraded. The report, however, went on to recommend restrikes on four DMPIs at the site—if the objective was to totally eliminate facility functions.

As illustrated in table XI.1, F-117s conducted strikes on an additional 7 nights following the strike on day 6, the last not occurring until day 38.

Table XI.1: Number of Days, Total Aircraft, and Total Bombs Employed Against the Baghdad Nuclear Research Center During Desert Storm

Aircraft	Air campaign days of attack	Total Aircraft	Bombs
F-117	2, 3, 6, 12, 14, 19, 22, 34, 35, 38	59	84
F-16	2, 3, 5	77	170
F-111F	19	7	4

Source: Our analysis of the 37th TFW Desert Storm and Missions databases.

---

[1]DOD 1992 appropriations hearings (Apr. 30, 1991), p. 490.

Appendix XI
The Experience of F-16s and F-117s at the
Baghdad Nuclear Research Facility

As successful as the F-117 strikes may have been on day 6, an additional 48 F-117s were tasked seven more times against the target over the next 32 days, dropping 66 more bombs. Moreover, on day 19 of the campaign, 17 F-111Fs were tasked to strike the site. Therefore, the scenario described by the Air Force—an unsuccessful, large conventional package strike using unguided munitions, followed by a successful, small package of stealth aircraft using guided munitions—neither fully presents the results of the two missions, nor fully presents the weight and type of effort expended to achieve success at this target.

Appendix XII
Comments From the Department of Defense

Note: GAO comments supplementing those in the report text appear at the end of this appendix.

OFFICE OF THE ASSISTANT SECRETARY OF DEFENSE
2900 DEFENSE PENTAGON
WASHINGTON, D.C. 20301-2900

March 28, 1996

STRATEGY
AND
REQUIREMENTS

In Reply Refer to:
I-96/35381

Mr. Kwai-Cheung Chan
Director, Program Evaluation
  in Physical Systems Area
Program Evaluation and
  Methodology Division
U.S. General Accounting Office
Washington, DC 20548

Dear Mr. Chan:

This is the Department of Defense (DoD) response to the General Accounting Office (GAO) draft report "OPERATION DESERT STORM: The Air Campaign," February 12, 1996 (GAO Code 973364), OSD Case 1094-X. The Department partially concurs with the report.

The DoD continues to believe the coalition victory was impressive militarily and "our air strikes were the most effective, yet humane, in the history of warfare." (President George Bush, May 29, 1991). Similarly the DOD acknowledges (Title V Report) the shortcomings of PGMs, PGM capable aircraft, TLAM and TLAM strike-planning, and our combat strike assessment capabilities. The DoD is well along in its programs to correct these shortcomings:

See comment 1.
- The acquisition of improved and new PGMs (e.g., AGM-130, CALCM, TLAM, SLAM ER, JDAM, and JSOW) is on track.

See comment 2.
- Under ASD(S&R)/D,S&ST/D,PA&E/J-8 co-sponsorship, the DoD has undertaken the Deep Attack/Weapons Mix Study (DAWMS) which will give insight and answers into the proper mix of munitions, and insight into the value to force structure of adding different platforms (fighters, bombers, naval aviation).

See comment 3.
- The Precision Strike Architecture study and several of the proposed FY1997 ACTDs (Counter CC&D, Integrated Sensor Tasking, Operator/ Intelligence, Precision Identification/ Engagement, Rapid Battlefield Visualization, Survivable Armed Reconnaissance on the Digital Battlefield, and Unattended Ground Sensor) will give insight into improvements to the DoD's ability to locate targets, discriminate among them in varying weather and environmental conditions, assess damage done by prior attacks and the need for re-attack, and rapidly provide targeting-quality data to weapons/delivery platforms.

See comment 4.
The DoD shares the GAO and Congressional interest in the effectiveness of the nation's aircraft and munitions. The aforementioned programs and the FY1996 authorizations and appropriations, providing funds to retain the Operational Test & Evaluation function at the OSD-level, will ensure rigorous testing of our weapons and weapon systems.

Appendix XII
Comments From the Department of Defense

Technical corrections to the report were provided separately. The Department appreciates the opportunity to comment on the draft report.

Sincerely,

Frederick L. Frostic
Deputy Assistant Secretary of Defense
Requirements and Plans

Appendix XII
Comments From the Department of Defense

GAO DRAFT REPORT - DATED FEBRUARY 12, 1996
(GAO CODE 973364) OSD CASE 1094-X

"OPERATION DESERT STORM: THE AIR CAMPAIGN"

DEPARTMENT OF DEFENSE COMMENTS

* * * * *

RECOMMENDATION

RECOMMENDATION: In light of the shortcomings of the sensors in Desert Storm, we recommend that the Secretary of Defense analyze and identify DOD's need to enhance the capabilities of existing and planned sensors to effectively locate, discriminate, and acquire targets in varying weather conditions and at different altitudes. Furthermore, the Secretary should ensure that any new sensors or enhancements of existing ones are tested under fully realistic operational conditions that are at least as stressful as the conditions that impeded capabilities in Desert Storm.

DOD RESPONSE: PARTIALLY CONCUR.

See comment 5.
    The DoD is actively researching new or enhanced target search, acquisition, and discrimination sensors. The physical limitations of all sensors including Lasers and FLIRS were known prior to Desert Storm. The DoD continues to seek new and improved technology to overcome these limitations. Testing will continue over the entire range of operational conditions, to ensure that we understand the limitations of all current and future systems.

See comment 3.
    The Precision Strike Architecture study and several of the proposed FY97 ACTDs (Counter CC&D, Integrated Sensor Tasking, Operator/Intelligence, Precision Identification/Engagement, Rapid Battlefield Visualization, Survivable Armed Reconnaissance on the Digital Battlefield, and Unattended Ground Sensor) will give insight into solutions to the DoD's ability to locate targets, discriminate among them in varying weather and environmental conditions, assess damage done by prior attacks and the need for re-attack, and rapidly provide targeting-quality data to weapons/delivery platforms.

RECOMMENDATION: In light of the shortcomings in BDA exhibited during Desert Storm and BDA's importance to strike planning, the BDA problems that DoD officials acknowledge continue today despite DoD postwar initiatives, problems such as timeliness, accuracy, capacity, assessment of functional damage, and cultivating intelligence sources to identify and validate strategic targets, need to be dealt with. We recommend that the Secretary of Defense expand DoD's current efforts to include such activities so that BDA problems can be fully resolved.

See comment 2.

See comment 6.
DOD RESPONSE: PARTIALLY CONCUR.
    Under ASD(S&R)/D,S&ST/D/PA&E/J-8 co-sponsorship, the DoD has undertaken the Deep Attack/Weapons Mix Study (DAWMS). This study involves an end-to-end analysis that provides insight and answers on the proper mix of munitions; the value to force structure of adding different platforms (fighters, bombers, naval aviation) and munitions; and the C4ISR architecture necessary to underpin our future attack operations. The scope of this study is sufficient to fully address all facets of combat strike damage assessment.

See comment 7.
    The BDA problems will never be fully resolved. As long as hostilities exist, perfect BDA will not exist. Current investments in platform and munition improvements and new acquisitions reflect lessons learned from DESERT STORM and shortcomings addressed in the Title V report and this and previous GAO reports.

Appendix XII
Comments From the Department of Defense

RECOMMENDATION: In light of the quantities and mix of guided and unguided munitions that proved successful in Desert Storm, the Services' increasing reliance on guided munitions to conduct asymmetrical warfare may not be appropriate. The Secretary should reconsider DoD's proposed mix of guided and unguided munitions. A reevaluation is warranted based on Desert Storm experiences that demonstrated limitations to the effectiveness of guided munitions, survivability concerns of aircraft delivering these munitions, and circumstances where less complex less constrained unguided munitions proved equally or more effective.

DOD RESPONSE: PARTIALLY CONCUR:

See comment 2.

The Department is currently conducting a comprehensive review of weapons and platforms required to perform assigned missions. The Deep Attack Weapons Mix Study (DAWMS) under ASD(S&R)/D,S&ST/D/PA&E/J-8 co-sponsorship has undertaken a study of the DoD's aircraft and weapons mix. This study's end-to-end analysis will provide insights and answers on the proper mix of munitions; the value to force structure of adding different platforms (fighters, bombers, naval aviation) and munitions; and the C4ISR architecture necessary to underpin our future attack concepts of operations.

See comment 8.

Concurrently, the DoD is aware of the capabilities of our highly-trained pilots and smart aircraft to achieve effectiveness similar to smart and expensive weapons. Innovations in tactics and weapons fusing are allowing our aircraft today to use unguided munitions where guided munitions were previously required. Unguided munitions will always be an important part of our munitions inventory mix. The DoD will continue to evaluate and balance new, more accurate, and more survivable weapons for those targets where they are required.

Appendix XII
Comments From the Department of Defense

The following are GAO's comments on the DOD's letter dated March 28, 1996.

GAO Comments

1. The acquisition of new precision-guided munitions may well provide new capabilities that overcome the limitations observed in Operation Desert Storm. However, the degree to which these new munitions may overcome the limitations of existing munitions can only be determined after rigorous operational test and evaluation of both new and existing munitions.

2. The Deep Attack/Weapons Mix Study will not fully address the implications of our findings concerning the strengths and limitations of guided and unguided munitions. DAWMS is an analysis of the full range of precision-guided munitions in production and in research, development, test, and evaluation that will determine the number and types of precision-guided munitions that are needed to provide a complementary capability against each target class. By analyzing only precision-guided munitions, the study does not address the benefits realized from 92 percent of the munitions delivered in Operation Desert Storm. The premise of the DAWMS does not acknowledge the ambiguous results from Desert Storm regarding munitions effectiveness, the cost and operational trade-offs between guided and unguided munitions, and the demonstrated preference for unguided over guided munitions against several strategic target categories.

3. The Precision Strike Architecture study was designed to define a "system of systems" for precision strike by

- defining the mission,
- identifying the component systems,
- developing a concept of operations,
- facilitating opportunities for system evolution,
- creating criteria for establishing choices among alternatives, and
- determining costs.

The resulting architecture for precision strike is a plan that addresses the limitations in strike capabilities demonstrated in our report. However, the degree to which the sensor and other precision strike shortcomings are alleviated cannot be known until a new precision strike architecture is implemented and tested.

Appendix XII
Comments From the Department of Defense

4. We strongly acknowledge the need to maintain a rigorous operational test and evaluation capability to ensure that commanders, planners, and operators are aware of both the strengths and weaknesses of existing and new weapon systems under a variety of combat conditions.

5. While the physical limitations of all sensors, including laser and forward-looking infrared, may have been known before Desert Storm, they were not necessarily fully acknowledged by DOD or its contractors either before the conflict or in reports to the Congress after the coalition's victory.

6. Our recommendation addresses the demonstrated intelligence shortcomings in performing BDA and in identifying strategic targets in Operation Desert Storm. It is not apparent that the scope of the Deep Attack/Weapons Mix Study is sufficient to address DOD's need to cultivate intelligence sources that can identify and validate strategic targets in future scenarios.

7. Part of the significance of the munitions use data from Desert Storm is that it reveals patterns of use when perfect BDA does not exist. For example, we found in Desert Storm that multiple strikes and weapon systems were used against the same targets; more munitions were delivered than peacetime test capabilities would indicate as necessary; determinations of whether target objectives were met were frequently unknown; and when objectives were met, the specific system responsible could not be determined. These observations should temper one of the primary expectations of the DAWMS: that a growing inventory and increasing capabilities of weapons will reduce the sorties required for deep attack missions.

8. We recognize that where DOD concurs with the premises of our recommendations, it does so based on information other than the analyses we conducted of the Desert Storm air campaign. Owing to these differences, the solutions pursued by DOD may not fully address the needs we perceived. Therefore, although the scope of the specific studies and ACTDs indisputably address our recommendations, the degree to which they result in solutions to Desert Storm shortcomings and limitations cannot be known until the resulting changes and innovations are operational.

Appendix XIII
Major Contributors to This Report

Program Evaluation and Methodology Division, Washington, D.C.	Kwai-Cheung Chan Winslow T. Wheeler Jonathan R. Tumin Jeffrey K. Harris Carolyn M. Copper

Glossary

Aimpoint	Desired location of bomb impact on target.
Air Superiority	The degree of dominance in the air battle of one force over another, which permits operations by the former and its related land, sea, and air forces at a given time and place without prohibitive interference by the opposing force.
Air Supremacy	The degree of air superiority wherein the opposing force is incapable of effective interference.
Battle Damage Assessment	An analysis of the damage inflicted on a target from a bombing or missile strike.
Black Hole	The Special Planning Group established by Gen. Glosson in Riyadh during Desert Shield to design the air campaign.
Breach	To create a break or opening in a line of defenses.
Center of Gravity	The economic, military, and political pillars of an existing regime.
Effectiveness	The level of functional damage achieved for a given munition or strike.
Fully Successful	A bomb damage assessment determination that the target objective was achieved and a restrike was unnecessary.
Imagery	Intelligence derived from visual photography, infrared sensors, lasers, electro-optical systems, and radar sensors such as synthetic aperture radar.
KARI	A French-design computer network for Iraq's air defense components. (KARI is Iraq spelled backward in French.)
Kill Box	A 30-mile by 30-mile geographic designation within the Kuwait theater of operations in which autonomous strike operations were conducted.

Glossary

Laser-Guided Bomb	A bomb that uses a seeker to detect laser energy reflected from a target and, through signal processing, guides itself to the point from which the laser energy is being reflected.
Lines of Communication	Land, water, or air route that connects an operating military force with a base of operations and along which supplies and military forces move.
Munition	Explosive projectiles (such as missiles) or items (such as bombs) with a fuse.
Not Fully Successful	A bomb damage assessment determination where the target objective was not achieved and a restrike was necessary.
Operation Order	A directive, usually formal, issued by a commander to subordinate commanders to effect the coordinated execution of an operation.
Operation Plan	A plan for a single or series of connected operations to be carried out simultaneously or in succession.
Platform	An aircraft or missile that delivers a munition to a target.
Sortie	One flight by one aircraft.
Strategic Target	A target integral to the source of an enemy's military, economic, or political power.
Strike	The delivery of munitions on one target by one platform during one sortie.